Key Terms in Stylistics

Nina Nørgaard, Rocío Montoro and Beatrix Busse

continuum

Continuum International Publishing Group
The Tower Building
11 York Road
London SE1 7NX

80 Maiden Lane
Suite 704
New York, NY 10038

www.continuumbooks.com

British Library Cataloguing-in-Publication Data
A catalogue record for this book is available from the British Library.

ISBN: 978-0-8264-1288-1 (hardcover)
978-0-8264-1948-4 (paperback)

Library of Congress Cataloging-in-Publication Data
Nørgaard, Nina.
Key terms in stylistics / Nina Nørgaard, Rocío Montoro and Beatrix Busse.
p. cm.—(Key terms)
ISBN 978–0–8264–1288–1 (hardcover)
ISBN 978–0–8264–1948–4 (pbk.)
1. Language and languages—Style. 2. Style, Literary. I. Montoro, Rocío. II. Busse, Beatrix. III. Title. IV. Series.
P301.N56 2010
410—dc22 2010000323

Typeset by Newgen Imaging Systems Pvt Ltd, Chennai, India

Contents

Introduction

What is stylistics?

Stylistics is the study of the ways in which meaning is created through language in literature as well as in other types of text. To this end, stylisticians use linguistic models, theories and frameworks as their analytical tools in order to describe and explain how and why a text works as it does, and how we come from the words on the page to its meaning. The analysis typically focuses qualitatively or quantitatively on the phonological, lexical, grammatical, semantic, pragmatic or discoursal features of texts, on the cognitive aspects involved in the processing of those features by the reader as well as on various combinations of these. While some stylistic approaches primarily show an interest in the producer of the text, investigating the style of a particular author, for instance, other stylisticians focus more on the text itself (broadly understood to encompass all types of discourse) and still others devote their attention to the reader and the role readers play in meaning construction. New developments in stylistics emphasize that the production of meaning needs to be accounted for as a double exercise encompassing as much text-informed inferences as the mental processes that allow text comprehension.

Stylistics is often regarded as a linguistic approach to literature – and understandably so, since the majority of stylistic attention so far has been devoted to literary texts. In actual fact, however, the range of discourses that stylisticians are currently engaged with has expanded considerably to include non-fictional forms such as advertising, academic writing, news reports as well as non-printed forms such as TV and pictorial advertising, film, multimodal publications, etc. With its base in linguistics, stylistics is (ideally) characterized by an informed, systematic, retrievable, and (usually also) contextual analysis, which is rigorous, consistent and open to falsification. Because of the 'scientific' nature of linguistics as compared to other fields in the humanities, the stylistic approach to text analysis may seem more objective than other branches of literary criticism. It is important to note, however, that in spite of stylisticians' concern with rigour, no stylistic analysis can be totally objective, but it will always be influenced by a myriad of factors, such as the stylistician's individual preferences and foci, as well as the linguistic paradigm employed for analysis or the chosen methodology. Notwithstanding this reservation, stylistics has proved itself to provide useful tools and methods which allow its practitioners to conduct informed analyses of the ways in which meaning is created in texts by linguistic means. Stylistics is interdisciplinary in scope – most obviously so by its bringing together linguistics and literary studies. Yet, the eclectic claims of the field have furthermore allowed views borrowed from disciplines such as philosophy, cultural theory, sociology, history and psychology to find their way into the stylistic analyses of literature. While sometimes criticized for its interdisciplinariness, stylistics has been praised by others for its interdisciplinary character which is considered one of the advantages and inspiring potentials of the approach.

Branches of stylistics – a brief historical overview

Historically, stylistics may be seen to date back to the focus on the style of oral expression, which was cultivated in rhetoric following the tradition of Aristotle's *Rhetoric*. The real flourishing of stylistics, however, was seen in particular in Britain and the United States in the 1960s, and was largely spurred by work done in the field by proponents of Russian Formalism such as Roman Jakobson and Viktor Shklovsky. The Russian Formalists wished to make literary inquiry more 'scientific' by basing it firmly on explicit observations about the formal linguistic features of the texts under scrutiny. They were particularly interested in 'literariness' and devoted their stylistic study to phonological, lexical and grammatical forms and structures such as parallelism and linguistic deviation which would make a text 'poetic' (see *formalist stylistics* and *foregrounding*). The formalists focused their stylistic investigations almost solely on poetry. While praised – at least in stylistic circles – for their devotion to the linguistic aspects of literary meaning-making, and for the systematic and rigorous nature of their work, formalist stylisticians were sometimes criticized for their overriding focus on linguistic form at the expense of the function and effects of the formal features put up for examination, and for their tendency to ignore the significance of contextual factors such as the pragmatic, social and historical contexts of these texts.

The focus on literature in general and poetry in particular, on the one side, and the interdisciplinary character which was visible even in the early years of stylistics, on the other, made some see stylistics only as a sub-branch of literary criticism. Also, it was questioned whether stylistics could be regarded as anything other than a method and whether, due to its eclecticism, it contained any ideological or theoretical foundations. Therefore, matters relating to function and context were increasingly addressed from the late 1970s, which witnessed a functional turn in stylistics (see *functionalist stylistics*). Of particular impact was Halliday's functional model of language, with its focus on language as a 'social semiotics', that is, a model of linguistic meaning-making as a social phenomenon influencing and influenced by the context in which it occurs. With Halliday, every linguistic choice came to be seen as functional, and the analyst, whether linguist or stylistician, would consequently investigate the (experiential, interpersonal and textual) functions of language as it is actually used in a specific context (see *M. A. K. Halliday*). The functionalist approach furthermore entailed an interest in longer stretches of text, which provided analytical tools for stylisticians who wished to devote their attention to longer texts such as narrative fiction and play texts.

Due to its focus on social context and the realization by any given text of contextual factors such as register, genre and ideology, Hallidayan linguistics came to play a significant role in branches of stylistics with an interest in the linguistic manifestation of ideology, like those of feminist stylistics (see entry) and critical stylistics (see entry). Feminist stylisticians are especially concerned with the realization and maintenance of (unequal) gender relations in literary as well as other types and texts and may, in fact, be seen as a variant of critical stylistics whose focus lies with the linguistic embodiment of social inequality, power structures and ideology more generally.

Also basically functional in nature are various pragmatic approaches to text analysis (see *pragmatic stylistics*), which emerged in the 1960s, but only really came to play a role on the stylistics scene from the late 1980s and the beginning of the 1990s. Like functionalist stylistics, pragmatic stylistics is concerned with language in use and the significance of contextual factors such as, for example, the linguistic, social, cultural and authorial contexts of the production and reception of texts. At the crux of pragmatic stylistics is the focus on conversation as exchange, or 'interpersonal meaning', and a devotion to linguistic features such as speech acts, discourse markers, politeness strategies, etc., which makes it a useful approach to drama and other types of text characterized by dialogue. In spite of the more focused stylistic attention thus paid to play texts, the relative neglect of this literary genre in stylistics is still apparent when compared to the stylistic analyses of other narrative genres.

Another, major turn in stylistics is that spurred by the recent rise and growth of cognitive linguistics. Of central interest to cognitive linguists and stylisticians alike is the role played by human cognition in the creation of meaning. Cognitive stylistics (see entry), or cognitive poetics, fuses cognitive science, linguistics and literary studies in analyses where meaning is seen as a product of the text *and* the human conceptualization of it, meaning that equal importance is ascribed to the text and the reader.

Corpus stylistics (see entry), which has developed along with corpus linguistics and technological advances, is another recent trend in the field. Corpus stylisticians apply the methods of modern corpus linguistics to the analysis of large amounts of literary texts and other linguistic data and fuse it with the major tenets of stylistics. Where linguists and stylisticians alike were previously restricted to searching texts manually for various linguistic phenomena, this can now be done by computers, provided that the phenomena sought for can be recognized by the available computer software. It can be no surprise that the corpus approach to literary analysis has spurred a fair deal of scepticism among some literary critics who basically worry that the handling of Literature (capital L intended) by a computer will fail to capture the special nature of literary art (for an informed and critical discussion of the advantages and disadvantages of a corpus-based stylistic approach, see Toolan, 2009). Notwithstanding such and similar criticism, corpus linguistics methods are increasingly acknowledged in stylistics today as a practical tool for handling large amounts of text and identifying the style of particular texts, authors or genres – a tool which can qualify the analysts' intuitions about the text and perhaps even make them aware of lexical and grammatical features and patterns which may not otherwise have come to their attention.

A relatively new actor on the stylistics scene is that of multimodal stylistics (see entry). Proponents of this branch of stylistics are interested in the meaning-making done not only by wording, but also by other semiotic modes involved in literary as well as other types of text. Based on research in multimodality more generally, multimodal stylistics aims to develop and apply 'grammars' for all the different semiotic modes which may be involved in a literary work of art, that is, modes such as typography, layout, colour and visual images, in order to be able to deal as systematically with all these modes and their interaction as more traditional stylistic branches have previously dealt with wording.

Finally, certain branches of stylistics combine elements from some of the branches mentioned above. Historical stylistics (see entry) is one such branch. With the aim of exploring historical texts from a stylistic perspective, or of examining linguistic aspects of style as they either change or remain stable over time, historical stylisticians draw on concepts, methodologies and models from corpus stylistics, cognitive stylistics and pragmatic stylistics, for example.

Stylistics in education and academia

In Britain as well as in other European countries such as Germany, Spain and Denmark, stylistics has found a place in the educational system as a discipline that bridges the traditional gap between literature and linguistics in different language degree programmes. In this context, courses in stylistics are typically implemented to increase students' awareness of different features of language and the ways in which they are employed in various types of text with different effects. In addition to improving students' analytical skills at a linguistic level, stylistics is also utilized with the aim of increasing students' own general linguistic performance or in specific courses on creative writing, for instance. A special branch of stylistics, pedagogical stylistics (see entry), is concerned with exploring the pedagogical implications of stylistics in the teaching of literature as well as in first and second language acquisition.

Over the years, stylistics has gained a significant following in academia in different parts of the world, from Europe to Africa, from the United States to Japan. Among other things, this has led to the formation of various groups and associations for stylisticians of which the most prominent are currently the *Poetics and Linguistics Association* (*PALA*) and the *International Association of Literary Semantics* (*IALS*) (see entries), both international associations with considerable memberships world-wide. The foremost stylistics journals of international scope are *Language and Literature, Journal of literary Semantics* and *Style* (see entries).

The stylistic tool box – an outline of the book

A metaphor often used to describe stylistics is that of the 'tool kit' or 'tool box'. This metaphor reflects a conception of the field as a big tool box which contains a broad range of linguistic tools available to critics who wish to anchor their analysis of literature and other types of text firmly in the actual language of these texts. As new linguistic paradigms emerge, new compartments and new tools are added to the tool box. While some stylisticians may prefer to stick to the tools from one compartment (the functionalist, the cognitive or the corpus compartment, for instance), others may choose to combine tools more freely from the entire tool box; hence, the interdisciplinary character of stylistics. It is the aim of *Key Terms in Stylistics* to provide the reader with an overview of the stylistic tool box, the tools available in it, the different linguistic paradigms and branches of stylistics which have produced and/or employ the tools as well as key thinkers in the field.

The book is organized into four sections. The first section, 'Key Branches in Stylistics', provides an overview of the diverse field of stylistics and comprises entries on different stylistic approaches to text such as cognitive stylistics, feminist stylistics, corpus stylistics and multimodal stylistics. The second section, 'Key Terms in Stylistics', consists of an extensive list of terms and concepts of relevance to the field with useful cross-references between the different entries. The third section, 'Key Thinkers in Stylistics', provides a list of important thinkers and practitioners in the field as well as summaries of their work, ideas and overall contribution to stylistics. In addition to key stylisticians, this section also lists other scholars who, while not stylisticians themselves, have had an impact on the field of stylistics because of their contribution to the linguistic paradigms which have informed the field over the years. This list is, by no means, intended as an exhaustive collection as many other scholars could have made it into the final inventory. Authors without entries in the 'Key Thinkers' section have been amply referred to in the bulk of the book so the reader is asked to check the 'Key Texts' section for further information on them. The final section, 'Key Texts in Stylistics', consists of a comprehensive list of core texts in stylistics. Here, the stylistic texts referred to in the previous sections of the book are listed as well as a considerable number of further texts in stylistics, covering the various branches of the field. At the end of this section, the reader also finds a list of the primary sources such as novels, poems or films which are quoted for exemplification in the book.

Key Branches in Stylistics

Cognitive stylistics/Cognitive poetics

Despite cognitive stylistics, also known as cognitive poetics, having only relatively recently been embraced by mainstream stylistics, it has rapidly become an ever-expanding, entrepreneurial and extremely productive branch. At its most basic, a definition can comprise a single sentence: 'Cognitive poetics is all about reading literature' (Stockwell, 2002, p. 1). On a more complex level, Stockwell expands it to:

> That sentence looks simple to the point of seeming trivial. It could even be seen simply as a close repetition, since cognition is to do with the mental processes involved in reading, and poetics concerns the craft of literature. (Stockwell, 2002, p. 1)

Viewed from this perspective, cognitive stylistics/poetics highlights the aspects of reading that literature consumers operate when they process literary texts. Cognitive stylistics, essentially, has emanated from the application to literature of models originally used in disciplines such as cognitive linguistics, cognitive psychology and artificial intelligence. Of special relevance are the multiple frameworks in which this branch has managed to capture issues such as 'what do people do when they read' and 'what happens to people when they read' (Burke, 2006a, p. 218).

Because of the data that cognitive stylistics is concerned with, i.e., literature, this branch is intricately linked to literary stylistics, alternatively known as literary linguistics. In fact, cognitive stylistics is said to have derived directly from it (Burke, 2006a, p. 218). By prioritizing the textual components of literature, literary stylistics embodies the most traditional ways of stylistic analysis based on the interface between form, function, effect and interpretation whereas cognitive stylisticians argue that the mental component of the meaning creation process should be included. Influences from disciplines such as psychology, cognitive psychology and cognitive linguistics are responsible for shifting the emphasis to take into consideration the mental aspects of reading too.

For instance, schema theory is one of such disciplines that, although originating from Gestalt psychology, has been extremely influential in bringing stylistics to the cognitive camp. Schema theorists claim that meaning is not only contained in the text; meaning needs to be built up by the reader using the text in negotiation with their own background knowledge. These two essential facets of understanding, which are complementary and dependable on one another, are known as bottom-up or stimulus-driven processes and top-down or conceptually-driven processes (Rumelhart and Ortony, 1977, p. 128). The former prompt the reader to construct a particular mental world thanks to the linguistic characteristics of the text, whereas the latter mobilize the background knowledge that the reader is already in possession of and that becomes activated when prompted by the specific linguistic props. Most sub-branches within cognitive stylistics accept that this negotiation is essential if we are to provide an accurate account of how understanding actually takes place.

Although the terms cognitive stylistics and cognitive poetics can and are used interchangeably, certain practitioners point out some slight differences in meaning. The first edited collection on cognitive stylistics research, published by Semino and Culpeper (2002), defends the former term:

> This collection aims to represent the state of the art in cognitive stylistics – a rapidly expanding field at the interface between linguistics, literary studies and cognitive science. Cognitive stylistics combines the kind of explicit, rigorous and detailed linguistic analysis of literary texts that is typical of the stylistics tradition with a systematic and theoretically informed consideration of the cognitive structures and processes that underlie the production and reception of language. (Semino and Culpeper, 2002, p. ix)

By maintaining the term 'stylistics' in the label, the rigour and replicability of stylistic methods is also safeguarded because it is underscored. These differences, however, appear unnecessarily fastidious to some scholars that consider both labels totally interchangeable. The variety of frameworks and models of analysis found under the umbrella term cognitive stylistics/poetics also evidences the healthy status of the discipline. Some of these frameworks include blending theory (Dancygier, 2005, 2006), conceptual/cognitive metaphor theory (Steen, 1994), contextual frame theory (Emmott, 1997), schema theory (Cook, 1994; Semino, 1997) and text world theory (Gavins, 2007; Werth, 1999). Although these frameworks differ as to how they explain the relationship between bottom-up and top-down processes (contextual frame theory uses 'frames', schema theory uses 'schemata' and text world theory uses 'text worlds', for instance), all models rely on the notion of mental constructs. Apart from the two edited collections by Semino and Culpeper (2002) and Gavins and Steen (2003), there are numerous other monographs and articles; see Freeman (1993, 1995), Freeman (1995), Gibbs (2003), Jeffries (2008), Sanders and Redeker (1996) and Tsur (1998, 2008).

See also *blending theory*, *conceptual metaphor*, *contextual frame theory*, *schema theory*, *text world theory* (Key Terms).

Corpus stylistics

Corpus stylistics has only recently entered the landscape of stylistics, but it has all the more forcefully begun to exploit the potential of combining corpus linguistics and stylistics. Defining corpus stylistics as the cooperation between corpus linguistics and stylistics or as the application of the methods of modern corpus linguistics to (literary) texts and fusing these with the tenets of stylistics involves some challenges.

If style is the essence of a text or displays characteristic features of a genre, of the language of a person/character, of a period or of a particular act in a play and corpus linguistics focuses on the repetitive patterns that can be attested in corpora, then there is a productive interplay on both sides. Also, the focus in stylistics on how a text means and what makes it distinctive in terms of norms allows for a productive interplay between corpus linguistics and stylistics, especially with regard to the theory of foregrounding, which discusses aspects that account for patterns and structures such as deviation and parallelism.

Both stylistics and its offshoot corpus stylistics focus on the interdependence between form and meaning/function. It is only possible to establish marked deviation and parallelism if we are able to identify – with the help of the analysis of large amounts of data – what the norms and conventions are. Yet, we cannot assume that a corpus, just because it is large or specialized, constitutes the norm against which the linguistic features in the text under investigation can be measured on a one-to-one basis. This is because frequently a corpus consists of text samples of, for example, different periods or genres rather than of one complete set of texts by one author, for example. In addition, complex contextual parameters in both texts – that to be investigated and the reference corpus that the text is measured against – need to be considered to establish a style, what is conventional, and what is creative or foregrounded (see also *historical stylistics*). However, there is no such distinction between literary and non-literary language; in fact scholars such as Carter (2004) stress that literary language has to be seen on a continuum, a cline of 'literariness'. The interplay between stylistics and corpus linguistics gives us some additional ways to 'measure, describe and handle this creativity' (Mahlberg, 2007, p. 221; see also Mahlberg, 2006).

Earlier quantitative attempts at identifying style by Fucks (1955, 1968, 1970/71) described, for example, the distribution of particular length of sentences of a variety of authors. A corpus stylistic analysis embraces the language of individual texts by providing frameworks against which these features can be identified, in terms of tendencies, intertextual relations, etc. This is a feature of corpus stylistics that will help stylistics to defend itself from attacks coming from linguistics proper that disapprove of stylistics and say that stylistics apparently simply prioritizes interpretation and is too unsystematic. Corpus stylistics focuses on interpretation and on answering the question of how a text means, which is appropriated from stylistics. This will then advance corpus linguistic procedures by not only describing achieved results, but also by interpreting them and answering the question of 'So what?'. If then similar findings to those already claimed within literary critical interpretations can be found, this is not a problem, because at least it can be proved that the methodology employed was right (Stubbs, 2005, p. 6).

Another point of intersection between stylistics and corpus linguistics is that by using a corpus of texts to be investigated with, for example, some corpus tools like *Wordsmith* (Scott, 2004), one needs to be as precise, comprehensive and detailed as possible (see also Hoover, Culpeper and Louw, 2007). It may bring to the fore linguistic features of levels of language – especially lexical, but also discoursal – which might otherwise not have been noticed. These observations can then be related to a particular style of a text or a corpus. A corpus stylistic approach is retrievable and also aims at providing patterns of particular linguistic phenomena, which can be established with the help of a quantitative/statistically representative framework. As such, corpus stylistics sees qualitative and quantitative analyses as interdependent and aims at testing the stylistician's intuition as well as respective models. If necessary, it helps generate modification or generalizations, because the results are based on large amounts of data.

To support descriptive adequacy, corpus stylistics also involves the construction of corpora and their annotation. It provides additional tools and frameworks by which texts can be analysed from a corpus stylistic point of view. These include such topics as, for example, the identification of collocation, key words, semantic fields or clusters and the correlation of those features to textual interpretation. For example, due to the digitization of various texts, it is possible to annotate larger corpora for their use of discourse presentation: Semino and Short (2004) and Busse (2010a) investigate speech, writing and thought presentation in twentieth-century and nineteenth-century corpora. Louw (1997) uses a corpus-based approach to show how what he calls the 'semantic prosody' of the word 'utterly' is used by Philip Larkin to induce feelings of threat in 'First Sight'. Hori (2004) investigates Dickens's style from a corpus stylistic perspective. Mahlberg (2007) investigates key clusters in Dickens's work as pointers of local textual functions. Toolan (2009) uses a corpus stylistic approach to investigate reader-progression and aims at understanding how the lexico-grammatical patterning contributes to narrativity and how useful a corpus approach is when the sequentiality of a text is the main issue.

See also *historical stylistics* (Key Branches), *collocation, foregrounding* (Key Terms), *John Sinclair* (Key Thinkers).

Critical stylistics

Critical stylistics is a term used to refer to stylistic work investigating the ways in which social meanings are manifested through language. This stylistic tendency is largely inspired and informed by critical linguistics and critical discourse analysis.

Critical linguistics and critical discourse analysis (CDA) are closely related, with the latter often employed as an umbrella term for both (see entry Critical linguistics originated with Roger Fowler and his colleagues at University of East Anglia, most notably Robert Hodge, Gunther Kres and Tony Trew, who set out to uncover how social meanings, such as po ideology, are expressed through language and how language in this respect may impact on the way we perceive the world (Fowler, Hodge, Kress and Trew, 1979; Fowler, 1991). This work was continued a decade later in what was now termed critical discourse analysis, with Norman Fairclough as the most prominent proponent (Fairclough, 1989, 1995, 2000). Much of the work in linguistic criticism and critical discourse analysis is based on M. A. K. Halliday's Systemic Functional Linguistics (see *M. A. K. Halliday*). Because of its focus on linguistic constructivism (i.e., the claim that language constructs, or 'construes', rather than represents meaning), and its claim that all texts through their linguistic choices realize contextual factors such as register, genre and ideology, the Hallidayan approach to language has been considered particularly suited for investigations of the ways in which social meanings are created through language. Another central concept in critical discourse analysis is that of 'naturalization', that is, the claim that certain discourses and the ideologies they reflect have become so ingrained (and thereby naturalized) in society that language users tend not to notice them as ideologies at all. A good example of this is provided by Jeffries (2010):

> The idea that children should be looked after and are not required to work 13-hour days in factories is now a very common ideology that has been naturalized in the United Kingdom for many years, and as a result seems to us to be self-evident. However, to those Victorian families who relied on children's wages and to those families in the developing world who do so today, this ideology would perhaps be surprising. (Jeffries, 2010, p. 9)

In stylistics, Fowler was one of the first and most prominent proponents of a critical stylistics. In *Linguistic Criticism* (1986), he explores phenomena such as the representation of experience through language, meaning and world view, the role of the reader as well as the relations between text and context. From a feminist perspective, Burton's (1982) analysis of the linguistic con- truction of the powerlessness of the female protagonist of Sylvia Plath's *The ll Jar* (1963) is frequently quoted (see *Deirdre Burton*). Through an analysis ansitivity patterns (see *transitivity*), Burton demonstrates how the novel's onist is constructed linguistically as passive and powerless when going electric shock treatment at the mental-health hospital to which she admitted. In *Language, Ideology and Point of View* (1993), Simpson, in turn, conducts linguistic analyses of the realization of (psychological and/or ideological) point of view in a number of literary and non-literary texts:

> By developing a particular style, a producer of a spoken or written text privileges certain readings, certain ways of seeing things, while suppressing or downplaying others. [. . .] The purpose, in other words, is to probe under the surface of language, to decode the stylistic choices which shape a text's meaning. (Simpson, 1993, p. 8)

For this probing, Simpson explores linguistic phenomena such as, for instance, the manifestation of attitude through language (*modality*; see entry), the linguistic construction of experience (*transitivity*; see entry) as well as pragmatic aspects of meaning-making. Finally, Jeffries in *Critical Stylistics* (2010) fuses critical discourse analysis and stylistics with a strong emphasis given to – and tools provided for the analysis of – the actual linguistic manifestation of social meanings.

See also *critical discourse analysis* (Key Terms), *Roger Fowler, M. A. K. Halliday* (Key Thinkers).

Emotion: stylistic approaches

Affective and emotional approaches to stylistics are recent additions to the eclectic range of formulations that stylistics feeds on. Such up-to-datedness, however, does not imply a totally novel way of looking at (mainly although not exclusively) literary texts as proved by Aristotle's concerns with the emotional aspects of reading (i.e., his theory of *catharsis* or 'purging'). This historical perspective notwithstanding, stylistic approaches to emotion have recently received a new impetus as more and more scholars have started to incorporate affective components into their analyses. The first hurdle to negotiate, though, is a disambiguation of the label itself. 'Emotion', 'affect', 'feelings' and 'mood' are terms amply discussed and defined in psychological and cognitive circles where they are not treated as synonymous. 'Affect' is generally considered to be the most general term, 'used to include emotions, moods and preferences' (Oatley et al., 2006, p. 412). 'Emotion' refers to a more complex set of affairs, 'typically a multi-component response to a challenge or an opportunity that is important to an individual's goals' (Oatley et al., 2006, p. 415). Some of these multi-faceted components include a conscious mind, bodily changes, face expressions, gestures or a marked tone of voice and finally readiness for action. Despite these two terms invoking different meanings in disciplines such as cognitive psychology and psychology, stylistics has generally conflated the two and treated them synonymously: 'Basically affective refers to feelings, hence it means "emotional"' (Wales, 2001, p. 10). Besides, stylistically-informed analyses have succeeded in looking into the emotional components of literary discourse as a whole, whether these affect the production level (author-induced emotion), the textual level (linguistic means) or the reception level (reader response).

Initially, the views propounded by traditional affective criticism gave rise in the 1940s and 1950s to what the New Critics called the 'affective fallacy' (Wimsatt and Beardsley, 1954). On the one hand, the traditional affective views following the Aristotelian tradition investigated the potential of a given text to raise some kind of emotional reaction in the reader, including a physical one, so the focus for the inducing of emotions was identified as emanating from the text. The New Critics dismissed such stance as unnecessarily subjective and called it the 'affective fallacy' as an evaluation of literature solely based on the emotional impact it would have on readers was considered methodologically and formally inappropriate. This position does not seem tenable nowadays, though; as Burke states, this 'anti-subjective view is completely implausible because of what is now known about the crucial role that top-down processing also plays in reading procedures' (Burke, 2006b, p. 127). The belief in the potential of texts for raising emotions was carried through and picked up by the formalist scholars of the 1960s as exemplified in Roman Jakobson's formulations on language (1960). Despite a reticence to deal with emotional issues openly because of his formalist background, Jakobson famously identified six different functions of language among which the 'emotive' is to be found alongside the 'conative', 'metalinguistic', 'poetic', 'phatic' and 'referential' . It could be argued, therefore, that even those movements that claim to define themselves as devoid of 'subjective' content seem to have incorporated some emotional component in their formulations. It is not until the 1980s that the affective aspects of the reception level of discourse (that is, that of the reader) are highlighted, particularly in reader response criticism. The label 'affective stylistics' was famously coined by Stanley Fish (1980), who states:

> I have argued the case for a method of analysis which focuses on the reader rather than on the artefact [...]. The chief objection, of course,

> is that affective criticism leads one away from the 'thing itself' in all its solidity to the inchoate impressions of a variable and various reader [...]. In the category of response I include not only 'tears, prickles', and 'other psychological symptoms' but all the precise mental operations involved in reading, including the formulation of complete thoughts, the performing (and regretting) of acts of judgement, the following and making of logical sequences. (Fish, 1980, pp. 42–3)

Fish's innovative interpretation not only shifts the focus of attention onto the reader, but also underscores the importance of including an account of the psychological processes involved in reading. Nevertheless, his initial defence of an investigation into readers' emotional concerns became weakened and never developed into a fully-fledged theory of emotional responses to literature. Moreover, interest in emotional aspects waned after Fish's initial surge despite the fact that cognate disciplines such as Systemic Functional Linguistics and discourse analysis embraced the challenge fully (Burke, 2006b, p. 127). The branch of stylistics known as cognitive stylistics or cognitive poetics has more recently become the catalyst for a rekindling of the interest in the role of affect. Semino's analysis of schema theory (1997), on the one hand, and van Peer's appraisal of a poetics of emotion (1997), on the other, are a case in point:

> Emotions, then, are intimately related to cognition. Thus, in assessing the emotional potential of literature, we shall have to take this relation into account [...]. Reading literature is [...] one such form in which our emotional involvement has clear cognitive overtones. (van Peer, 1997, p. 227)

Van Peer signals here the intricate connections existing between cognitive components of human comprehension and their emotional counterparts, something that has not always been accepted as a given in the field of psychology. Van Peer's adamant emphasis on the existence of such connections seems to explain the newly accepted take on emotional concerns emanating from cognitive analyses of literature. Finally, it is worth noting that a great deal of recent work on affective responses to literature has highlighted emotional aspects at the reception level of discourse, that is, the reader's emotional reaction rather than the encoding of emotion in language. For further developments of the branch see Burke (2001, 2010), Downes (2000), Montoro (2011) and Tsur (1978, 1992, 2002, 2008).

See also *cognitive stylistics/cognitive poetics*, *reader response criticism* (Key Branches).

Empirical study of literature

Empirical perspectives on the study of literature advocate the implementation of a rigorous, primarily, although not exclusively, quantitative study of literary texts by adopting an observational and analytical perspective. The empirical study of literature (ESL) feeds directly from methodologies employed in the social sciences such as anthropology, psychology, cognitive psychology and psycholinguistics and argues for the applicability of their most characteristic tools of these methodologies to literary analysis. This interest in rigour highlights that analyses of literature and the arts in general can actually be conducted in as scientific a way as those carried out in the social sciences. This way of looking into literary concerns is a newly taken enterprise, especially adopted by the members of the *International Society for the Empirical Study of Literature and Media (IGEL)* founded in 1987.

Despite this defence of the use of testable methods for the analysis of literature, literary empiricists maintain that their work falls well within the boundaries of literary analysis:

> We shall argue in the next pages that the empirical study of literature embodies a shift of perspective and emphasis in comparison with more traditional literary scholarship, but that it remains within the bounds of literary studies proper. (Schram and Steen, 2001b, p. 2)

As such, these empirical studies deal with issues of literature as a cultural and social artefact, comparable to other artistic and media forms. Of special importance in this approach is the emphasis placed on the role of the reader as a cultural and social participant, which has subsequently resulted in a much tighter and methodologically sound treatment of studies of reader response. It is not surprising, thus, that empirical studies tie in especially well with general stylistic interests as the principles of applicability, testability, falsifiability and retrievability that characterize stylistics are particularly enhanced by an empirical perspective. As with the former, stylistics, in general, maintains that any methodology that encourages a rigorous perspective to look at form in combination with function, effect and interpretation will be of benefit.

The fruitful nature of empirical approaches is also reflected in the interdisciplinarity that characterizes this take on literary texts. Scholars whose work falls well within the remit of stylistics have collaborated closely with colleagues in psychology and cognitive psychology departments. One clear case of this collaboration is the STACS project (Stylistics, Text Analysis and Cognitive Science: Interdisciplinary Perspectives on the Nature of Reading) (Emmott et al., 2007, p. 213) at the University of Glasgow, which has been successful in bringing together tools traditionally used in stylistics such as foregrounding, and psychological testing methods, such as 'anomaly testing' and 'text change detection method' (Emmott et al., 2007, pp. 204–5). As Hakemulder states, 'the empirical study of literature (ESL) concerns all aspects of literary communication' (2006, p. 274); so, empirical testing functioning at the levels of production and reception is especially conducive to the integration of all these diverse disciplines and methodologies. As a result, quite a lot of empirical work has focused on aspects of linguistic foregrounding in relation to its effect on the reader. Emmott et al. (2007), for instance, analyse how traditional stylistic takes on fiction tend to focus on the way salient features can underscore 'key plot and thematic moments [. . .] guiding the interpretation of readers at these points' (2007, p. 205). They argue that looking at those salient features tends to be done by enticing readers to produce accounts of those features they consider to be especially striking. The main problem arising out of assessing foregrounding effects in this way is the inevitable subjectivity colouring respondents' accounts. Moreover, as Emmott et al. point out (2007, p. 207), such technique might provide significant results as far as the overall impression of the text is concerned, but not in relation to the actual way in which psychological processing takes place. When the effect on the reader is measured by employing the rather more accurate and strict methods generally used in the social sciences results can be not simply different but sometimes even contradictory to those based on subjective evaluation of text saliency (see Emmott et al., 2007, for a critique of van Peer, 1986).

As is common practice in academia, though, some discordant voices claim that empirical approaches to literature also have their disadvantages. Schreier (2001, p. 35), for instance, points out that the perspective of over 25 years that empirical studies now enjoy has allowed some much needed objectivity on the (ironically!) objective claims made by ESL practitioners:

> There have been voices of scepticism or even discontent from within ESL, voices focusing on the question of fit between the subject matter of ESL

> and the methods used to study it. Brewer (1995), for instance, has criticized that the methods used in ESL for data collection have focused on the cognitive-instrumental aspects of reception to the exclusion of, for instance, affective or aesthetic ones. Groeben (1994) has stressed the necessity of adapting methods so as to suit current changes and extensions of the subject matter of ESL, such as the inclusion of other media; and Ibsch has repeatedly expressed concern over the neglect of complex issues, such as the reception of longer texts or text reception by experts (1994, 1998). (Schreier, 2001, p. 35)

To the above, Schreier also adds the problem of how to analyse longer stretches of text (indeed, novels), how to control the variables respondents are being assessed on (questionnaires and multiple choice forms to be filled in on computer screens) and how to collect 'think aloud protocols' (Schreier, 2001, p. 35). In sum, there have been suggestions that vouch for an inclusion of 'the so-called qualitative methods as they have been developed in the social sciences (Andringa, 1998; Groeben, 1994; Ibsch, 1998)' (Schreier, 2001, p. 35). For further work by ESL scholars see Cupchik and Leonard (2001), Hakemulder (2000, 2004), Hanauer (2001), Steen (2003), van Peer and Hakemulder (2006).

See also *corpus stylistics* (Key Branches), *Catherine Emmott*, *Willie van Peer* (Key Thinkers).

Feminist stylistics

Feminist stylistics aims at utilizing stylistic tools for the investigation of those concerns and preoccupations traditionally identified in feminist approaches to the study of language. Like feminist studies in general, a feminist stylistic perspective is keen to flag up gender issues although the focus crucially shifts to the linguistic (and also multimodal) manifestations of these concerns. As Mills puts it: 'Feminist stylistics is concerned with the analysis of the way that questions of gender impact on the production and interpretation of texts' (Mills, 2006, p. 221). She goes on to describe the way this branch has developed from its incipient applications to the present moment and highlights its main focus as being the following:

> Rather than assuming that notions of gender are simply a question of discriminatory messages about sex difference embedded in texts, feminist

> stylistics is concerned with unravelling the complex messages which may be deduced from texts and also with analyzing the way that readers piece together or resist these messages. (Mills, 2006, p. 221)

Contrary to what might have been the case in the past, recent feminist views on the crucial role of language to project social and political standpoints is not circumscribed to perpetually alleging the existence of discriminatory values. Instead, feminist stylistic views are more interested in spelling out those values that do exist in texts, whether these may be prototypically patriarchal or not. In addition, recent feminist stylistic positions also acknowledge that binary considerations of gender as simply male or female are deeply reductive as neither males nor females form a homogeneous or discrete group.

If a feminist perspective is to continue being successful, Mills claims (2006, p. 221), it is necessary that scholars are capable of moving on from an exclusive textual analysis performed at the micro-level of language (that is, the use of the generic 'he', or generic nouns to encode sexism), to a more comprehensive discourse level which will ensure, for instance, the investigation of linguistic structures such as direct or indirect speech, and the way these are exploited with reference to male and female characters, or the study of lexical collocations in relation to the prototypical language patterns associated with male and female textual entities (Mills, 2006, p. 221).

Feminist stylistics scholars have been particularly prolific at producing accounts of the way the micro-level of language encodes ideologically-loaded messages, especially those in which female characters are presented in a disadvantageous social position. The now classic study by Burton (1982), for instance, illustrates this point clearly. Her analysis of Sylvia Plath's semi-autobiographical novel *The Bell Jar* (1963) highlights the main protagonist's lack of control when, due to her precarious mental state, she is taken to a mental institution and is subjected to electric shock treatment. Burton uses a transitivity analysis to illustrate the protagonist's powerlessness as she is never presented as an actor in the text. Instead, most of the many material action processes used in the extract discussed by Burton identify the female protagonist as the goal of those actions in a way that underscores her incapacitated state. As Simpson confirms, 'Burton argues provocatively for a political dimension in textual interpretation and suggests that links between literary analysis and political standpoint can be articulated clearly through systematic and principled methods of analysis' (Simpson, 2004, pp. 185–6), for which endeavour feminist stylistics seems especially suited.

This focus on the marriage of political and social dimensions to literary-linguistic analysis has been taken on successfully elsewhere. In a collection of essays on female writing edited by Wales (1994), female scholars investigate not only the advantages but also the necessity of looking at feminism from the perspective afforded by linguistic means:

> They present an original and close analysis of a 'literary' text, or range of texts, by applying the methodology or framework of linguistic (grammatical, lexical, pragmatic, discourse) theories, in order to address directly questions and ideas that have been raised in feminist literary theory, criticism and linguistics about gender and style. (Wales, 1994, p. vii)

The tradition established by Burton can be felt in this volume as the contributors discuss the pervasiveness of gender concerns in different types of discourse as well as across various periods in time, all the time striving to account for such concerns via linguistic frameworks. Thus, Jeffries (1994) analyses the issue of 'apposition' in contemporary female poetry, Wareing (1994) looks at the submissive, passive roles generally associated with popular fiction protagonists and Calvo (1994) concentrates on the discourse tactics used by the character Celia in Shakespeare's *As You Like It* (1599), especially as far as her positive politeness strategies are concerned. This focus on textual practice typically seen in the 1990s has not waned as can be seen in Jeffries's (2007) recent work on the textual manifestations of the female body. Faithful to a primarily linguistic focus, this monograph looks at the way women's bodies are characterized, discussed and textually constructed in women's magazines. Jeffries argues that such construction both mirrors and projects twenty-first-century preoccupations such as appearance, looks or weight concerns. Mills (1995) has previously done some work on the construction of the female self, but has successfully also included multimodal analyses of printed adverts in which textual features are combined with various other graphological and photographic components to similarly embed prototypically patriarchal values in advertising for women.

Finally, because of their widespread impact, feminist positions have also been appropriated and exploited in narratological approaches to fiction:

> In its broadest sense, feminist narratology embraces the study of narrative (including its formal features, interpretation, and function) with particular

> attention to the ways in which these might inform or be informed by aspects of feminist theory. (Page, 2006, p. 482)

Further to the above, Page (2007b) advocates elsewhere for the complementarity of feminist narratological and feminist stylistic perspectives on fiction. She states that whereas feminist narratology has traditionally been saturated with preoccupations on aspects such as plot, focalization or voice, feminist stylistics has opted to concentrate on what Mills defines above as the micro-level of language, that is, the use of pronouns, nouns and phrases, among other linguistic structures. Other stylistic scholars prefer to merge the two branches or simply to place them in a continuum rather than seeing them as discrete categories. For further work on feminism and linguistic issues in general see Jackson (1993), Jones (1986), Litosseliti and Sunderland (2002), Montoro (2007, 2011) and Walsh (2001).

See also *critical stylistics* (Key Branches), *narratology*, *transitivity* (Key Terms).

Film stylistics/The stylistics of film

The application of traditionally textual tools of analysis to the study of film and moving images has resulted in a new approach within stylistics known as film stylistics or the stylistics of film. Some stylistics practitioners have claimed that many of the frameworks used in textual analysis can in fact be used to explicate formats other than the printed text. As is the case with textual stylistics, film stylistics aims for a more retrievable way of analysing cinematic forms based on frameworks which have already proven successful in the study of textual forms. McIntyre (2008), for instance, points out that this interest should hopefully result in a better understanding of the general construction of meaning in a variety of formats:

> It is also the case that stylisticians should consequently find themselves better able to describe and explain how particular textual effects are realized, how readers' interpretations are constructed and how these can be supported through analysis. Some stylisticians have already begun to engage with such issues, providing analyses of texts which incorporate significant multimodal elements (see, for example, Boeriis and Nørgaard, 2008 [sic]). Nonetheless, there remains a substantial amount of work to be done in this area. (McIntyre, 2008, p. 310)

It is also hoped that by incorporating new forms into the broad spectrum of textual material already used by stylisticians the discipline as a whole will benefit from the new challenges that these new formats will no doubt bring along. Nevertheless, such a recent interest on the part of stylisticians to look at cinematic varieties does not mean that filmic forms have not been previously investigated by other scholars. On the contrary, 'film studies' is a well-established discipline that has been concerned with the structural and functional features of film for quite some time. Some of its main proponents have, rather successfully, applied a variety of approaches to the study of films such as considerations of aspects of the theory of film (Carroll, 1996a, 1996b; Tredell, 2002), evaluations of movies as cultural constructs (Kellner, 1999; O'Regan, 1999), or assessments of filmic forms from a psychoanalytic perspective (Allen, 1999; Hochberg and Brooks, 1996), among others. A stylistic slant on the analysis of cinema cannot and should not do away with all these approaches; instead, it should incorporate all the findings from film studies as the basis on which to build further perspectives.

A particularly rich area of study for film analysts has been that of cinematic adaptations of (mainly, although not exclusively) fictional novels. One of the topics that adaptation scholars tend to raise is the way in which the original textual versions are transposed into a new medium, which also generally gives rise to the issue of fidelity of the latter towards the former. For instance, McFarlane (1996, 2000), Thomas (2000) and Whelehan (1999) all consider the relationship between the two forms but, as McFarlane (2000) points out, this is a question on which even the general public feels entitled to pass comments:

> It is [...] quite common to come out of a cinema after viewing an adaptation or to engage in casual conversation about it afterwards and to hear such comments as 'Why did they change the ending?' or 'She was blonde in the book' or, almost inevitably, 'I think I liked the book better'. (McFarlane, 2000, p. 165)

Besides this concern with the faithfulness with which textual forms are translated into cinematic formats, film scholars interested in incorporating stylistic approaches into their analyses have focused on the way existing stylistic frameworks can aid to explain fiction's potential for trans-medial manifestations. For instance, Forceville (2002a) suggests that the already-existing models for narrative analysis should be re-evaluated in light of the increasing multimodal manifestations of fictional forms:

> Since stories increasingly take on pictorial and mixed-medial forms, narratology needs to investigate to what extent narrative devices exceed the boundaries of a specific medium. One way to examine this issue is to focus on film adaptations of narratologically complex novels or stories. (Forceville, 2002a, p. 119)

Forceville succeeds in achieving such an aim by looking into the way non-verbal means are exploited in the filmic version (Schrader, 1990) of Ian McEwan's *The Comfort of Strangers* (1981) to convey the same sense of confusion created via free indirect speech and thought in the printed form. Other traditionally stylistic phenomena whose film manifestations have been analysed are mind style (Montoro, 2010a, 2010b), character dialogue (McIntyre, 2008), the functioning of speech acts in film dialogue (Short, 2007b) and the possible pedagogical-stylistic applications of film (Montoro, 2006b).

Finally, stylisticians are also beginning to pay attention to the rather enriching research output emerging from scholars working within a systemic-functional tradition and multimodal texts. Of special interest are the new attempts at combining computerized methods of analysis with the study of the moving image, broadly understood as those formats which employ dynamic pictures, be it in the form of films, adverts, documentaries, computer-generated imagery, etc. For instance, Baldry and Thibault (2006) have devised a rather exhaustive way of looking at multimodal texts based on multimodal concordancers which are capable of monitoring several items (sound, movement, colour or verbal input) in the various semiotic modes which can simultaneously be at work in the formats encompassed by the notion of the moving image, that is the sonic, the musical, the pictorial or the linguistic modes. Their rather thorough annotated descriptions of multimodal texts allow for a more comprehensive analysis of film, adverts or documentaries as multi-layered pieces of discourse. For further work on film stylistics from a systemic-functional perspective see Baldry (2004), O'Halloran (2004), Pun (2008) and Tseng (2008). For further issues concerning the interface between literature and film see the recently launched journal *Adaptation*.

See also *mind style*, *multimodality* (Key Terms).

Formalist stylistics

Formalist stylistics refers to the type of stylistic work done from the 1910s to the 1930s by a diverse group of theoreticians known as the Russian Formalists and later taken up by stylisticians, especially in Britain and the United States, in the 1960s and early 1970s. The Russian Formalists were a fairly heterogeneous group of people consisting primarily of members of the Moscow Linguistic Circle (founded 1915) and the Petrograd Society for the Study of Poetic Language (founded 1916). Common to these were an interest in poetic language and a wish to make literary inquiry more 'scientific' by modelling it on linguistics and thereby anchoring it solidly in observations about the formal features of the texts in question. The overriding interest of the formalist approach was in poetic form, or 'literariness' in Jakobson's terminology (1960), which led to a focus on elements of the literary text which made it 'literary' and set it apart from other types of text.

According to Jakobson's model of communication (1960), the poetic function of language is dominant in texts which 'focus on the message for its own sake', i.e., in texts where lexical, grammatical or phonological choices, for instance, draw attention to themselves and hence to the poetic nature of the text. Formal features such as parallelism and deviation from the linguistic norm are seen as stylistic features which would mark the text as literary, or poetic. While the poetic function is seen as the dominant function of poetry, it is not exclusive to that genre, but may also occur in other types of text as in Jakobson's own example of the political slogan for Dwight D. Eisenhower: 'I like Ike'. A similar approach to the poetic function of language is expressed by Victor Shklovsky, who introduced the concept of 'defamiliarization' (*ostranenie*,'making strange') as a central aspect of the technique of art:

> The technique of art is to make objects 'unfamiliar', to make forms difficult, to increase the difficulty and length of perception because the process of perception is an aesthetic end in itself and must be prolonged. *Art is a way of experiencing the artfulness of an object; the object is not important*. (Shklovsky, [1917] 1988, p. 20; Shklovsky's italics)

In Shklovsky's terms, the function of art is thus to defamiliarize the familiar to make us re-perceive what we have stopped noticing because of its familiarity and to make us recognize the artfulness of the expression itself. In line with formalist thinking, the Russian folklorist, Vladimir Propp, broadened the scope of formalist enquiry by setting out to identify the basic plot components and structures of folk narrative, resulting in his *Morphology of the Folktale* (1928).

Without doubt, the work done by the Russian Formalists was seminal to the growth of stylistics in the 1960s and early 1970s, but the formalist approach to stylistic analysis has also had its critics. In particular, formalist stylistics has been criticized for its overriding interest in linguistic form at the expense of considerations about the function and effects of the formal features put up for examination. Another point of criticism concerns the tendency in formalist stylistics to investigate literature in isolation from contextual factors such as the social and historical contexts of the text. In Weber's words,

> the problem with these formalist stylistic analyses is that they strike one as mechanical, lifeless, sterile exercises, and largely irrelevant to the interpretation of the literary work that they are describing. And if the critics try to ascribe some function or meaning to the formal patterns that they have uncovered, then a huge leap of faith is required to move from description to interpretation. (Weber, 1996, p. 2)

Others, as, for instance, Stanley Fish (1973), have criticized formalist stylistics for its claim to scientific objectivism and for ignoring the role of the reader in the identification of stylistic effects.

Later examples of formalist stylistics were those inspired by Chomsky's generative grammar. Here the focus was likewise placed on form, but the analysis now pivoted on the rules which lie behind the generation of grammatical sentences. Altogether, the Chomskyan approach never grew to have many practitioners in stylistics except from a US-based branch investigating the application of generative ideas to the study of metre.

See also *foregrounding* (Key Terms), *Noam Chomsky*, *Roman Jakobson* (Key Thinkers).

Functionalist stylistics

After a period of stylistic concern with poetic form relatively detached from considerations about the contexts, functions and interpretational significance of the formal phenomena under investigation (see *formalist stylistics*), stylistics took a functional turn in the late 1970s. According to Leech:

> Functionalism (in the study of language) is an approach which tries to explain language not only internally, in terms of its formal properties, but also externally, in terms of what language contributes to larger systems of which it is a part or subsystem. Whether we call these larger systems 'cultures', 'social systems', 'belief systems', etc. does not concern me. What is significant is that functionalist explanations look for relations between language and what is not language, whereas formalist explanations look for relations between the elements of the linguistic text itself. (Leech, 1987, p. 76)

The stylistic shift in focus towards functionalism was largely due to the emergence in linguistics of different functional approaches to language, and, in particular, to the development and general popularity of Halliday's functional model of language, now known as Systemic Functional Linguistics (Halliday, 1994; see also *M. A. K. Halliday*). At the crux of Hallidayan linguistics is an interest in language in use and a recognition of the fact that all language use takes place in context – situational as well as cultural. Every linguistic choice is seen as functional and meaningful and the grammatical labelling employed for linguistic analysis is intended to reflect semantic function rather than form (see *transitivity*). With the functionalist approach also came an interest in longer stretches of text (see, for instance, Halliday and Hasan, 1976) which enabled stylisticians to turn their attention more easily to longer texts such as narrative fiction and play texts.

The functionalist approach to language has had an impact in many corners of stylistics. Due to its focus on meaning-making in context, various contextually and/or ideologically oriented branches of stylistics such as feminist stylistics and critical stylistics (see entries) are indebted to the functionalist approach, as is much of the work done in pragmatic stylistics (see entry), which, among other things, subscribes to the functionalist concern with language in use.

See also *critical stylistics*, *feminist stylistics*, *formalist stylistics*, *pragmatic stylistics* (Key Branches), *M. A. K. Halliday* (Key Thinkers).

Historical stylistics

Historical stylistics is the application of stylistic approaches, tools and methods in order to investigate diachronically changing or stable styles of particular linguistic phenomena in historical (literary) texts, a particular situation, or a particular genre, for example. It also refers to the synchronic investigation of a particular historical (literary) text from a stylistic perspective (Adamson, 1995, 2001; Busse, 2006a, 2006b, 2007). The stylistic framework may include any of the approaches to which stylistics has branched out. It also embraces the description of the interplay between language usage and contexts as well as its theorizing, and a focus on how a historical text means what it does. As such, historical stylistics can be seen as an 'interdiscipline' (Leech, 2008, p. 1) between linguistic description and (literary) interpretation. Historical stylistics approaches have shown that the language-literature divide is a myth.

The dominating influence of the new technologies has also had an impact on historical stylistic approaches. Due to digitization, more historical texts are electronically available now and there are new ways of engaging with texts because the procedures we can take on to search, browse or link texts have been enormously simplified. For some, academic interest in the linguistics of older stages of English has in fact been revived, kept alive and eventually increased through the availability of corpora and through computerized texts analysis. However, number-crunching for its own sake does not constitute a complex historical stylistic framework, but the investigation of corpora may reveal phenomena which would otherwise have gone unnoticed. Yet, the potential of historical corpora for an explicit historical stylistic investigation has only been explored rather tentatively. This is despite the fact that literary texts constitute an important part of historical corpora and not simply due to the lack of spoken sources for historical periods.

Busse (2010a) introduces the term 'new historical stylistics' and argues that it is time to take stock and to describe the methodological, theoretical as well as practical challenges involved in this new enterprise. She also stresses that new historical stylistics can and should consolidate the potentials for stylistic investigation of historical texts with more traditional approaches. Furthermore, by explicitly pointing to the *stylistic* aspects of new historical stylistics and emphasizing the stylistic notion of *how* a historical text means, she stresses that 'new historical stylistics' contributes to issues at stake in modern historical linguistics alike.

The challenging task for a historical stylistician is that of the historical linguist in general: how do we make our interpretations valid (Fitzmaurice and Taavitsainen, 2007; Taavitsainen and Fitzmaurice, 2007). The historical stylistician also has to ask in what ways it is possible for us, as modern historical stylisticians, to reconstruct the past and establish the styles of a particular genre, a linguistic phenomenon, etc. Fitzmaurice and Taavitsainen (2007) draw our attention to the methodological flaws when investigating older stages of the English language through corpora or by means of form-to-function approaches. The focus of stylistics on an informed, systematic, retrievable and contextual analysis, which aims at describing and explaining how we come from the words on the page to its meaning, meets the need for securing the validation of data.

A new historical stylistic analysis of texts dating from older stages of the English language presupposes a comprehensive knowledge of the period, context and the language in which the text was produced. It also assumes knowledge of genre conventions, existent editions, copy texts and spelling variation, and the role of the editor as a mediator (Taavitsainen and Fitzmaurice, 2007, p. 21). In addition, a good starting point for a new historical stylistic analysis of a particular linguistic phenomenon, thus, would be to use findings of the phenomenon (or related features) in contemporary English, for example, and then investigate whether these findings can also be transferred to historical data. For example, for an investigation of speech, writing and thought presentation in a corpus of nineteenth-century narrative fiction (Busse, 2010a) it is necessary to use Modern English findings and investigations, but, at the same time, it is also necessary to put these results for Present-day English into a historical perspective of nineteenth-century discourse presentation and to account for nineteenth-century particularities. This includes a variety of contextual information which guides our reading: generic knowledge and encyclopaedic background knowledge as well as knowledge of historical schemas and scripts, belief systems, which may all lead to what Toolan (2009, p. 7) calls a 'colouring by the reader' – in the historical stylistic sense, the said modern reader reconstructing the past. But our modern assumptions about a historical text can also easily lead us astray. Language change always happens. It is visible in such grammaticalized forms as 'actually', which used to be an adverbial of time before it changed into a pragmatic epistemic stance marker indicating actuality and reality (Biber et al., 1999, p. 870; Busse, 2010b).

In the process of interpretation of historical (literary) data the creative interaction between quantitative and qualitative investigations is crucial to the new historical stylistic approach (Busse, 2010a). This interplay must avoid circularity, a research question which only matches the data, and number-crunching for its own sake (Taavitsainen and Fitzmaurice, 2007). However, it cannot rely only on individual and purely subjective readings alone. Cooperation between intuition and corpus linguistic methods (Semino and Short, 2004; McIntyre, 2007) is paramount for a new historical stylistic approach. Corpus-based investigations aim at identifying forms and repetitive patterns, but we need to situate them within their contexts, otherwise we only establish their frequency (Taavitsainen and Fitzmaurice, 2007, p. 18). It takes a human analyst to make sense and interpret the discourses at stake (Toolan, 2009, p. 16). Yet, the investigation of large amounts of data also provides us with a framework and a norm against which the results of a new historical stylistic investigation are measured to establish the discourses of a particular genre, the stylistic realization of a particular linguistic feature or text or to establish creative language in general.

Establishing (historical) linguistic and stylistic norms and irregularities relates to another highly crucial concept within stylistics that is also indispensable for new historical stylistics, namely the theory of foregrounding. The interplay between the analysis of a linguistic phenomenon in a historical text and the various contexts in which it occurs is highly complex. It allows the analyst to establish what changes, what remains constant, or, in other words, it allows analysts to establish the relationship between the conventional and the innovative (Taavitsainen and Fitzmaurice, 2007, p. 27). In order to measure and describe the levels of foregrounding (including deviation and parallelism) on a historical dimension, it is impossible to argue on a one-to-one basis that what occurs in a big historical reference corpus constitutes the ordinary or the norm. A more delicate and contextually based analysis is necessary, which deals with context(s) and envisages the notion of 'emergent grammar' or emergent styles (Taavitsainen and Fitzmaurice, 2007). Styles in historical texts are not always stable in terms of form-to-function or function-to-form, but may be constantly modulated within a historical framework. What constitutes a writer's motivated choice may, in the course of time, be a norm and become highly frequent. In addition, Leech's (2008) distinction between deviation on a primary, secondary and tertiary level needs to be seen as interdependent when exploring the effects of linguistic processes in historical contexts. Language norms, discourse specific norms as well as text-internal norms play a role when evaluating stylistic change and stability within a historical dimension.

In historical pragmatics (Jacobs and Jucker, 1995) and historical sociolinguistics much has been said and done to illustrate the usefulness of functionally situated approaches for broadening their scope and to illustrate what we know about the usage of English in former times. Written data has been accepted as a valuable and necessary source, and the time-span for the investigation of 'spoken' language is no longer restricted to Present-day English as can be seen, for example, in the extensive body of studies on the historical development of speech acts in English (for example, Jucker and Taavitsainen, 2000, 2008; Kohnen, 2000). An investigation of the relationship between language form and meaning within a new historical stylistics framework (Busse, 2010a) uses and enhances methods and terminology from historical pragmatics and historical sociolinguistics in order to discover both change and stability. Both a pragma-philological and a diachronic approach (Jacobs and Jucker, 1995), including a form-to-function and a function-to-form mapping, are seen in new historical stylistics as interdependent and too complex to be set apart from one another.

See also *corpus stylistics* (Key Branches).

Multimodal stylistics

Multimodal stylistics is a fairly new branch of stylistics which aims to broaden the modes and media to which stylistic analyses can be applied. Thus, the (extended multimodal) stylistic toolkit, in addition to being useful for the analysis of the printed word, can illuminate how other semiotic modes such as typography, colour, layout, visual images, etc. do also construct meaning (see e.g., Gibbons, 2010; Nørgaard, 2010b). From this stylistic perspective, all communication and all texts are considered multimodal – even conventional literary narratives without special visual effects, since written verbal language automatically and without exception involves both wording and typography (or graphology) as well as realization in space in terms of layout. Multimodal stylisticians furthermore broaden out the concept of, for instance, the novel to include not only the narrative of the wording and possible visual images, typography and layout but also the book cover, the paper quality and other aspects of the book's material realization. With its focus on meaning-making as a multi-semiotic phenomenon, multimodal stylistics thus also allows for more comprehensive stylistics analyses of drama and film (see Simpson and Montgomery, 1995; McIntyre, 2008; Montoro, 2010a; and entry on *film stylistics*).

The aim of multimodal stylistics is to develop as systematic descriptive 'grammars' of all semiotic modes as those already developed for the mode of wording (i.e., the lexical and grammatical aspects of verbal language). Much of the work in multimodal stylistics is based on research done more generally on multimodality by scholars like Kress and van Leeuwen (1996, 2001), O'Toole (1994), O'Halloran (2004), Baldry and Thibault (2006) and Bateman (2008), who base their theoretical and methodological framework on Halliday's 'social semiotics' (see *M. A. K. Halliday*); as well as by scholars like Forceville (1996) and Currie (2004), whose work on filmic multimodality is informed by cognitive theory. Multimodal stylisticians draw on the descriptive apparatus that these pioneers of multimodal thinking have developed for modes other than the verbal. In addition to wording, the semiotic modes most prominently involved in literary meaning-making are those of typography, layout and visual images.

The analysis of typography, for instance, focuses on the meaning-making potential of the visual side of verbal language. In this connection, the meanings created by various typographic features such as the use of italics, boldface and majuscules (i.e., capital letters) as well as of different typefaces and of lettering in different colours are considered and systematized. To this end, multimodal scholars (e.g., van Leeuwen, 2006b) have developed a system of characteristic typographic features to enable a detailed description of different typefaces and the characteristics that set them apart from other typefaces. To reflect the methodological affiliation to linguistics, these characteristic features are sometimes referred to as *distinctive features* (van Leeuwen, 2006b, pp. 147–52). Another way of systematizing typographic meaning-making involves the categorization of typography according to the semiotic principles behind the meanings created by the visual side of verbal language (van Leeuwen, 2005b; developed further by Nørgaard, 2009). One example of this is the use of majuscules to create the meaning of 'shouting'. Here the typographic salience of majuscules may be seen as *iconic* in that it visually imitates the sonic salience of someone shouting. Another example is the use of a typical typewriter font such as Courier to create the meaning of 'typewritten'. Here the relation between the typographic signifier and the signified may be characterized as *indexical*, since the typeface may be seen as a (fictive) indexical marker that the text has been produced by a typewriter. Other semiotic principles involved in typographic meaning-making are those of *symbol* and *discursive import*. Arguably, plain black typography in literary texts may be regarded as symbolic (in Peirce's sense of the word; see Peirce, 1931–58), since the relation between the visual side of the typographic signifier and that which is signified can be seen as unmotivated and arbitrary (see Nørgaard 2009 for a critical discussion of this). Discursive import, on the other hand, occurs when typographic signs and their associated meanings are 'imported' into a context where they did not previously belong (van Leeuwen, 2005b, p. 139). A good example of this is provided by Owens and Reinfurt (2005), who, albeit in different terms, discuss the discursive import of the typeface 'Data 70' from the electronic processing of cheques into entirely different contexts. Based on the typography of 'E13B' (known from cheques), which was designed as a typeface that could be read by machines, Data 70 is a fully fledged alphabet, which, with its associations of automated systems and computerization, has been imported discursively into the context of book covers, music albums, film titles, etc.

The analysis of layout aims to systematize the meanings created by the arrangement of text and images in the spatial layout of the page. One of the things examined in relation to layout is *information value* (Kress and van Leeuwen, 1996, pp. 186–211), that is, the question of whether special meaning is ascribed to the top and bottom, left and right, centre and margin of the page. A second issue concerns *linking* (van Leeuwen, 2005a, pp. 219–47), which refers to the ways in which different layout units are linked, whether they be verbal or visual, as well as the status the different modes hold in the communication: Do visual images, for instance, illustrate the verbal text, or do they create meanings that are not expressed verbally, and, if so, to what extent? Further compositional resources are those of *framing* and *salience*. Framing is a resource for connecting or disconnecting elements in a visual layout and is typically realized by lines, colour and/or blank space. The most frequent type of framing in literary texts is probably that constituted by margins and blank space. These layout features may, for instance, play a part in the construction of the meaning of 'different text', such as that of a letter, by demarcating the separation, and hence special status, of such text from the rest of the narrative. Salience, on the other hand, concerns elements which stand out, for instance, in the layout of the page. In written prose, such as that of Foer's novel, *Extremely Loud and Incredibly Close* (2005), photographic images and other visual effects are hence salient against the background of the rest of the text, and against the background of the genre conventions of the novel altogether. At the same time, however, elements in these photographic images may be salient in themselves such as the figure of a falling man in one of the photographs (Foer, 2005, p. 205), who is conspicuously distinctive against a black and white background, which is respectively suggestive of one of the sides of the Twin Towers of the World Trade Center and the sky. The salience of the falling man in this image is arguably strengthened by him being the only human figure in the image and by the (for a human, unusual and fateful) process of falling – or floating – mid-air itself, of which he is represented as the participant (see Nørgaard, 2010a).

For the analysis of visual images, whether they be drawings or photographic images, Kress and van Leeuwen's *Reading Images. The Grammar of Visual Design* (1996) provides a fairly comprehensive grammar delineating how the visual, like the verbal, may be seen to express ideational, interpersonal and compositional (Halliday's 'textual') meaning (see *M. A. K. Halliday*). According to Kress and van Leeuwen, visual images construct ideational meaning through the representation of participants, processes and circumstances (1996, pp. 43–118). Interpersonal meaning is created by the positioning of the viewer and is analysed in terms of what Kress and van Leeuwen call gaze, size of frame/social distance, perspective and visual modality (1996, pp. 119–80). Compositional meaning, in turn, is realized through information structure, linking, framing and salience (1996, pp. 181–229). By combining aspects of Kress and van Leeuwen's visual grammar with a more traditional stylistic analysis of the dialogue of McKellen's (1995) film version of *Richard III*, McIntyre (2008) demonstrates how the visual may be described as systematically as the verbal, how the verbal and the visual interact and, ultimately, how a multimodal approach allows the analyst to make a more comprehensive analysis of a filmed play than that captured by a stylistic analysis of the verbal text only.

From a cognitive perspective, Forceville (1999, 2002a), for instance, works on the interface of novels and their cinematic adaptations. He illustrates how multimodal formats need to be viewed as manifestations of the same mental constructs responsible for the realization of linguistic forms, the particular ones he looks into being linguistic metaphors (1999) and representations of free indirect thought (2002a). Forceville (1996) also analyses advertising discourse as it appears in print and in billboards from a cognitive multimodal perspective and concludes that verbo-pictorial metaphors are clear examples of how conceptual metaphors are indeed mental constructs capable of manifesting themselves in more than one semiotic mode.

Altogether, the multimodal take on stylistics would seem a promising approach for analysts who acknowledge that all texts, including literary ones, are multimodal, and who wish to employ and further develop tools for the description of multimodal meaning-making which are as delicate and systematic as those traditionally employed in stylistics for analysis of verbal forms.

See also *film stylistics* (Key Branches), *multimodality* (Key Terms), *Charles Forceville, M. A. K. Halliday, Theo van Leeuwen* (Key Thinkers).

Narratology

Narratology, far from being a subdomain of stylistics, is a fully-fledged discipline in its own right. Narratological approaches to the study of texts have been included in the work of humanities scholars since Russian Formalism took hold of literary studies, although the beginnings of narratology are generally acknowledged to have primarily been informed by the structuralist views of the 1960s. Thus, although not to be classified as a sub-branch of stylistics, this discipline has traditionally offered plenty of working tools to stylisticians, especially to those concerned specifically with narrative fiction. Herman (2007b) broadly defines the discipline as follows:

> An approach to narrative inquiry developed during the heyday of structuralism in France. Instead of working to develop interpretations of individual narratives, narratologists focused on how to describe narrative viewed as a semiotic system – that is, as a system by virtue of which people are able to produce and understand stories. (Herman, 2007b, p. 280)

We would be wrong, however, to assume that narratology can be conceived of as a univocal body of research. Instead, the multifarious interpretations as to how to best describe the boundaries of this scholarly enterprise are sometimes dictated by a definition of the object of study this discipline is interested in, that is, the notion of narrative itself, but such endeavour is not an easy task either: 'Since narratology is the science of narrative (or a theory of narrative), its very scope depends on the definition of the latter' (Prince, 2003b, p. 1). As is customary in the humanities and the arts, it seems more profitable to avoid a stern definition of narrative and narratology so that the various trends, sub-branches and developments can be accommodated. There seems to be some consensus, though, as far as the various phases that narratological studies have lived through. These delimitations are, once more, made very broadly and with lots of scope for further fine-tuning, but most scholars (for instance,

Cornils and Schernus, 2003; Darby, 2001; Kindt and Müller, 2003) appear to agree on the existence of three major stages in the development of narratology, sometimes re-distributed and amalgamated into two. Herman (2007a) opts for the latter option and distinguishes two main periods which he terms the 'classical' and 'postclassical' (p. 13) approaches to the study of narrative:

> I use the term *classical approaches* to refer to the tradition of research that, rooted in Russian Formalist literary theory, was extended by structuralist narratologists starting in the mid 1960s, and refined and systematized up through the early 1980s by scholars such as Mieke Bal, Seymour Chatman, Wallace Martin, Gerald Prince, and others. I also include under the rubric of classical approaches work in the Anglo-American tradition of scholarship on fictional narrative; some of these scholars were influenced by and in turn influenced the Formalist-structuralist tradition. (Herman, 2007a, p. 12)

In this camp, we find the work of authors such as Tomashevsky, Shklovsky and Propp; Shklovsky's distinction ([1925]1990) between *fabula* and *sjuzhet*, for instance, or Propp's *Morphology of the Folktale* ([1928]1968) became some of the referents on which further perspectives on narrative were subsequently built. Kindt and Müller (2003) are among those scholars that prefer to divide the classical stage into two separate phases:

> The first phase, beginning in the mid-nineteenth century in Europe and the USA [. . .] took its material from three main sources: the remnants of normative rhetoric and poetics, the practical knowledge of novelists and the observations of literary critics [. . .]. It was only in its second phase that 'narratology' became a distinct subdiscipline of textual studies, after the term first used in 1969 by Tzvetan Todorov in his *Grammaire du Décaméron* found wide international acceptance. Todorov's account of the aims and themes of narratology was heavily influenced by Russian and Czech Formalism and structural linguistics [. . .]. Subsequently, however, the 'high structuralism' of these generative grammarians achieved far less international currency than the 'low structuralism' of Gérard Genette. (Kindt and Müller, 2003, pp. v–vi)

Whether the first stage is divided into two sub-groups or considered as a unified whole does not detract from the fact that the scope of the so-called classical narratology extends well into the 1980s, when its focus on traditional structuralist methodologies and concerns starts to wane under the influence of new trends emerging from other humanities and social science disciplines such as anthropology, psychoanalysis, cognitive linguistics and cognitive psychology. Irrespective of whether the initial stages are amalgamated or not, most scholars claim that the revival of the discipline took place in the 1990s when the third period of narratology is said to have started:

> Narratology, it is argued, is now more alive than ever before, having undergone something of a renaissance since the 1990s after a period of stagnation and crisis during which its demise was repeatedly proclaimed. The 1990s produced such a proliferation of heterogeneous approaches that narratologists such as David Herman find it more appropriate to speak of 'narratologies' in the plural. (Cornils and Schernus, 2003, p. 138)

Whether scholars refer to this new era as the third stage or whether they adopt the 'postclassical' term coined by Herman, most of them convene in acknowledging that the new phase is fraught with influences and interdisciplinary links with cognate areas. This has permitted new forms of inquiry into the nature of narrative forms to be incorporated into the already existing frameworks. Of special interest to stylisticians, in particular to those exploring the cognitive dimensions of literary processing, is the new application of cognitive theories to the study of narratives:

> Study of the cognitive dimensions of stories and storytelling has become an important subdomain within the field of narrative analysis. Concerned both with how people understand narratives and with narrative itself as a mode of understanding, cognitive approaches have been brought to bear on stories in a variety of media [. . .]. Equally various are the disciplinary traditions from which cognitive approaches borrow descriptive and explanatory tools. Source disciplines include cognitive linguistics; pragmatics; discourse analysis; narratology; communication theory; anthropology; stylistics; cognitive, evolutionary, and social psychology; rhetoric; computer science; literary theory; and philosophy. (Herman, 2006a, p. 452)

This acceptance of influences from such a wide spectrum of disciplines is positively conducive to cross-fertilization and general enriching of both narratology and stylistics as the latest work on narrative carried out by stylisticians, as much as the publications by narratologists on stylistic issues, proves (Gibbons, 2010; Herman, 2005b, 2006b; McHale, 2007; Page, 2007b).

See also *cognitive stylistics/cognitive poetics* (Key Branches), *narrative*, *narrator* (Key Terms).

Pedagogical stylistics

Pedagogical stylistics has at least two facets. One embraces the pedagogical usefulness and potential of stylistics for teaching (the language of) literature. The other includes the role of stylistics in L1 and L2 pedagogies, that is, the teaching of (English) language through literature.

The complex developments within literary criticism over the last 20 years have affected the interplay between literature, language and language education in the language classroom. Reflections on the author's intentions, textuality, measurements of responses of readers as well as discussions about literary texts to be included in the canon formation influence approaches to the way literature is taught and the view that in learning a foreign language its literature should be read. In turn, because of the role of English in the world and the status of World Englishes, there has been a growing awareness of the need for highly profiled environments in which English is taught as a Foreign Language (EFL), for example. Research in second and foreign language studies and in pedagogical stylistics has increased immensely. The pedagogical aim of stylistics in teaching (literary) language and how this language functions is based on how we as readers – native and non-native – come from the word on the page to its meanings. Stylistics as a method can help explain how a particular use of language works within a text for both the native and the non-native speaker and how texts are interpreted and understood by the reader.

According to Carter and Stockwell (2008, p. 249), pedagogical stylistics developed in the 1970s and became very practical as one way of evading the attacks levelled at stylistics (see *critique of stylistics*). To a large extent, language was then taught also using literary texts which represented a rather attractive option for some L2 learners as contemporary literature was often chosen. Some language teachers were of the opinion that works that prominently made a foregrounded use of linguistic tools were especially suited to show language in action. For others the former would only be appropriate for advanced learners. But also lately a more concerned view has been voiced which stresses that stylistics has contributed to methodologies in the teaching of literature and that, therefore, L1 and L2 methods are embedded in stylistics.

Textual transformations, which highlight the stylistic notion of meaning as choice and the theory of foregrounding, are crucial. For example, cloze procedures, where students are asked to insert a missing word in a verse line to later evaluate the author's choice, are commonly used. Alternatively, comparative analysis and re-writing texts from different perspectives are also widespread in L2 environments and in stylistics. These demand a different set of linguistic choices and knowledge of the linguistic features of a variety of genres and text types in order to transform, for example, a poem into a blog. Readers are guided through an active process of reading and learners become explorers of linguistic, textual and cultural transformations in which the text is seen as a corrective of complex linguistic structures. These observed linguistic choices construe meaning and they make the interpretation by the reader as reader or the reader as learner retrievable.

The notions of creativity and literariness are explained against the background of various norms and conventions (see Brumfit and Carter, 1986; Carter and McRae, 1996; Cook, 1994, 2000; Carter, 2004; Pope, 1994, 2002). Furthermore, Carter (2004) stresses the fact that everyday language is also creative and that this has an impact on the understanding of literature: 'the teaching of literature in a variety of cultural contexts may be better informed by understandings of the pervasively creative character of everyday language [. . .]. The idea that creativity exists in a remote world of literary genius can be demotivating to the apprentice student of literature, especially in contexts where a second or foreign language literature is taught' (2004, p. 213). Stylistics has contributed to the methodologies of teaching literature and this in turn has affected developments in L1 and L2 pedagogy.

As Carter (2007a) explains, the new developments within stylistics present not only new challenges but also new exciting opportunities for the teaching of stylistics:

> The intellectual excitement of cognitive poetics (with its re-tuning of the significance of language processing), the awesome power of corpus linguistics, the depth and richness of studies in narrative analysis, the ever

> new angles on the literariness of language – all now take place routinely alongside developing opportunities for web-based teaching and learning, the pedagogic possibilities afforded by hypertexts, more refined rhetorical-analytical tools, enhanced paradigms for greater empirical investigation, more and more successful integration of quantitative and qualitative methodologies. (Carter, 2007a, p. viii)

The new branches within and influences on stylistics certainly need to be addressed from a pedagogical perspective. Issues that are now investigated as a result of so many new perspectives are, for example, how learners appropriate themselves of other discourses, how stylistics helps show the contextual nature of all texts and a need for close investigation and how a stylistic analysis of a literary text can be used to promote identity and feeling (Watson and Zynger, 2007). Also, Mick Short's (2007c) web-based learning environment (http://www.lancs.ac.uk/fass/projects/stylistics/), which introduces students to stylistics, illustrates not only the versatile didactic and pedagogical potential of stylistics, but also discusses the challenges of introducing students to stylistics in a web-based format (Short, Busse, Plummer, 2006). For further references and investigations see Cook (1994), Carter and McRae (1996), McCarthy and Carter (1994), Short (1989, 1996).

See also *critique of stylistics* (Key Terms).

Pragmatic stylistics

Pragmatic stylistic approaches combine approaches from pragmatics and stylistics to answer questions about how (literary) language is used in context and how it contributes to the characterization of the protagonists in a literary piece of art or how power structures are created and so on. Pragma-stylistic investigations have influenced general pragmatic approaches, methods and theories on both a synchronic and a diachronic dimension, too. Especially in historical pragmatic investigations, which include a pragma-philological and a diachronic pragmatic analysis, literary texts have been a source frequently drawn on, because there is no spoken data available for historical periods, and play texts constitute an important source to explore 'the spoken', although admittedly, this is the 'constructed' spoken language. Other points of intersection between pragmatics and stylistics include the focus on context and on the effects of the interactional strategies used in context. Furthermore, pragmatic stylistics has stressed a comprehensive holistic approach to conversational interaction and includes the complex interplay between norms and deviations as well as forms and meanings. On the assumption that norms and conventions from natural language usage are built upon in literary conversation, those pragma-stylistic findings have something to say about linguistic realizations of politeness strategies in general. The same holds true for the realization of speech acts or discourse markers in literary texts. Pragmatic-stylistic approaches and multimodal stylistics have also drawn attention to the need for including other semiotic modes in order to account for the interplay between language and the visual, etc. in films, for example (Busse, 2006b; McIntyre, 2008). More recent approaches combine pragma-stylistic investigations with corpus stylistic approaches and relate the identification of linguistic patterns to interactive features. In addition, within a broad and comprehensive framework that resulted also from the pragmatic analysis of historical texts, the pragma-stylistic focus on language as exchange and the contextual features of language also embraces the analysis of fictional narrative passages, e.g., the relationship between narrative passages and discourse presentation or a combination of pragma-stylistic and cognitive stylistic considerations (see also Toolan, 2000).

Underlying a pragma-stylistic investigation of dialogue are some central questions of stylistic analysis: Why and how does a play text/dialogue mean what it does? What is the specific style of a conversational exchange? How can it be analysed? What are the effects of the linguistic choices made? What do these choices say about the characters'/speakers' interpersonal relations and their inherent power structures? How is humour created? Why do we perceive interactional exchange as, for example, impolite? The systematic, rigorous application of pragma-linguistic concepts and tools helps answer those questions. Short (1989, 1996, 2007b) illustrates the systematic investigation of play texts, their specific style(s) and the relationship of play texts with performance. Short (1989) develops a stylistic tool kit for the exploration of conversational exchange and draws on areas of pragmatics and discourse analysis (areas which do not play a major role in the analysis of poetry, for example).

Major foci of the pragma-stylistic tool kit are on contextual features of language use and on seeing conversation as exchange. The notion of context may of course include various aspects: for example, what Schiffrin (1987) has described as the physical, personal and cognitive context, or what we would generally understand as social, cultural, linguistic, authorial or editorial contexts of production and reception.

Norms and conventions of authentic everyday communication can be seen as a base for the interpretation of fictional characters' use of speech. Otherwise, it would not be possible to detect foregrounded use of politeness markers, irony, over-decorous greetings or comedy. Dialogue in drama or in passages of speech presentation in narrative fiction is clearly 'constructed' (or purpose-built) dialogue because the author has been in control and the mediator of it. Nevertheless, pragmatic findings can be applied to its analysis because the principles of social interaction are exploited. 'Dramatic action, as Herman (1995, p. 6) points out, becomes meaningful in relation to the "authenticating conventions" that are drawn from the wider world of affairs in which the dramatic activity is embedded' (cited in Simpson, 1998, p. 41). This process of identification is of course rendered more complex in the case of historical stylistic investigation of e.g., play texts from older stages of the English language (see *historical stylistics*).

The question of how a reader perceives conversational exchange and interprets it also leads us to an illustration of the discourse architecture of prototypical dramatic texts. According to Short (1996), these comprise two discourse levels. One relates to the discourse level between writer and reader (or audience in the case of a performance), the other is embedded and relates to the discourses exchanged between character and character.

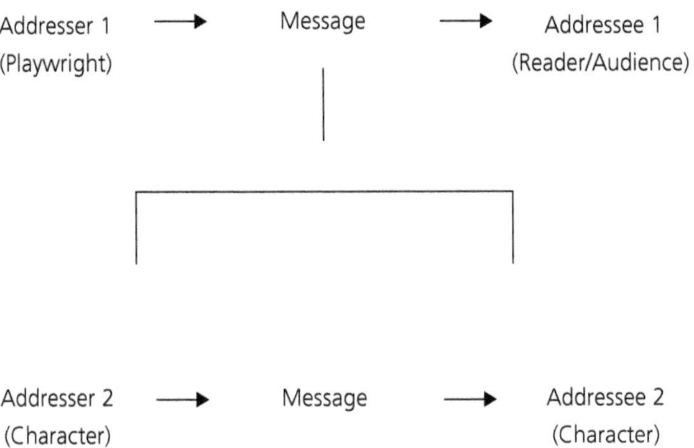

An example from Shakespeare's *Hamlet* will exemplify this:

King But now, my cousin Hamlet, and my son,
Ham. [Aside] A little more than kin and less than kind
King How is it that the clouds still hang on you?
Ham. Not so, my lord, I am too much in the sun.

(*Hamlet* 1.2.64–7)

The inherent nature of conversation – that of exchange – can be seen here, because we find four turns, one of which, as the stage direction from the edition taken – the *Riverside Shakespeare* (Evans, 1997) – informs us, is explicitly uttered with the writer-audience level in mind, as it is an 'aside'; the other three are relevant to the character-character interaction, but are also addressed to the reader or the audience during a performance. The interactive features of these utterances are also expressed by means of the address forms exchanged. However, the lexical choices are different: King Claudius chooses a personal name, 'Hamlet', and two kinship terms, 'cousin' and 'my son'; Hamlet only resorts to the conventional title 'my lord' (Busse, 2006b). The choice of address terms construes, at least superficially, their power structures. Even if we did not know the social relations between Hamlet and Claudius, their choice of address forms would allow us to infer that, conventionally speaking, Claudius's position is higher up the social ladder than that of Hamlet, because King Claudius is allowed to address Hamlet by his personal name. Yet, the frequency by which Claudius uses these forms of address also illustrates how much he tries to gain favour with Hamlet. The King alludes to both of Hamlet's roles within his nuclear family: that of being his nephew and his son, a kinship relation which results from King Claudius's marriage to Gertrude, Hamlet's mother. Hamlet's reply is cautious and reserved. He uses a very conventional and frequently used form of address, 'my lord', which denies any intimate and personal kinship relations. With his use of positive politeness strategies, on the one hand, and his severe moral criticism of their marriage, on the other, Hamlet also tries to redress his sadness about his father's death/murder. Hamlet's homophonous pun on 'son' and 'sun', which stresses that he is too much in the light of the present King, with 'sun' being the royal emblem, is an indicator of his realization of evil. This last point draws our attention to the need for including in the interpretation process contextual information of Early Modern England as well as of the linguistic context. At the same time, it would have been ideal for the historically situated interpretation of those lines to include editorial considerations. But for ease of understanding, a modern spelling edition is drawn on.

This example also shows another fundamental question to be addressed in the pragma-stylistic analysis of play texts: that is the relationship between the play as a text and as performance. A pragma-stylistic point of view stresses that a sensitive analysis of drama can be achieved through the analysis of the text and that this stylistic analysis provides the analyst with a framework as to how a text should be performed. Productions of plays are then seen as variations of the same interpretation of a play, but not as new interpretations (each performance of a production is then a set of different instantiations) (Short, 1998, p. 8). In the example above, the stage directions inform us that the utterance 'A little more than kin and less than kind' is addressed to the audience, who is in the know about Hamlet's real state of mind. Claudius also criticizes Hamlet for still mourning his father's death, which gives an additional clue as to Hamlet's visual expressions during the performance.

Next to the classic stylistic tool kit of investigating graphological information, sound structure, grammatical structure or lexical patterning, pragmatic models like speech act theory, Grice's (1975) 'Cooperative Principle', politeness, implicatures or turn-taking management (see entries) are among the pragma-stylistic approaches frequently applied to the language used in play texts. The individual or multiple application of these discourse areas addresses such questions as how conversation functions as exchange and how it reveals (power, social or interpersonal) relations among participants. Background knowledge of the world, which is also frequently arranged in schemata, plays as important a role for the pragma-stylistic analysis of play texts as does knowledge of sociolinguistic conventions or of the various contexts – social, cultural, political, production, linguistic, editorial – in which the play (text) is set.

Due to space restrictions, it is impossible to elaborate on all pragmatic concepts that lend themselves fruitfully to a pragma-stylistic investigation. Therefore, only some of the major (and most frequently applied concepts) will be explained, although this does, by no means, entail that what linguists call the establishment of 'phatic communion' or 'adjacency pairs' is less important for the identification of fictional dialogue as exchange.

The 'turn' is one of the central concepts of interaction and conversation analysts of the ethnomethodological school have illustrated that, unlike our expectations, in ordinary conversation, turn-management is systematic (Sacks et al., 1978) and rule-governed (see entry *turn-taking*). The order of speech in drama suggests itself to an analysis of the turn-taking management. Important questions to be asked are then, for example, who speaks to whom or who interrupts and who has the longest/shortest turns (Short, 2007c). In the example mentioned above, King Claudius switches topics and attempts to initiate a conversational exchange with Hamlet and to gain favour with him.

Another important concept to be drawn on for a pragma-stylistic analysis of a play text is that of Grice's (1975) cooperative principle, which also explains why, as readers, we are able to draw inferences (see entry). Conversation is assumed to be goal-directed. These goals are usually fulfilled because we co-operate in conversation and follow the maxims of quantity, quality, manner and relation. Failing to observe one of those maxims (violating or flouting it, for example) is due to the fact that speakers often say something indirectly. In order to understand the irony of Hamlet's reply 'I'm too much in the sun' it is useful to explain how the maxim of quality is flouted on the discourse level of writer and audience and violated on the character-character level, when seen from Claudius's perspective. Claudius must perceive Hamlet's reply 'I'm too much in the sun' as uncooperative (violating the maxims of quality and quantity as well as relevance), because Hamlet does not initially confirm that he is mourning his father's death. On the contrary, his reference to the 'sun' superficially refers to him as being allegedly in good spirits. But, as mentioned, it also ambiguously criticizes Claudius's usurpation of the throne and of fatherhood, which is indicated by the noun 'sun'. The audience, however, knows that the Ghost of Hamlet's father has shown Hamlet Claudius's murder of Hamlet's father. Hence, the audience will understand the pun on 'sun' and 'son'.

The stylistic application of Grice's (1975) cooperative principle frequently goes hand in hand with the identification of politeness strategies. Among the frequently used models are Brown and Levinson's (1987) work on politeness (see entry). Claudius's choice of vocative forms could be seen as address strategies that are directed both at Hamlet's positive and negative face, while Hamlet's choice of 'my lord' is rather unmarked because this address form is one of the most frequently used forms in the Early Modern English period (Busse, 2006b), which also undergoes a process of semantic generalization. As such, it is not addressed at Claudius's social position or aims at establishing a bond between them.

The identification of politeness strategies also involves the ability to relate linguistic realizations of utterances to their illocutionary forces. In other words, it involves knowledge of speech acts (see entry *speech act theory*). The pragma-stylistic analysis of speech acts and determining their illocutionary force through the way they are linguistically realized is not an easy task, especially if non-contemporary drama is observed (see *historical stylistics*). Politeness phenomena in historical texts cannot be compared on a one-to-one basis to Present-day realizations of speech acts because, for example, in Early Modern English requests there was less hedging and less indirectness (Culpeper and Archer, 2008). Furthermore, felicity conditions for the realization of a speech act need to be carefully considered. In the example from *Hamlet*, it is essential to realize the homophony between 'sun' and 'son', and at the same time, to know about the meaning of 'sun' as an indicator of royal status. Otherwise, Hamlet's utterance cannot be identified as an insult on the writer-audience discourse level, and it cannot be understood why, on the character-character level, initially at least, Hamlet's utterance is ambiguous between a compliment and an insult.

Due to the attention paid mainly to poetry by early stylisticians, stylistic investigation of fictional/literary text types containing dialogue and (inter-) action first emerges as late as the 1980s. Pragmatic approaches were certainly around at the end of the 1960s, but the tardiness in applying them within a stylistic framework may be a result of the character of spoken conversation, which has for a long time been seen as debased when compared with written expository or literary texts. Also, stylistics had to get used to investigating pieces of texts larger than poems. To date, the stylistic investigation of literary play texts or (constructed, fictional) dialogue has not as frequently been pursued as that of narrative fiction or poetry. Yet, especially since the 1990s, there has been a more extensive pragma-stylistic investigation of play texts and an extensive broadening of the pragma-stylistic tool kit, which also interplays with corpus, cognitive and multimodal stylistic approaches.

See also *historical stylistics* (Key Branches), *cooperative principle cooperation*, *politeness*, *presupposition and entailment*, *speech act theory*, *turn-taking*, *vocatives and naming* (Key Terms).

Reader response criticism

Reader response criticism is a label that encompasses a series of critical approaches to literary studies popular since the 1960s and 1970s. Reader response criticism does not, in fact, refer to a unified body of work but embodies a series of theoretical strands all linked by their concern with the role of the reader in literary interpretation. As Wales summarizes:

> There was the affective stylistics of Fish (1970f) in the United States and of Riffaterre (1959f) in France; the structuralist poetics of Culler (1975) with his literary competence; and the semics of Eaton (1966f). [. . .] Reader response criticism, like post-structuralism, tried to move away from the text as critical focus, and even more so from (the intentions of) the author. (Wales, 2001, p. 331)

Most of these movements strove to separate themselves from the previous text-centred concerns of New Criticism and formalism. As a result, they all highlight, albeit in different ways, the central role played by the reader viewed as active participant rather than as simple 'recipient' of the product that is the literary text. For instance, Fish's famous 'affective stylistics' (1980) primarily considers the emotional response of readers, but also bears in mind the psychological processes involved in text processing. The strand known as Reception Theory, on the other hand, is associated with the work of the Constance School in Germany, more precisely with Jauss, Iser and certain other German scholars (Schneider, 2005c, p. 492). Whereas the former's preoccupations lie with issues of literary history, the latter's work boosted a new conceptualization of readers as active participants. Iser (1978), in turn, not only looks at meaning construction by assessing readers' mental input but also avoids neglecting the way the text itself predetermines how such meaning is actually constructed (see top-down and bottom-up processes in *schema theory*). Other perspectives normally considered under the label reader response are those proposed by Culler (1981), Eco (1979) and Holland (1968, 1975).

The various taxonomies of reader 'types' suggested by the different strands are a further commonality between these branches. The similarities end here, though, as the various scholars are prompt to put forward their own labels which, nonetheless and more often than not, appear to refer to similar concepts. Thus, whereas most authors accept the concept of 'ideal reader' (Iser, 1978) as the entity that most closely resembles what authors consider the perfect receptacle for their particular works, Riffaterre (1959) opts for the 'super-reader', Fish (1970) proposes the 'informed reader' and Eco (1979) suggests the 'model reader'. More recent narrative theory, however, appears to have abandoned a classification of 'types of reader' in favour of what Schneider calls 'reader constructs' (2005a, p. 482). Most of the theoretical considerations assessing the particular role of readers are, in fact, conceptualizing such entity as an abstract construct rather than as real individuals facing texts. The original approaches to the study of reader responses, thus, primarily remained theoretical assessments and it is only the new perspectives afforded by empirical studies of literature that have tried to redress this fact. The work done on issues of foregrounding has been particularly successful at reinterpreting what role the reader is actually endowed with:

> van Peer (1986) found that the attention of readers is indeed attracted by the deviations and parallelisms contained in a text, that readers find text passages containing a high concentration of such devices more important and more worthy of discussion. In replicating this investigation, Miall & Kuiken (1994a), Hakemulder (2004), and Sopcak (2004) also found evidence for the affective value foregrounding passages have for readers: they are read significantly more slowly and enhance aesthetic appreciation, they influence readers' perceptions of the world, and they are evaluated more highly on a second reading. In all these studies, moreover, readers' personalities played only a marginal role, confirming van Peer's earlier findings: apparently foregrounding devices operate partly independently of reader characteristics. (van Peer et al., 2007, p. 7)

Thanks to the new empirical perspective taken on by van Peer and his collaborators (van Peer, 1986; van Peer et al., 2007), a new lease of life has been injected into studies of reader response. The determining role of textual devices described in empirical assessments of literature is clearly reminiscent of Iser's preoccupation with the way the text predetermines the reader's understanding, but this new stance is characterized by a far more structured and rigorous methodology. Crucially, this new take on the reader's role also allows us to investigate the emotional involvement created by the presence of certain foregrounding markers, thus echoing the claims put forward by Fish in relation to his affective stylistics. Finally, despite van Peer et al.'s seeming dismissal of readers' personalities as non-essential components in the reading experience, work undertaken by stylisticians in conjunction with psychologists and cognitive psychologists (Emmott et al., 2007) has actually underscored the core role that readers' individual psychological characteristics play in the processing of texts.

See also *emotion: stylistic approaches*, *empirical study of literature* (Key Branches), *foregrounding*, *schema theory* (Key Terms).

Key Terms in Stylistics

Alliteration

Alliteration is a stylistic device consisting of the repetition of the same consonant sound in nearby words. To qualify as alliteration, in the strict sense of the word, the consonant sounds must occur in word-initial position. Alliteration has a cohesive effect, since identical sounds tend to tie words together if they occur in close vicinity. It can be employed for emphasis and mnemonic effects and is frequently used as a means of foregrounding in poetry, advertising, newspaper headlines, political slogans, etc. Examples of alliteration thus occur in the first line of Keats's poem 'To Autumn' ([1820] 1983): 'Season of mists and mellow fruitfulness!', as well as in the title of Gurinder Chada's film *Bend it Like Beckham* (2002).

Alliteration is sometimes used in a broader sense to refer also to what is otherwise known respectively as assonance and consonance. Assonance is the repetition of vowel sounds in nearby words, usually in stressed syllables. Consonance, on the other hand, is used by some to refer to the repetition of consonant sounds in nearby words irrespective of their position, while others employ the term to refer to the repetition of final consonant sounds only.

See also *assonance, cohesion, consonance, foregrounding* (Key Terms).

Arbitrariness, Arbitrary

It is a feature of human verbal language that – as a rule – the linguistic sign is arbitrary in the sense that no natural relation exists between the linguistic signifier and that which is signified (Saussure, 1916). There is thus no 'tableness' about the word 'table' and nothing 'bookish' about the word 'book'. Instead, the meaning of the linguistic sign is determined by convention, which means that a speech community has agreed on labelling a concept in a particular way, while another speech community calls it something else (English: 'table';

German: 'Tisch'; Danish 'bord'). Some linguistic items are exceptions to this rule due to a certain aspect of iconicity by which they somehow resemble what they signify. In fact, with the advent of functionalism and linguistic constructivism in the 1960s, the concept of the arbitrariness of the linguistic sign was questioned. Onomatopoeic words like 'cuckoo', 'splash' and 'rattle' are good examples of iconicity. Another example is syntactic iconicity where the word order and the sequencing of events reflect the meaning expressed by the text (De Cuypere, 2008; Willems and De Cuypere, 2008).

See also *signifier and signified, icon, iconic, iconicity* (Key Terms), *Ferdinand de Saussure* (Key Thinkers).

Assonance

Assonance is a stylistic device consisting of the repetition of the same vowel sound in nearby words, usually in stressed syllables. Assonance has a cohesive effect, since identical sounds tend to tie words together if they occur in a sequence of nearby words. Like alliteration and consonance, assonance can be employed for emphasis and mnemonic effects and is frequently used as a means of foregrounding in e.g., poetry, advertising, newspaper headlines and political slogans, as in 'I like Ike', the slogan for Dwight (Ike) Eisenhower in the American presidential campaign of 1952.

See also *alliteration, cohesion, consonance, foregrounding* (Key Terms).

Blending theory

Blending theory (also called conceptual blending theory or conceptual integration) is one of the most recent additions to the branch of stylistics known as cognitive stylistics. Blending theory (BT) emerges from two traditions within cognitive linguistics, conceptual metaphor theory (CMT) and mental spaces theory (MS). Blending theory, however, has now developed into a fully-fledged theoretical framework independent of both its parenting models. BT's main proponents are Fauconnier and Turner (1998, 2002) but extensive work has been done by Coulson (2001, 2006), Coulson and Oakley (2000), Grady (2005), Grady, Oakley and Coulson (1999) and Sweetser (2000) among others.

BT differs from both CMT and MS in the way it describes the cognitive process of meaning creation via the existence of certain emergent structures (the blends) not accounted for by either of the other two frameworks.

Whereas MS addresses understanding via the existence of mental spaces generated online because of the interaction of linguistic cues and background knowledge, among other things, in any current ongoing discourse, CMT is concerned with explaining the cognitive basis of conceptual metaphors via the mental correspondences or mappings between two distinct conceptual domains. BT's theoretical apparatus is built around the notion of conceptual integration networks, which are the mechanisms that enable the creation of meaning. Integration networks function when several spaces are interconnected by mental correspondences or mappings, which is clearly reminiscent of some of the theoretical principles of the two parenting models: the notion of spaces from MS and the mapping between spaces from CMT. Unlike the former, though, BT identifies four (sometimes more are also possible) primary spaces that ultimately give rise to the various emergent structures; the basic spaces that need to be present are the input space 1, the input space 2, the generic space and the blend itself.

A significant point of departure between BT and CMT is the possibility of coming across instances of backward projection. BT emphasizes the multidirectional nature of the creation of blends whereby any component of the whole integration network is susceptible to change at any moment. Compare this with the unidirectional structure of mappings between source and target domains in CMT which only allows setting up correspondences from the former to the latter. An example, the expression 'this surgeon is a butcher' taken from Grady et al. (1999, p. 103), can help us understand much better the workings of BT in practice. These authors state that, although, initially, this sentence might be thought of as a linguistic manifestation of the conceptual metaphor SURGEON AS BUTCHER, further insights underscore that the emergent meaning is more than the simple mapping from the source domain BUTCHER onto the target SURGEON. Conceptualizing this metaphor as a unidirectional mapping loses the crucial 'incompetence' element of the resulting metaphor. They argue that only certain components from each input space, that of SURGERY and BUTCHERY are actually called upon to form the final blend; for instance, from the former, we import the human nature of the entities performing and enduring the operation, the tools used to carry out the procedure (scalpel), the goal of healing the patient, and the means employed to achieve such goal, surgery. On the other hand, the BUTCHERY space also contains a human, the butcher, accomplishing the action of dismembering an animal; the butcher would also need some tools to implement such actions, a cleaver, for instance; the goal would differ from that of the surgeon as butchers do not intend to heal their subjects but mainly to dismember them and the means by which such a goal is achieved is through butchery. The resulting blend, Grady et al. (1999) conclude, is formed by combining some of the components from each input space, namely, the identity of a surgeon and the role of a butcher and by crucially adding elements of its own: the healing goal of the surgeon is somehow coupled with the butchery means employed by the butcher but not his skilfulness; therefore, a new meaning is generated, that of the surgeon being incompetent.

The number of input spaces that configure blends in BT is not necessarily always confined to two. Input spaces are typically 'structured by information from discrete cognitive domains' (Coulson, 2006, p. 190), that is, from the various areas that the blend feeds itself from. The generic space, on the other hand, contains some components common to all the inputs and, finally, the blend is created as a new and independent space with its own internal configuration. Blending theorists point out that the emergence of blends responds to a series of processes based on the dynamic aspects of meaning construction, as is the case in the formation of mental space lattices (see *mental space theory*). The active nature of blend creation is, nonetheless, not random but carefully monitored by the selective projection of the input spaces. Selective projection involves a careful evaluation of which components in the various inputs are actually relevant for the creation of the emerging blend (remember how the 'human' aspect of the surgeon was selected, but not his skilfulness). This procedure allows an economical handling of the rich cognitive material included in the various input spaces. Additionally, Fauconnier and Turner point out that blends are also governed by a series of constitutive processes called composition, completion and elaboration. Composition 'involves attributing a relation from one space to an element or elements from the other input spaces' (Coulson and Oakley, 2000, p. 180) so that elements from the various spaces would 'come together' in the new space. In Grady's example above some aspects of the domain of butchery are mapped onto some aspects from the domain of surgery. According to Evans and Green (2006) completion 'involves schema induction [...] schema induction involves the unconscious and effortless recruitment of background frames' (p. 409); so the initial composition process needs to summon already existing frames, that is, we know that both surgeons and butchers use particular tools in their professions. The role of the completion stage, thus, is to furnish and supplement the information gathered from the initial inputs. Finally, elaboration is the process that ultimately generates the unique features of the blend as we saw above.

Studying literature from the theoretical perspective afforded by BT is but one of the manifold applications of this framework. As Freeman says:

> Perhaps the most valuable aspect of blending theory as it is being developed and expanded is the way in which it is moving toward a unification of various strands of research in different disciplinary areas, from Charles Sanders Peirce's (1931–58) work on the significance of index, icon, and symbol and Susanne K. Langer's (1953, 1967) work on the importance of form in the mind feeling in philosophy to Antonio Damasio's (1999) work on emotion and consciousness and V. S. Ramachandran's [sic] (1998) work on culture and the brain in neuroscience. As blending theory begins to incorporate these and other cognitive linguistic studies, such as Langacker's (1987, 1991) work on foregrounding and deixis, Talmy's (2000) work on fictive motion, Lakoff, Johnson (1980, 1998), and others' work on conceptual metaphor, and Nänny and Fischer's (2003) work on iconicity, it promises to enrich our understanding of literary creativity. (Freeman, 2006, p. 116)

BT has become a theoretical proposition firmly embraced by practitioners of stylistics, which is not surprising considering the particularly creative nature of literary discourse and its inclusion of novel blends. For specifically stylistic analyses using BT see Canning (2008), Crisp (2008), Freeman (2003, 2005, 2006), McAllister (2006), Semino (2006c), Sweetser (2006), Tobin (2006) and Turner (2006).

See also *cognitive stylistics/cognitive poetics* (Key Branches), *conceptual metaphor theory*, *mental spaces theory* (Key Terms).

Cluster

See *corpus stylistics* (Key Branches).

Coherence

While cohesion refers to the linking of sentences into text (see Halliday and Hasan, 1976), coherence concerns the appropriateness of a given text (and the various choices involved in its composition) in its communicative context. Some choices may thus be more appropriate, and hence more coherent, than others in the situational and cultural contexts in which the text occurs. In a legal text, for example, expected choices would be linguistic markers typical of formal written language, whereas the use of informal conversational wording and structures would be considered inappropriate and consequently incoherent in a legal context.

See also *cohesion* (Key Terms).

Cohesion

Cohesion refers to the way sentences combine into text by means of text-internal ties. The concept of cohesion (as well as that of coherence) is largely owed to Halliday and Hasan, whose seminal study of the phenomenon, *Cohesion in English* (1976), has been greatly influential in stylistics as well as in linguistics more generally. Halliday and Hasan (1976) identify five main types of cohesive tie in English – four grammatical and one lexical. Grammatical ties are realized by conjunction, ellipsis, substitution and reference. Conjunction and conjunctive expressions such as 'but', 'then', 'accordingly' and 'nevertheless' work by explicitly signalling how different parts of the text relate to each other. Secondly, ellipsis links different parts of a text by means of omission as in 'I could offer her a lift. But no, I won't_' where a cohesive tie exists between the empty slot following 'I won't' and 'offer her a lift' in the previous sentence. Closely related to the cohesive resource of ellipsis is that of substitution. In an alternative version of the sentence above, a placeholder may thus occupy the empty slot, thereby linking the two sentences: 'I could offer her a lift. But no, I won't *do so*'. Reference, in turn, occurs when linguistic items 'make reference to something else for their interpretation' (Halliday and Hasan, 1976, p. 31). Prevalent examples of reference are pronouns ('you', 'she', 'his'), demonstratives ('this', 'that', 'those') and articles ('a', 'the'). The element referred to (i.e., the referent) may precede the referring item (anaphora) or follow it (cataphora) (see *referent*). Lexical cohesion falls into three subcategories: repetition, synonymy and collocation. Repetition and synonymy are both examples of reiteration. Where the former occurs when a lexical item is either repeated in its identical or near identical form ('run'/'run', 'run'/'running'), in the latter case a lexical item is reiterated by some kind of synonym ('car'/'automobile'), including hyponymy, that is from specific to general ('poodle'/'dog'), meronymy or part-whole ('finger'/'hand') and antonymy or opposition ('happy'/'sad'). Collocation, or expectancy relations, is cohesion created by means of words that have a tendency to co-occur. Certain words tend to come in pairs like 'make' and 'decision', 'freezing' and 'cold', 'waste' and 'time', but there may also be a broader sense in which words are likely to occur together, thereby forming lexical sets. When we read about 'computer', 'screen' and 'keyboard', for instance, we may expect to also encounter 'mouse pad' and 'desktop', since these lexical items tend to collocate and thereby tie the text together; we would, however, be rather surprised if we encountered words such as 'bedpan' and 'chainsaw' in the same context.

In their seminal work on cohesion in English, Halliday and Hasan (1976, pp. 297–8) briefly mention a cohesive phenomenon which they call 'unresolved cohesion'. Unresolved cohesion occurs when reference items such as pronouns and the definite article are employed, consequently implying a sense of familiarity, but without the reader being in possession of the right sort of knowledge to track the referent. Such a situation would affect the reader's ability to process the reference. According to Halliday and Hasan, unresolved cohesion is a common feature of the opening of short stories where it functions to (a) engage the reader's interest, (b) imply that what we read is not the whole story and (c) put the reader 'on the inside, as one who is assumed to have shared a common experience with the speaker or writer' (Halliday and Hasan, 1976, p. 298). It should be added that the use of unresolved cohesion is by no means limited to the opening of short stories. In fact, this stylistic device is often employed irrespective of genre and generic stage for focalization and the creation of narrative perspective with the implication that the cohesion that may seem unresolved to the reader is resolved to the fictional character through whose mind the narrative is filtered.

The amount and nature of cohesive ties in a text have a direct impact on the ease with which the text can be understood. Some texts display a high number of cohesive ties which are relatively easy to make sense of, while the cohesive nature of other texts is more complex. In the first chapter of Faulkner's *The Sound and the Fury* ([1929] 1978), cohesion plays a significant role in the creation of the narrative perspective and fictional microcosm of the novel. Here, extensive use of unresolved cohesive ties in the shape of personal pronouns such as 'they', 'them' and 'he' whose referents cannot be tracked in the nearby text makes the text difficult to understand, yet, at the same time, it helps establish the narrative perspective as that of thirty-three-year-old Benjy who is mentally retarded with a mind like that of a child. In the first paragraphs of the novel, Benjy is watching some people who are playing golf. This passage is characterized by a complete absence of nominal reference to the golfers and the golf course that he is watching, which may indicate that he does not know the word (or concept) of golf and hence does not understand what the people he is observing are doing. While the unresolved cohesive reference ties make Benjy's section of the novel difficult to read, another cohesive resource, i.e., collocation, plays a significant role in establishing the setting. In the first paragraphs, the lexical set of the collocating lexical items 'fence', 'flower spaces', 'grass', 'flower tree' and 'pasture' establishes the external physical setting of the narrative, while 'hitting', 'hit', 'flag', 'took the flag out', 'put the flag back', 'caddie' and 'balls' in combination gradually reveal that the people Benjy is watching are playing golf, thereby narrowing down the meaning potential of the outdoor setting to that of a golf course.

In addition to the lexical and grammatical means of cohesion listed above, elements such as alliteration, assonance, consonance and different kinds of rhyme likewise display the ability to establish cohesive links between different elements in a text. The cohesive effect of alliteration, assonance, consonance and rhyme is arguably a visual as well as an auditive phenomenon. When we read the text aloud, we hear the patterns of similar sounds and hence sense the cohesive ties which are established sonically, yet we may also spot the similarities as visual similarities when we read the text silently.

See also *alliteration*, *assonance*, *collocation*, *consonance*, *rhyme* (Key Terms).

Collocation

Collocation embraces the Firthian (1957) notion that a word can be described by the company it keeps: 'Meaning by collocation is an abstraction at the syntagmatic level and is not directly concerned with the conceptual or idea approach to the meaning of words. One of the meanings of *night* is its collocability with *dark*' (Firth, 1957, p. 196), similarly the adverb 'ago' frequently collocates with 'a week' or 'a month' to form the expression 'a week/month ago'. In order for an expression to be a collocation, the word needs to occur together with others in more than regular frequency.

Sinclair (2004, p. 14) defines a collocation as 'the co-occurrence of words with no more than four intervening words'. Hoey (2005, p. 5) adds an additional focus on psychology to his definition of collocation: 'A psychological association between words (rather than lemmas) up to four words and evidenced by their occurrence together in corpora more often than is explicable in terms of random distribution'. Toolan (2009, p. 19), in turn, re-stresses the textual basis of collocation. His definition follows from his corpus-stylistic analysis of narrative progression in twentieth-century short stories:

> Collocation is the far-greater-than-chance tendency of particular words to co-occur (adjacently or within a few words of one another). These co-occurrence tendencies have text-constructional and semantic implications. Proficient native language users are equipped, by their communicational experience, with the commoner collocational tendencies and implications. (Toolan, 2009, p. 19)

Frequently, collocation is mentioned hand in hand with the term 'colligation', which describes the ways grammatical words appear with particular lexical items 'to cover relationships between grammatical categories and particular lexical words' (Butler, 2004, p. 154). For example, the word 'ago' frequently functions grammatically as an adverb of time in initial position.

Sinclair (2004), Hoey (2005) and Toolan (2009) all relate collocation(s) (and colligation) to 'naturalness' and to the native speaker's competence to produce them, which makes them appear fluent and proficient. The concept of 'lexical bundles' developed by Biber et al. (1999) and Biber et al. (2004) also has to be mentioned here because it refers to extended collocations of three-, four-, five- or even six-word sequences that occur in a statistically marked frequency. Biber et al. (1999) used a large corpus as well as computer analysis for identification of those multi-word units. This is an area of corpus linguistic research which also focuses on so-called n-grams with 'n' standing for the number of words that can be seen to occur in more than just random frequency. It also correlates to what Sinclair (1991, 2004) has called the 'idiom principle', which means that what we hear, read or use are often fabricated multi-word phrases. This principle interacts with the 'open choice principle', which relates to the ability of a speaker to constantly fill a slot within a sentence, a process which is only governed by grammatical rules. From both a syntagmatic and paradigmatic point of view it should also be stressed that one principle to which collocations can be related is that of compositionality (Kortmann, 2005, p. 193). Often the meaning of expressions and their syntactic relations can be inferred from their parts and refers to what is named after the German philosopher and mathematician Gottlob Frege, that is, the 'Fregean Principle' (Kortmann, 2005, p. 5). However, idioms cannot be reconstructed from the parts of words they consist of.

Collocations can be identified for content words (like adjectives, adverbs and nouns) and function words (like articles, pronouns and so on) alike, even though the latter are usually more frequent than the former. Frequent words also have their own repetitive patterns. When we investigate collocational patterns of content words, there will be function words in their surrounding, which makes collocations one of the linguistic proofs of why the lexis-grammar interface cannot be separated.

Mike Scott's (2004) key words tool of the software *WordSmith* compares the keywords in one text with those in another, larger reference corpus. In other words, since we know that frequency is a relative concept, comparison and reference corpora and statistical procedures are needed in order to be able to establish collocation patterns. Frequencies of words have to be seen in relation to words in their context.

One tool for further analysis of collocations used in corpus linguistics is to build concordance lines based on large amounts of data, i.e., a corpus. A concordance line brings together and displays instances of use of a particular word from the widely disparate contexts in which it occurs. A collocation then consists of a core word combined with words on either side. These are called the right and left contexts respectively. This means that patterns of similarity can be detected in the words surrounding the core word. Some examples are 'the fact that' or 'in fact', which are frequently occurring collocations: here 'fact' is the core word and the other function words ('the', 'that' and 'in') surround it (Hunston, 2006; Hunston and Francis, 1999).

The question about the extent to which collocational investigations, both on a synchronic and a diachronic dimension, play a role in stylistic analyses need to be discussed. Bill Louw (2006, pp. 92–3) has criticized the base on intuition in stylistics and, via recourse to his concept of semantic prosody, adamantly stresses the potential of collocational investigations and corpus linguistics for reforming stylistics, because bottom-up studies are objective and allow the stylistician to be more precise about textual phrasings. Toolan (2009, p. 21), however, stresses that these aims may be laudable but 'in the meantime a more realistic but still difficult goal is the uncovering of some of the textual patternings that give rise to rich critical readings'. Also, the fact that 'it takes a human analyst to uncover insights and disclose things, using collocational analysis' (Toolan, 2009, p. 21) is important to stress, so there should ideally be a combination of qualitative and quantitative investigations (Semino and Short, 2004). In addition, there is the risk of neglecting certain other complex textual features which go beyond the lexical framework. A corpus-linguistic, bottom-up approach is lexically based, and collocations function as one example of that. And even that might not always do justice to the characteristics of the text under investigation.

Furthermore, the range of possible functionalities of a particular search programme cannot guide the research question. In addition, a particular programme cannot immediately detect complex discoursal phenomena. The real value of the identification of collocations is to highlight repetitive patterns and tendencies which a focus on reading and intuition alone would have missed. It is then possible to make use of Sinclair's (2004) theory of prospection and encapsulation or of Hoey's (2005) comprehensive model of lexico-(grammatical) priming. Toolan summarizes Sinclair (2004, pp. 82–101, pp. 115–27):

> a first segment of text raises implicit questions that subsequent discourse will address, wholly or in part, and that each succeeding segment of text may open or prospect further kinds of question or incompleteness for yet later text to resolve. (Toolan, 2009, p. 16)

Hoey's approach to lexico-grammatical priming is more comprehensive. He uses the psychological notion of priming and shows not only the lexical boundedness of particular frequent items, but also how those items tend to co-occur with specific sentence elements as well as in particular semantic and pragmatic roles and genres. For the stylistician, this raises questions of styles in general and specific norms as well as deviations of/variations on those norms. At the same time, the stylistician needs to address questions about the extent to which these primings are perceptible to the language user and what their effect is. Mahlberg (2007), choosing a corpus stylistic approach (see entry), has illustrated, for example, how four-word or three-word clusters can be related to functions in Dickens's narrative fiction. Toolan (2009) impressively uses these models to explore further to what extent narrative progression functions in twentieth-century short stories, but also points out that human intuition cannot be underestimated in the understanding of texts.

In their treatment of cohesion, Halliday and Hasan (1976) regard collocation as one of their categories of cohesion (see entry). Theirs is a broader sense of collocation, which includes, for example, lexical items typically belonging to the same lexical field such as the co-occurrence of *novel*, *plot* and *character* in relative close proximity.

See also *corpus stylistics*, *historical stylistics* (Key Branches).

Conceptual metaphor

Conceptual metaphor theory, also known as cognitive metaphor theory, is traditionally associated with George Lakoff and Mark Johnson, in particular with their seminal work *Metaphors We Live By* (1980, 2003). The theory of metaphor propounded by these scholars is not to be confused with more traditional perspectives, especially those that view metaphor as primarily a trope or a kind of linguistic embellishment. Conceptual metaphor theory (CMT, for short) defends that metaphorical patterns are a pervasive and fundamental component of the human thought process and not simply a linguistic device to enhance language, especially as found in literary discourses. Cognitive linguistics has fully embraced Lakoff and Johnson's proposal but has also expanded and reformulated many of the original principles of CMT. The basic tenets, however, are still in place nowadays and are considered not only valid but paramount by scholars from a diversity of disciplines; among those, stylistics has been a major contributor to the refocusing and enriching of CMT.

In cognitive linguistic terms a conceptual metaphor is not a mere trope. A very pedestrian attempt at a definition would be 'an understanding of concept A in terms of concept B'. This understanding, however, is not realized at the level of the utterance, sentence or word, but at a cognitive level. It is more accurate to define conceptual metaphors as the understanding of some conceptual domain in terms of another conceptual domain. Defining what constitutes a conceptual domain, nonetheless, is not free from controversy either. The initial work undertaken by Lakoff and Johnson identified a series of domains of thought which they found pervasively repetitive in human cognition, but later studies have underscored several problems associated with the way in which these conceptual domains had been arrived at, especially in relation to the lack of real data used by Lakoff and Johnson (as explained below).

Kövecses (2002, p. 4) provides a concise way of defining conceptual domains: 'A conceptual domain is any coherent organization of experience'. Some of these rich mental frames are 'journeys', 'war', 'games', 'money', on the one hand, and 'love', 'argument', 'thought' or 'morality', on the other. An example might help us here; consider the following expressions in English: 'Their relationship was on fire', 'They are old flames', 'I don't want to get burnt again', 'His consumption by love', 'My love for her never stopped smouldering'. According to CMT, these are all linguistic manifestations of a common conceptual metaphor, namely LOVE IS FIRE (note that conceptual metaphors are typographically distinguished by using small capitals). The two conceptual domains giving rise to this metaphor are LOVE and FIRE, the metaphor being the result of establishing a series of conceptual correspondences between the former and the latter. CMT calls this transference of constituents 'mappings'; in our case, some of the cognitive attributes of humans' experience of FIRE have been utilized to comprehend the domain of LOVE. The conceptual domain we use to draw elements from in order to establish the analogy (FIRE in our case) is known as 'source domain'; the domain we transfer the analogy onto is called 'target domain' (that is, LOVE). The transference always happens from the source to the target domain and tends to be non-reversible, that is, conventional conceptual metaphors do not appear to work in the opposite direction, as in *FIRE IS LOVE. This non-reversibility can be easily understood if we consider the contrast existing between those domains generally used as source and those commonly found as target. Whereas humans conceptualize 'journeys', 'war', 'games' or 'money' as fairly concrete organizational patterns of experience, 'love', 'argument', 'thought' or 'morality' convey, instead, fairly abstract meanings less easily related to the basic experiential aspects of humans' lives. The domain of 'journey', for instance, conjures up images of travelling entities, a starting point and a destination, means of transport or the possibility of eventualities taking place during the journey. Understanding the complex concept of LOVE as if it was a JOURNEY (LOVE IS A JOURNEY conceptual metaphor) simplifies the cognitive process and allows for various linguistic manifestations of this metaphor as in:

> Look how far we've come
> We're at a crossroads.

> We'll just have to go our separate ways.
> We can't turn back now. (Kövecses, 2002, p. 5)

If the opposite process was to take place, that is, understanding the more delineated, specific concepts (money, for instance) in terms of the less tangible, non-physical ones (such as morality), a considerable cognitive effort would be required. Some of the commonly identified source and target domains are the following:

> Source domains: the human body, health and illness, animals, plants, buildings and construction, machines and tools, games and sport, money and economic transactions, cooking and food, heat and cold, light and darkness, forces, movements and direction.
>
> Target domains: Emotion, desire, morality, thought, society/nation, politics, economy, communication, time, life and death, religion, events and actions. (Kövecses, 2002, chapter 2)

Recent studies on metaphor have refocused their efforts by highlighting certain flaws of the initial studies of the 1980s and 1990s. Lakoff and Johnson's conviction of the primarily cognitive, as opposed to linguistic, nature of metaphors has now been questioned by many scholars. Alongside this concern lies the total reliance shown by CMT scholars on made-up examples as well as their lack of consideration of data emerging from real discourse and from large corpora. Authors such as Cameron (2003), Deignan (1999, 2005), Low (2003), Semino (2008), Steen (1999), have openly moved away from compiling artificial examples in order to gather naturally-occurring data. Because of the new methodological approaches based on corpora analysis, new perspectives are emerging, especially in relation to the dichotomy 'thought vs. language' vehemently defended in the original formulations of CMT.

Nowadays, it is preferred to view metaphors as phenomena solidly anchored in cognitive processes but whose outward manifestations via linguistic or other means (see *multimodality*) also require due considerations. Similarly, scholars have also highlighted the need for a clear recognition of the previous analysis of metaphors having taken place for centuries before *Metaphors We Live By* (1980). Cameron (2003), Jäkel (1999) and Mahon (1999) remind us that some of the tenets adopted by CMT are not as ground-breaking as they were claimed to be for most of those principles had already been discussed or, at least, signalled by philosophers such as Aristotle, Kant, Blumemberg and Weinrich.

See also *cognitive stylistics/cognitive poetics* (Key Branches), *grammatical metaphor, metaphor, multimodality* (Key Terms).

Concordance

See *corpus stylistics* (Key Branches), *collocation* (Key Terms).

Connotation

See *denotation and connotation* (Key Terms).

Consonance

Consonance is a stylistic device consisting of the repetition of a series of consonant sounds in nearby words. While some use the term to refer to the repetition of consonant sounds irrespective of position, others employ the term to refer to the repetition of final consonant sounds only. Like alliteration and assonance, consonance has a cohesive effect, since identical sound tends to tie words together if they occur in close vicinity. Consonance can be employed for emphasis and mnemonic effects and is frequently used as a means of foregrounding in poetry, advertising, newspaper headlines, political slogans, for instance. Examples of consonance occur in the following verse lines from Poe's 'Annabel Lee' ([1849] 1983): 'For the moon never beams, without bringing me dreams/of the beautiful Annabel Lee/And the stars never rise but I feel the bright eyes/of the beautiful Annabel Lee'.

See also *alliteration*, *assonance*, *cohesion*, *foregrounding* (Key Terms).

Contextual frame theory

Contextual frame theory (CFT) emerges from the research carried out by Emmott (1992, 1994, 1995, 1996, 1997, 2002a, 2003a) on the way people read narratives, the fully-developed proposal appearing in *Narrative Comprehension. A Discourse Perspective* (1997). In the latter work, Emmott establishes the basic premises of this model and clearly argues that her primary focus is not 'literary style' or 'literary themes', nor is her book 'about specific texts' (1997, p. 4). She underscores that her model of narrative comprehension is related to the research undertaken by artificial intelligence scholars (as well as cognitive scientists in general), although additionally those issues are contextualized within a linguistic framework. As Emmott summarizes:

> My aim is to present a hypothesis about how people read narratives, focusing on some of the most basic aspects of story comprehension. The objective is to answer questions such as 'How do they know which characters are involved in the action at any particular point in a story?', and 'How do they monitor the location and time of the action?'. (Emmott, 1997, p. 4)

As such, CFT was primarily conceived to track the reference to characters and events in narrative fiction but it has subsequently been applied to other genres as well (see Stockwell, 2002 and McIntyre, 2006, for drama; Jeffries, 2008, for poetry). CFT shares with other cognitive stylistic and cognitive linguistic models the notion of mental representations or worlds (see *blending theory, mental spaces theory, possible worlds theory* and *text world theory*), here termed 'contextual frames':

> I use the term 'contextual frame' (or 'frame') to describe a mental store of information about the current context, built up from the text itself and from inferences made from the text. [...] I am suggesting that each contextual configuration needs to be retained in memory, at least temporarily. Without this, we could not create a context from the fragments of information provided in individual sentences. (Emmott, 1997, p. 121)

Reference assignment in narrative, thus, happens within the mental storage places that are contextual frames and which readers need to be able to monitor in order to make sense of the text. The information contained in these configurations can be episodic or non-episodic, that is, it can pertain simply to the locative, personal and temporal coordinates of the given frame or it can belong to the general knowledge background system of the whole narrative. Actions and events occurring during a particular frame would be episodic whereas characters' defining features such as their racial profile, their gender or their belonging to any particular social class, if relevant to the story, would be non-episodic. The process by which we are able to take stock of all the variations and permutations in frames is called 'contextual monitoring' and is achieved by a variety of means, binding being one of them. For Emmott binding means:

> Simply that 'episodic' links between entities (people and places) are established, thereby creating a context which is monitored by the mind [...]. For fictional narrative, therefore, 'binding' means the reader's awareness that one or more fictional characters are in one particular fictional place at one particular time. (Emmott, 1997, p. 123)

Characters are accordingly 'bound in' to a particular frame as soon as they are mentioned as entering a particular location and will remain bound into that frame until the text explicitly cues their exit. Unless otherwise stated, the rules of general logic that govern the real world (cf. the Principle of Minimal Departure in possible worlds theory) would also apply in the story-world, so the binding of characters in or out of particular frames necessarily needs to abide by these rules too. Sci-fi, ghost or fantasy narratives, on the other hand, would be exempt from complying with them, but simply because of the generic characteristics of these fictional forms. CFT is also concerned with the accurate and economical processing of information of the various frames. Such productive approach to tracking frames is achieved thanks to a selection process that foregrounds only one particular frame at a time, relegating, albeit not eliminating, the rest to a secondary plane. This is the process known as priming. Emmott argues that an effective survey of the movements within and between frames forces readers to retain just one main focus of attention, despite other contiguous frames existing in the background too. It follows, thus, that the elements of any particular primed frame are, by default, also bound. Reference assignment is also considered in relation to its textual presence as characters can be textually-overt or textually-covert. The cues to track the former type are primarily linguistic, so characters can be 'mentioned by a name, common noun, or pronoun or if there is a grammatical elision or some other indication at the textual level that a character is present' (Emmott, 1997, p. 124). The latter characters are those primed or unprimed characters that have not been explicitly bound out of the frame in question and hence still in the reader's mind. The complete set of characters in any one narrative, whether they are bound or unbound, primed or unprimed, forms the 'central directory' which is used by readers to follow the involvement of characters, their active participation or their tangentiality to the main story. Finally, CFT also describes the way the mental representations that are frames can be changed, resulting in various types of alterations named 'frame modification', 'frame switch', 'frame recall' and 'frame repair'. The first type occurs 'if the text explicitly states that a character enters or leaves the location' (Emmott, 1997, p. 142), although the reader must assume that the rest of the frame will stay unchanged. Should any character exit their current physical location, their status would be consequently affected as they become not simply unprimed but also bound out. Their being bound out similarly affects their textual status as they cannot be considered textually-covert either. Contextual monitoring also identifies that, on other occasions, frames are not simply modified but that readers totally abandon what was the primed frame up to that point and move to track the features of a different one, a process known as 'frame switch'. Frame switch is commonly found when new locative or temporal parameters are introduced as in, for instance, flashbacks or flashforwards. Switching frames also implies that the characters of the unprimed frame do not become bound out but simply primed out and could, hence, be brought back into focus if desired. Such scenario corresponds to the third form of alteration described in CFT, the so-called frame recall, which arises every time a frame is re-primed in the narrative. According to Emmott, frame recall 'provides an explanation of how pronouns can be decoded which lack a recent co-referential antecedent' (1997, p. 153). Finally, CFT also accounts for those instances in which readers need to retrospectively adapt their cognitive processing of a particular frame, either because new elements have emerged or because the narrator has purposely misled them. If this is the case, readers need to resort to frame repair to adjust their inferences to the newly arisen pieces of information. Additionally, CFT addresses the issue of characters' varying state of mind by introducing the notion of 'enactors'. This concept encompasses the various cognitive manifestations of any particular character along the narrative, that is, the same character can display distinct psychological traits at various points in the storyworld as in, for example, the psychological make-up of a character as a child or adult, or the psychotic and conventional characteristics of a bipolar patient as character. The ample scope for application of the framework is being proved by the way recent developments of cognate disciplines are incorporating some of the foundational tenets of CFT; for instance, Gavins (2007) has borrowed the notion of enactors for her reworking of text world theory and McIntyre (2006) has expanded deictic shift theory by adding the concepts of priming and binding to the original proposal. For reviews (albeit rather general) of CFT see Herman (2001) and Weber (2004).

See also *blending theory, mental spaces theory, possible worlds theory, text world theory* (Key Terms).

Conversation analysis

See *pragmatic stylistics* (Key Branches).

Cooperative principle; cooperation

The concept of a 'cooperative principle' (CP) is based on Herbert P. Grice's (1975) work on everyday communication and how we rely on certain principles of cooperation when we communicate. This principle is central within pragmatic approaches to language and has also had a crucial influence on the stylistic analysis of play texts and spoken conversation in narrative fiction, for example.

The focus on language usage and on pragmatics as the study of meaning in context was not initially promoted by linguists, but developed from a branch of philosophy. This branch criticized work in logic in which natural language was described by principles of formal logic, such as truth conditions and truth values. Language philosophers, such as John L. Austin, John R. Searle or Herbert P. Grice, advocated a countermovement to traditional logic and tried to explain the central features of natural language and ordinary communication. According to Grice (1975), for example, pragmatic inferences cannot be equated with semantic inferences of presupposition and entailment (see *presupposition and entailment*), because these are not based on the conventionally agreed meanings of words, phrases or sentences, but require additional contextual knowledge. From our experience of language we know that a similar utterance may have different meanings and effects in different contexts. It can be assumed, however, that different cultures and interlocutors in those cultures comply with certain principles of communication, 'Politeness' (see entry) being one of them and Grice's (1975) 'Cooperative Principle' (CP) another of those pragmatic principles.

Grice formulated his cooperative principle as: 'Make your conversational contribution such as is required at the stage at which it occurs, by the accepted purpose or direction of the talk exchange in which you are engaged' (Grice, 1975, p. 45). According to Grice (1975), every act of communication is cooperative in that interlocutors strive to be cooperative when they communicate. To answer such questions as 'What does the utterance mean?', 'How does it relate to what was said earlier?' and 'What is the intention behind it?', the CP eases the meaning inference process. Grice did not simply spell out his CP but he also formulated a series of general conversational principles that he calls 'maxims' and that allow for the CP to take effect. These are the maxims of quality, quantity, relation and manner (Kortmann, 2005, p. 237):

(a) Quality: Make your contribution one that is true. Do not say what you believe to be false. Do not say that for which you lack adequate evidence.
(b) Quantity: Make your contribution as informative as is required for the current purposes of the exchange and not more informative than required.
(c) Relation: Be relevant. Do not change the topic.
(d) Manner: Be perspicuous: Avoid obscurity of expression, avoid ambiguity, be brief and orderly.

Grice's maxims have been criticized for not taking account of the power structures that are reflected in and can be created through language (see *critical discourse analysis*). However, it seems plausible to say that Grice was right to observe that communication would be less successful without those maxims. Also, there are features, such as 'hedges' for example, which we use to soften what we say, that is, we try to maximize the degree of cooperation if we are in need of impinging on somebody's negative face (Kortmann, 2005, p. 238). Furthermore, the maxims are not rigid rules, they reflect communicative behaviour and may serve as guidelines. In addition, Grice also takes account of the fact that compliance with his maxims depends on the situation and the verbal behaviour involved. Finally, the maxims have been praised for their robustness (Kortmann, 2005, p. 238) and Grice's cooperative principle has always been seen alongside other principles, such as the politeness principle (Leech, 1983; see *politeness*).

The fact that Grice defines interaction via the existence of four maxims does not imply that speakers are obliged to adhere to these maxims all the time. In fact, it is a very common occurrence that interactants in conversations 'fail' to abide by such principles which are not to be seen as rules but rather as general expectations that underline communication. If those maxims are followed, they are said to be 'observed'; the non-observance of the maxims can be realized by 'violating a maxim', 'opting out of a maxim', 'a clash', 'flouting a maxim', 'suspending a maxim' or 'infringing a maxim' (Thomas, 1995). Of all these options, flouting is the only one that refers to the blatant and intentional non-observance of any of the maxims. This means that both interactants are aware of the fact that there must be a reason why maxims are disregarded which leads to the creation of 'conversational implicature'. Violation of a maxim, on the other hand, means that only the speaker is aware of the fact that he/she violates a maxim. Conversational implicature, thus, refers to the extra meaning generated by the non-observance of the maxims. For instance, if when sitting next to a window, somebody says to you 'it's quite hot in here', they most likely are implying that, because of your proximity, you should open the window for them. Instead of stating that in so many words, the meaning has been implied for the addressee to infer. 'Flouting', thus, is a breaking of the maxims that is known to both speaker and hearer, that is deliberate and ostentatious.

The 1980s saw a high proliferation of models of implicatures based on Grice's principle. These are, arguably, reductionist in outlook. Among them are Horn (1988), who developed Grice's notion of a scalar implicature, and Sperber and Wilson's (1996) relevance theory.

See also *pragmatic stylistics* (Key Branches), *critical discourse analysis, politeness, presupposition and entailment* (Key Terms).

Corpus

See *corpus stylistics* (Key Branches).

Critical discourse analysis

Critical discourse analysis (CDA) investigates the relations between language and society. It assumes that language plays a crucial role in creating, maintaining and legitimating inequality, injustice and oppression in society. The most important aims of CDA are to raise awareness of the power of linguistic constructivism (language construing reality) and of its impact on society and to trigger change.

Although critical discourse analysis does not follow a particular school of thought (Wodak and Meyer, 2001), Halliday's (1994, 2004) systemic functional grammar (see *M. A. K. Halliday*) is most frequently drawn on. This is visible in the works by CDA proponents such as Norman Fairclough (1989) or Theo van Leeuwen (2005a), for example. Halliday's grammar is particularly suited for CDA because of its orientation towards context, that is, situational, generic and ideological. Furthermore, its three-dimensional approach to language – the textual, interpersonal and ideational – provides CDA with a broad range of grammatical tools for analysis as well as a theoretical framework. These allow the analyst to disclose the ideologically loaded as well as constructed nature of discourses and 'enact[ed] hegemonic genres – specific ways of using language to achieve purposes of social domination' (van Leeuwen, 2006a, p. 290).

Critical discourse analysts like Ruth Wodak, for example, also use other methods, such as argumentation strategies and forms of conversation analysis. Van Dijk (1993), however, has also illustrated that a multi-disciplinary approach is necessary which 'chooses and elaborates theories, methods and empirical work as a function of their relevance for the realisation of socio-political goals' (van Dijk, 1993, p. 252). This also affects the ways that critical discourse analysts engage with critical social theory as proposed by Foucault, Bourdieu, Habermas, Harvey or Giddens – to name but a few. CDA shows how discourses create power structures, but key concepts like that of ideology are sometimes defined and used in slightly different ways by the various analysts. For example, van Dijk (1993, p. 258) considers ideologies to be 'worldviews' that create 'social cognition': 'schematically organised complexes of representations and attitudes with regard to certain aspects of the social world, e.g. the schema [. . .] whites have about blacks'. Fairclough's (1997, p. 26) view of ideologies is, in turn, based on Marxism. The topics that have been explored by critical discourse analysts range from racism and anti-semitism (Wodak et al., 1990), immigration and asylum seeking (van Leeuwen, 1999), the business world and the language of politics (Fairclough, 1995), to gender, education, doctor-patient scheme and so on.

Stylistics shares with CDA the focus on the identification of styles as well as a number of similar tools for analysis, although CDA's data is usually non-literary language. In turn, Hallidayan grammar has been crucial for stylistics analysis, but the stylistic analysis is often less politically motivated. A CDA analysis of literary texts can be seen in Birch (1991) and Weber (1992). Widdowson has criticized proponents of CDA for imposing their (usually left-wing) interpretation of a text on the linguistic analysis (see Widdowson, 1995, 1996b, 2000 and Fairclough, 1997).

See also *M. A. K. Halliday* (Key Thinkers).

Critique of stylistics

For a long time, stylistics has been considered to be neither entirely part of linguistics nor of literary criticism. Therefore, it has been attacked by linguists as well as literary critics. According to Carter and Stockwell:

> Some linguists have felt stylistics is too soft to be taken too seriously, tending to introduce irrelevant notions such as performance data and readerly interpretations; some literature specialists, by contrast have felt that stylistics is too mechanistic and reductive, saying nothing significant about historical context or aesthetic theory, eschewing evaluation for the most part in the interest of a naïve scientism and claiming too much for interpretations that are at best merely text-immanent. (Carter and Stockwell, 2008, p. 291)

In order to understand Carter and Stockwell's evaluation in more detail, it makes sense to elaborate on some of the developments of stylistics and its foundations. Although stylistics has never solely drawn on a rhetorical basis, it has been considered to be not only a direct descendant of rhetoric, but also part of rhetoric alone, because of its focus on form of usage (*elocutio*) and on the effects and appropriateness language has in a given context. Stylistics, however, has also been affected by a number of other developments. Its interdisciplinary status, which is highly productive today and has turned stylistics into an accepted linguistic discipline, is probably based on three founding and foundational strands (Carter and Stockwell, 2008, p. 291):

(a) Anglo-American literary criticism
(b) Structuralism
(c) Emerging field of linguistics

From Anglo-American literary criticism, for example, stylistics received a(n initial) focus on literature; from structuralism the notion of style as motivated choice; and from the emerging field of linguistics the rigour of descriptive analysis. The 1960s, for example, saw the formation of these elements into a set of conventions for analysis. Areas of focus were related to the concept of literariness. Poetry received most of the initial analytical attention and foregrounding was discussed in theoretical terms as well as practically through the identification of deviating and parallel linguistic features. For instance, the same deviation and parallelism were eventually also discussed in relation to narrative fiction and drama. The focus on literature in general and poetry in particular, on the one side, and the interdisciplinary character which was visible even in the early years of stylistics, on the other, made some see stylistics only as a sub-branch of literary criticism. Also, it was questioned whether stylistics could be regarded as anything other than a method and whether, due to its eclecticism, it contained any ideological or theoretical foundations. This is a pertinent critique that has been persistently levelled at stylistics: '[it] has neither established a sound theoretical position of its own, nor grafted itself securely onto either of its parent disciplines' (Sinclair, 2004, p. 51). Perhaps because others have found this to be the attraction of stylistics (McIntyre, 2007b, p. 567), stylistics has thrived since its beginnings and has rigorously employed new developments in pragmatics and sociolinguistics, for example. Also, it has become a widespread discipline to teach (English) language through literature (see *pedagogical stylistics*) and in L1 and L2 pedagogies. Yet, it had to go through periods of serious attacks.

The controversies over stylistics receive their first expressions in the debate between the stylistician Roger Fowler and the literary critic F. W. Bateson: 'the Fowler-Bateson debate' (see Fowler, 1971), who discussed the alleged discrepancy between rigorous descriptiveness and literary sensibility. The attack by Stanley Fish and defence by Michael Toolan (see Fish, 1980; Toolan, 1990), which is a debate over the status of interpretation in literary reading, also illustrates this. Mackay (1996) argues that the attempt of some stylisticians to be more objective is an illusion. This was influentially refuted by Mick Short, Donald Freeman, Willie van Peer and Paul Simpson (1998). The debates led to discussions about whether stylistics had better be labelled 'literary linguistics', because the name 'stylistics' and its associations with 'style' and the difficulties of defining the polyphony of possible meanings of style (see *style*) have led to wrongly delimiting stylistics to the mere task of identifying the style of an author, which is reductionist and exclusive.

Perhaps the attacks testify to the value of stylistics as a discipline. No matter what, there can be no doubt that stylistics will be facing new exciting intellectual challenges, which result from the power of the new technologies, for example, or further research in the cognitive sciences and new (historical) approaches to literature and literariness. In Carter's words: 'The first decade of the twenty-first century is witnessing less concern with bridges and dividing lines and more a sense that there is much to be done within the interdisciplinary field of stylistics in and for itself with no longer any overriding need to explain, to attack or to defend' (Carter, 2007a, p. viii). Stylistics has overcome these debates and there is no longer a need to justify what it does and how it does it.

See also *style* (Key Terms), *Introduction*.

Defamiliarization

See *foregrounding* (Key Terms).

Deictic shift theory

In order to understand the principles of deictic shift theory (DST), it is essential to consider the notion of deixis itself (see *deixis*). Deixis is a term derived from Greek which means 'pointing'. In linguistics, this concept has been used to refer to the way in which language can 'point', not merely in a locative and temporal manner (via the adverbs 'here', 'there', 'now' and 'then', for instance), but also as a means of signalling personal, social or psychological distance (by using address terms, vocatives, titles or demonstratives). Deictic shift theory, however, is less concerned with establishing the ways in which spatio-temporal parameters (among others) are marked in language but more with the cognitive repositioning into the story world of fiction that readers are able to experience. DST came about as the interdisciplinary product of the work undertaken by a number of scholars from the State University of New York at Buffalo. Although their research backgrounds were different (artificial intelligence, philosophy, linguistics, psychology, communicative disorders, education, English and geography), the DST version put forward in *Deixis in Narrative. A Cognitive Science Perspective* (1995) primarily reflects their shared concerns with narrative fiction. Central to DST is the notion of the deictic centre. As McIntyre says, 'This refers not just to a speaker or hearer's location in space and time, but also to their position in a social hierarchy, and this complex deictic centre is the position from which they interpret deictic terms' (2006, p. 92). The deictic centre frames speakers' reality and allows them to assess other deictic indicators from this core perspective. Speakers tend to assume that, by default, they always inhabit the deictic centre, so any reference to other locations or time will be conceptualized in relation to their current *here* and *now*. The speaker and their circumstances, thus, form the origo from which shifts in deictic coordinates will take place. DST claims that readers embark on a very specific kind of cognitive exercise when they approach narratives for their current *here* and *now* loci are transposed to the particular parameters of the world of the narrative. Segal summarizes DST as follows:

> The Deictic Shift Theory (DST) argues that the metaphor of the reader getting inside of a story is cognitively valid [. . .]. We suggest that when one reads a narrative as it is meant to be read, he or she is often required to take a cognitive stance within the world of the narrative. A location within the world of the narrative serves as the center from which the sentences are to be interpreted [. . .]. DST is a theory that states that the deictic center often shifts from the environmental situation in which the text is encountered, to a locus within a mental model representing the world of the discourse. (Segal, 1995, p. 15)

Stockwell (2002, p. 46) highlights that DST is able to ascribe a cognitive dimension to the concept of deixis which earlier classifications had neglected to acknowledge (Bühler, 1982; Levinson, 1983; Lyons 1977). Readers of fiction are, thus, capable of taking a cognitive stance within the mental construct which is the story world, temporarily abandoning the referential parameters of their immediate reality. According to Stockwell, this cognitive ability to shift dimensions also indicates that speakers, in general, and readers, in particular, are capable of what he calls 'deictic projection' (2002, p. 46). The idiomatic expression 'putting yourself in someone's shoes' neatly summarizes the notion of deictic projection, as speakers/hearers can modify their deictic indicators to accommodate the other party's deictic centre instead. For instance, consider the way the temporal reference in a post-it note on a tutor's office door ('Back in 5 minutes') needs to be conceptualized by students: on the one hand, the note's temporal frame can be understood from the perspective of the writer who expects to be away from her office no longer than the time stated; on the other, students reading that note can assume that their tutor has left her office some time in the immediate past and will be back in less than five minutes from ('their') now, in which case they would be projecting their temporal frame to that of their lecturer. If they fail to project their temporal parameters, then they can expect to be waiting outside their tutor's office for at least five minutes counting from the moment they read the note.

In this respect, McIntyre (2006, p. 93) emphasizes that the notion of 'deictic projection' has consequences for the understanding of the concept of 'point of view' which can be manipulated by authors, narrators and/or characters to entice readers to implement a particular set of transpositions into the deictic centres of others within the story world. Galbraith (1995) uses the term 'deictic fields' to refer to a series of cognitive deictic dimensions sharing the same deictic centre; in fiction, unlike what happens in everyday communication, such deictic fields do not have the speaker as origo, but some entity within the story world which is dictating that world's deictic parameters. The move between ontological planes, that is, from our everyday lives to the fictional account of the story world is, according to McIntyre 'the first deictic shift' (2006, p. 99) and, once the leap through the gate of fiction has been instantiated, further shifts can take place.

Galbraith discusses two ways in which such shifts occur, which she calls (borrowing terms from artificial intelligence) PUSHes and POPs. The former move happens when we 'submerge' ourselves into a 'less available deictic plane' (Galbraith, 1995, p. 47), whereas the latter follows a process of 'emerging' back from a particular deictic field. According to Galbraith, PUSHes are shifts typically found in flashbacks, when stories are embedded within stories, or when the narrative includes episodes of fantasy. POPs, by contrast, are associated with episodes in which a character, for instance, wakes up from a dream, or when the narrator makes a remark (the POPping move) within the story that might point towards a particular *dénouement*. The narrator's intervention will eventually lead to a desire, on the part of readers, to an eventual return to the story world from which the narrator departed, that is, out of that POP and PUSHing back into the story (Galbraith, 1995, p. 47). Stockwell suggests that picking up a novel and 'moving from being a real reader to perceiving yourself in a textual role as implied reader or narratee' (2002, p. 47) also constitutes an instance of PUSHing, while closing a novel signals the final POPping out of the story world and onto reality. Galbraith (1995) finishes her account of the way deictic fields are exploited in fiction by discussing what she calls 'deictic decay', which refers to the decline in prominence of those fields which are not regularly activated after having been previously set in motion.

The work undertaken by stylisticians on the notions initially propounded by the researchers at the State University of New York has underscored a series of problems with the original model. McIntyre (2006) has questioned several aspects of the framework as initially formulated, in particular the rather vague way in which the core components of the model, the notion of POPping and PUSHing, are dealt with. For instance, he critiques this aspect of the framework as slightly underdeveloped and underscores that there should be a clear difference between shifts that happen at the discourse level, that is moves in and out of distinctly different ontological planes, and those transitional moves between deictic fields within the story world. Furthermore, McIntyre emphasizes that there is no clear indication as to which particular textual clues indicate how instances of POPping or PUSHing come about, or how deictic fields are seemingly delineated by speakers and hearers. Finally, he also comments on the unfortunate choice of terminology to describe the shifts between fields as the terms PUSH and POP appear to create a kind of parallelism with the latter being merely the opposite process to the former, although such is not necessarily always the case. For further applications of DST, see Jeffries (2008) and Herman (2001, 2009).

See also *deixis* (Key Terms).

Deixis

Consider the following two definitions of the term:

> Deixis, a term which is derived from the Greek word δείζις (meaning pointing), concerns the use of certain linguistic expressions to locate entities in spatio-temporal, social and discoursal context. In English such deictic expressions typically include first- and second-person pronouns, demonstratives, tense, certain place and time adverbials and some verbs such as 'come', 'go', 'bring', 'take' and 'fetch'. Such deictic expressions encode specific aspects of the speech event and cannot be interpreted unless contextual parameters are taken into account. (Marmaridou, 2000, p. 65)
>
> Deixis is the encoding in an utterance of the spatio-temporal context and subjective experience of the encoder. It is primarily linked with the

> speech or discourse event. It is the phenomenon whereby the tripartite relationship between the language system, the encoder's subjectivity and various contextual factors is foregrounded grammatically or lexically. (Green, 1992, p. 121)

The first of these definitions comes from a work with a primarily pragmatic slant (*Pragmatic Meaning and Cognition*, 2000) whereas the second follows more closely the concerns of the stylistic tradition ('Deixis and the poetic persona', 1992). Both explanations, however, highlight that the notion of deixis conveys the meaning of 'pointing or situating' understood both in a literal sense ('pointing in space', 'pointing in time', 'pointing in discourse') and in a metaphorical sense ('placing in the social scale' or 'situating yourself psychologically and emotionally'). Green (1992, p. 128) states that deixis can be encoded linguistically in two main ways, via 'deictic terms' and 'deictic elements'. Deictic terms are a set number of linguistic items capable of projecting deictic parameters which include the personal pronouns ('I', 'you', 'she'), demonstrative determiners and pronouns ('this', 'that'), certain adverbials ('here', 'there', 'now', 'then'), definite referring expressions (introduced by the definite article 'the'), a few lexical verbs ('come', 'go', 'bring', 'take') and the vocative. Deictic elements, on the other hand, are not, in and of themselves, capable of displaying deixis; they can be used deictically in very specific situations so their deictic function is completely context-dependent. Green (1992) discusses the role of tense in relation to its possibility as deictic element (cf. Marmaridou's quotation above where tense is considered a deictic marker): if the sentence 'The sky is blue' is uttered when leaving your place in the morning and actually confirming that the day is bright and clear (hence referring directly to the contextual circumstances surrounding the production of your utterance including the time of production), then, the present tense is said to be used deictically. If, on the contrary, you simply produce that utterance as a statement concerning a general state of affairs (that is, the fact that skies tend to be that colour) then you are using the present tense generically and no deictic encoding should be inferred from that use.

The diverse ways in which deictic terms and elements alike can encode literal and metaphorical 'positioning' give rise to the various types of deixis generally discussed by scholars. There are only slight discrepancies as far as terminological variations go, the main categories generally acknowledged being 'place deixis', 'temporal/time deixis', 'person deixis', 'social deixis', 'empathetic deixis' and 'discourse deixis' (Green, 1992, 1995; Levinson, 1983; Lyons, 1977; McIntyre, 2006, 2007a).

The first type, place deixis, allows speakers to anchor their utterance spatially; the speaker's position is, by default, the deictic centre or origo (see also definition of 'deictic centre' in entry on *deictic shift theory*), so locative parameters are always established in relation to this core spot. The clearest spatial deictic terms are 'here' and 'there' and the determiners/pronouns 'this' and 'that' (plus their corresponding plural forms). The fact that the speaker is the one deciding on the closeness and remoteness of the objects, events or circumstances referred to is indicative of their egocentric assumptions as deictic centres. That the speaker is, by default, the origin of any deictic encoding has also further consequences for the analysis of empathetic deixis, as described below. Time deixis, as Levinson states, 'concerns the encoding of temporal points and spans relative to the time at which an utterance was spoken (or a written message inscribed)' (1983, p. 62). The purest temporal deictic terms are the adverbs 'now' and 'then', but tense is often found as deictic projector too. Person deixis, thirdly, highlights the way the role of the participants (speakers/writers, listeners/readers) is encoded in the actual speech event, for which function, personal pronouns are the preferred option. Whereas first-person pronouns are generally used by speakers to refer to themselves and second-person to the listener, third-person pronouns invoke those entities fulfilling neither of these roles. In the case of literary texts (although not exclusively), personal pronouns' function as deictics is intricately linked to their potential as focalization and point of view markers.

Social deixis highlights the social viewpoint of interactants and is inscribed in the so-called terms of address. Items such as vocatives ('hey John'), honorifics (Sir, Lady) or title markers (Dr, Professor, Mr, Ms) can project the type of relationship held between speaker and hearer, so much that the misuse of these forms could have significant social consequences. For instance, if, on meeting the person you know to be your university lecturer, you address her inappropriately by using the vocatives 'mate', 'honey' or 'babe', or fail to acknowledge her institutional rank by dropping her correct title, 'Professor', you could seriously compromise your relationship with this person by having ignored differences in academic status. The next category is that of empathetic deixis which appears to be closely linked to the positioning of the speaker/writer as physical centre, so it is realized by forms also employed to indicate place deixis such as the determiners/pronouns 'this' and 'that'. Unlike place deixis, though, empathetic deixis encodes psychological and emotional closeness or distance towards the person, object, events or circumstances referred to. For instance, compare the use of the determiners in (a) 'I prefer this way of life' and (b) 'I can't stand that attitude'. Finally discourse deixis can be defined as:

> The use of expressions within an utterance to refer to some part of the discourse that contains this utterance (Levinson, 1983, p. 85). Therefore, discourse deixis is deixis in text. A text, whether in its written or oral realization, is closely related to the concepts of space and time [. . .]. Discourse deixis is expressed with terms that are primarily used in encoding space or time deixis. (Marmaridou, 2000, p. 93)

Marmaridou deftly explains the way discourse deixis works with the examples (a) 'Listen to this joke' and (b) 'Do you remember that story'. Both forms can be said to be used discoursally because their referent is part of the discourse itself, but the temporality of the discourse as it unfolds is also invoked. In the examples above, therefore, (a) indicates temporal closeness for the 'joke' is about to be disclosed after uttering the sentence, whereas (b) suggests remoteness in that the story-telling being referred to took place sometime in the past. There are numerous studies exploiting the concept of deixis and its further applications to other stylistic issues; see, for instance, Cockcroft (2005), Green (1995), McIntyre (2006, 2007a), Tsur (2003), van Peer and Graf (2002) and Werth (1995b).

See also *deictic shift theory* (Key Terms).

Denotation and connotation

Terms employed in linguistics, semiotics and literary criticism to distinguish between two facets of meaning. Denotation is the generally-agreed-upon 'dictionary definition' or 'literal meaning' of a word, while connotation refers to the various associations and secondary meanings that the word may evoke. Denotation and connotation thus concern the relationship between the signifier and the signified. While Saussure (1916) tended to focus on denotative meaning in his model of the sign, theorists after him – notably among them, the French semiotician Roland Barthes (1915–80) – have argued for a more nuanced view of the signified which acknowledges that the signified concept of a given signifier comprises denotative as well as connotative meaning. A popular example of this is the signifier 'home' which denotes the meaning of 'a place where one lives', yet at the same time it may also connote concepts such as 'privacy', 'security', 'comfort' and 'family'.

The denotation and connotation of a word or expression may vary according to the context in which it occurs. In one context, the lexical item 'bank' will be employed to denote 'a financial institution where people can borrow or keep money', while in another, the denotation of the same word will be 'a raised area of land along the side of a river'. Similarly, the word 'feminist' may carry positive connotations such as 'independent', 'progressive', 'aware of gender issues' for some people, but negative connotations such as ' aggressive', 'militant' and 'man-hater' for others. It is generally believed that the denotation of a given signifier is more fixed and less open to interpretation than its connotative meaning. It is important to note, however, that the connotations of a given word are not completely subjective, and that even the denotative meaning of words, as well as of other semiotic signs, is socio-culturally specific and never completely neutral.

In semantics and philosophy, 'reference', 'referent' and 'referential meaning' are employed to describe what is termed denotational meaning above, i.e., the use of language to represent the extra-linguistic world. The referent of the lexical item 'book' is thus a real, physical, book, which is consequently referred to by linguistic means. In these fields, 'reference' contrasts with 'sense', which concerns the linguistic meaning of a lexical item and its relations to other linguistic items in the system to which it belongs.

See also *referent, signifier, signified* (Key Terms).

Deviation

See *foregrounding* (Key Terms).

Diachronic

See *historical stylistics* (Key Branches), *Ferdinand de Saussure* (Key Thinkers).

Discourse presentation

Discourse presentation is a ubiquitously used term and seems to refer to a variety of linguistic and socio-cultural phenomena. For some, it may allude to the presentation of speech or conversation. For others, it may refer to the linguistic approach of discourse analysis or discourses in general and their contexts. And still others who use the term 'discourse presentation' do not clearly differentiate between speech or thought presentation categories. The term discourse presentation is used here as a cover term to refer to the strategies reporters or narrators use to present other people's speech, thought or writing. It is also employed to describe the possibilities of labelling those modes and their functions. The term 'presentation' instead of 'representation' is the preferred choice because it is less ideologically loaded. Toolan remarks that:

> [y]ounger readers, fully of the digital age, may be puzzled that these opening remarks about the power to record and represent speech are not focused on audiotape recording and digitised sound files, now very widespread means of representing speech. But this [. . .] is about an affordance of the much earlier and culture-changing technological breakthrough, the development of writing, and literary authors' rich repertoires of means for presenting characters' words on the page. (Toolan, 2006c, p. 698)

This section will use Leech and Short's (1981) and Semino and Short's (2004) model of discourse presentation. The earlier model by Leech and Short (1981) is mainly based on the analysis of literature. Yet, it should be stressed that the model and its underlying principles can be transferred to other varieties and genres (Toolan, 2006c). In fact, it has been applied to journalism, parliamentary debates and magazines.

Because the presentation of other people's speech seems to be most pervasive (and easiest to understand), it makes sense to begin with some examples from this mode of discourse presentation to illustrate in general what it entails if other people's speech is presented. It is possible for a reporter to present the words of a speaker in a direct way, by means of the so-called direct speech (DS). This can be done with the help of a reporting clause (1) 'he said', which is sometimes also called the *inquit* clause or 'framing clause'. It can also be done without it (2), which is labelled free direct speech (FDS):

(1) 'She is a lovely person,' he said.
(2) 'She is a lovely person.'

In example (1), the distinction is between the reporting clause, which identifies the speaker of the reported clause and the verb of communication, and the reported clause, which presents the speaker's message. The stretch of direct speech is marked by inverted commas/speech marks. The reporting clause helps the reader to understand that this stretch is reported *verbatim*. In addition, all deictic markers (pronouns, tense, time and place expressions (Toolan, 2006c, p. 699)) construe the speakers' position and their deictic centre. Often the reporting clause also contains paralinguistic information or reference to the speaker's mood or attitude. These additional linguistic markers function as evaluation or indexical cues (Toolan, 2006c, p. 699). We may also report the words of others in a more indirect way (3).

(3) He said that she was a lovely person.

Although the reporting clause in (3) is still used ('he said') the inverted commas have disappeared and there is also a tense shift from 'is' as in (1) to 'was'. The stretch 'she was a lovely person' is indirect speech (IS). The reported clause is usually introduced by a complementizer or subordinator, among which 'that' is most common in Modern English (others are 'if' or 'whether'). While in direct speech (DS) all deictic elements mark the position of the speaker, in indirect speech (IS), the narrator controls them both with reference to space and time. Spatial and temporal markers like 'here', 'today', 'this' and 'now' will be replaced by 'there', 'on that same day' and so on. Here the foreign language learner of English might be reminded of the complicated rules that had to be studied to understand 'reported speech'. In IS, the speaker's real words used in the antecedent discourse are often not reported on a one-to-one basis. But the 'content, gist or illocution of the actual or implied DS utterance' (Toolan, 2006c, p. 699) is given. It is especially in narrative fiction that a variation of source is assumed because a variety of possible antecedent versions of DS are possible. In 'real' or 'non-fictional' discourses a need for what is called faithfulness is more important, because even in IS, it is assumed that what is presented is very similar to the antecedent wording. For example, as readers of newspaper reports about political speeches or decisions made by politicians we assume that the words reported are the exact words used by the speaker.

Toolan (2006c, p. 699) points out that 'When contemplating Direct Speech [. . .] at least two binary distinctions need to be considered: is the text in which it appears literature or non-literary; and is it hypothetical or actual'. Despite Toolan's distinction between literary and non-literary forms, it should be stressed that DS is still considered the most faithful category of speech presentation for fiction and non-fiction alike.

All the examples presented so far illustrate the presence of a 'teller' who has purposely decided to report the speech of somebody else. Direct speech and indirect speech differ in terms of their realization, propositional content and function, and such differences are carried through for the presentation of thought and writing alike. Leech and Short (1981) claim that these three varieties of reported discourse work on parallel scales although their functions in language are different. So although thought presentation is utterly different in function (especially in terms of faithfulness claims, in terms of effects, in terms of the construal of thought in linguistic form and in terms of the possibility of summarizing thought), Short (2007a) stresses that it makes sense to display the three presentation modes on parallel scales.

Semino and Short (2004) extend the discourse presentation model from that in Leech and Short (1981/2007) by not only making a distinction between speech, thought and writing presentation, but by also introducing new parallel categories on each scale which result from their analysis of a corpus of twentieth-century narrative fiction, autobiography and newspaper reports. As can be seen in the diagram below, the new categories are the narrator's representation of voice (NV) on the speech presentation scale, narrrator's representation of writing (NW) in the writing scale and internal narration (NI) in the thought presentation scale. Category N (narration) often occurs in brackets on the left-end scale of the respective categories because it is closely connected with NV and the narrator's report of a speech act (NRSA), but it is not real speech presentation. Most recently, Short (2007a) has suggested considering NI to be part of narration (like Toolan, 2001) rather than part of the thought presentation scale, and he introduces the category of NT, narrator's presentation or reference to thought.

The order of the different speech presentation scales reflects the linguistic features involved in indirect and direct forms and the faithfulness claims between anterior and posterior discourse or, in other words, the rising degree of narrator involvement moving to the left-hand side and the character involvement moving to the right-hand side of the model.

NV	NRSA	IS	FIS	DS	FDS
narrator's presentation of voice	narrator's presentation of speech acts	indirect speech	free indirect speech	direct speech	free direct speech

Diagram 'Speech presentation scales'

NW	NRWA	IW	FIW	DW	FDW
narrator's presentation of writing	narrator's presentation of writing acts	indirect writing	free indirect writing	direct writing	free direct writing

Diagram 'Writing presentation scales'

NI	NT	NRTA	IT	FIT	DT	FDT
internal narration	narrator's presentation of thought	narrator's presentation of thought acts	indirect thought	free indirect thought	direct thought	free direct thought

Diagram 'Thought presentation scales'

Speech presentation

As can be seen in the diagram, 'Speech presentation scales', the presentation of the speech of others can take on different forms depending on the relationship between posterior and anterior discourse. NV contains presentations of minimal speech or verbal activity as well as its manner or style as reported by the speaker, but no mention of the actual form or content of the utterance is made. NV is different from NRSA to the extent that, in NRSA, the narrator provides information about the illocutionary force of the reported utterance (Semino and Short, 2004, p. 44); Page's (1973) idea of *submerged speech* and Short's (1996) *Narrator's Representation of Speech* are similar concepts. An example is 'To her voluntary communications' (Austen, [1816] 1985, p. 262) from Austen's *Emma* where the reader is informed that speech has taken place. In terms of effect it can be said that it illustrates the point of view of a particular character and that it functions as an introductory statement to speech. It has a signalling function to what follows. It may also be used as reference which summarizes what a group of people has said.

NRSA often consists of one clause where the speech report verb is followed by a noun phrase or a prepositional phrase indicating the topic. Hence, the speech act value is provided, but not the exact content. It is often used to summarize or to give background information. An example is 'went on to express so much wonder at the notion of my being a gentleman' (Dickens, [1860] 1999, p. 109), where the speech act verb 'express' is followed by a nominal group after the preposition 'at': 'the notion'.

The following utterance from Charles Dickens's *Great Expectations* is an example of IS: 'Once more, I stammered with difficulty that I had no objection' (Dickens, [1860] 1999, p. 109). The reporting clause is 'Once more, I stammered with difficulty' and the reported clause is 'that I had no objection'. As mentioned, indirect stretches of speech presentation are often introduced by conjunctions like 'that', 'if' or 'whether' and the reporting clause conventionally precedes the reported clause. In addition, the relationship between reporting and reported clause is that of hypotaxis (that is, of dependence), while for DS it is often claimed that reported clause and reporting clause stand in a paratactic relationship (that is, they are clauses at the same level). According to Lubock (see Short, 2007a and Toolan, 2001), indirect discourse forms *tell* a character's words whereas direct discourse forms *show* them. Nevertheless, in comparison to NRSA, indirect speech (IS) seems closer to the character because it contains the speech act, the topic and the propositional content, but not necessarily the precise words of the utterance. As such, it is more faithful to the original, but it also foregrounds the act of reporting.

FIS carries linguistic features from DS and from IS. Other terms used are *erlebte Rede* or *style indirect libre*. While the reporting clause from IS and the quotation marks from DS do not often occur, it may contain deictic features from both DS and IS. Therefore, its claims of faithfulness in relation to the words and structures used in the anterior discourse are not always clear and FIS and FIT are not always easy to distinguish, because often they both share the linguistic feature of modality (Toolan, 2001, p. 131). According to Semino and Short (2004, p. 13), FIS often creates ironic effects, because it is perceived by the reader as distancing him/her from what the character said. An example is when Mr. Woodhouse in Austen's *Emma* worries about a ball. His inference of Emma's disappointment is somewhat diminished by his pessimistic conviction that they should stay at home anyway: 'and as for the ball, it was shocking to have dear Emma disappointed; but they would all be safer at home' (Austen, [1816] 1985, p. 41). Here the reporting clause is missing and the deictic orientation is that of reporting (past tense and back-shifted pronouns).

DS and FDS are the modes of speech presentation in which a character's words are *shown.* The effect is that of mimesis. DS contains both a reporting and a reported clause, which is marked in inverted commas. DS brings with it a further faithfulness claim as it reports verbatim the speech act value, the grammatical structure and the words of the utterance as well as its propositional content. An example is '"Emma knows I never flatter her," said Mr. Knightley' (Austen, [1816] 1985, p. 42), where the reported clause is distinguished from the reporting clause ('said Mr. Knightley') by inverted commas. The effect of DS is that of vividness and dramatization, as the exact words of the character are given (Toolan, 2001, p. 120). Toolan also points out that 'the choice of direct speech reporting is also to accept a scenic slowing of pace, an enhanced focus on the specificity and detail of an interaction, and a greater pressure on the author to make such text redeemingly interesting' (2001, p. 129). According to Leech and Short (1981/2007) and Semino and Short (2004), the norm for speech presentation in their corpus of twentieth-century narrative fiction is direct speech.

FDS, on the other hand, must contain the direct reported clause (mostly in inverted commas), but it does not need to include the reporting clause. FDS is most faithful as it presents the words of the character/or the original with no obstruction from the narrator or the reporter. As most investigations of DS and FDS have differentiated between DS and FDS, Semino and Short (2004, p. 49) have maintained that distinction in their annotation of the various discourse presentation categories, although they see the difference between DS and FDS (and likewise between DW and FDW) as a variation of the same category. Also, Semino and Short (2004) notice that it is not uncommon for a stretch of direct speech presentation to move to free direct speech presentation which, therefore, aggravates the annotation process and highlights the danger of making arbitrary decisions. Although Short (2007a) suggests the inclusion of FDS in the category of DS, Busse (2010a) suggests annotating both categories separately and maintaining the traditional distinction.

Writing presentation

Writing presentation, in which the anterior discourse or the original is a piece of written discourse, is similar in function to speech presentation.

However, generally, it is stronger in relation to faithfulness claims because writing has been valued more highly than spoken language. In Semino and Short's (2004) corpus, writing presentation is more frequent in the news reports and (auto)biographies than in narrative fiction and also the quantitative distribution of the respective categories for writing presentation is different from those for the other discourse presentation scales (Semino and Short, 2004, p. 48).

In writing presentation, similar options to those for speech presentation are suggested (see diagram 'Writing presentation scales'). NW includes those cases where the narrator reports that the character engages in writing. NRWA is the most frequent category in the Semino and Short (2004, p. 105) corpus and describes the written act and the value of the writing act, but no further reference is made to the content. Often a prepositional phrase followed by noun phrases occurs. An example would be the summary of the advertisement which searches for Oliver Twist in Dickens's ([1837] 1966) *Oliver Twist* and which Mr. Bumble discovers while reading the newspaper: 'And then followed a full description of Oliver's dress, person, appearance, and disappearance: with the name and address of Mr. Brownlow at full length' (Dickens, [1837] 1966, p. 110).

IW contains the writing act, the topic and the propositional content, but not necessarily the precise written words of the utterance. IW is usually introduced by a reporting clause or a reporting signal. An example of IW is 'A letter arrived from Mr. Churchill to urge his nephew's instant return' (Austen, [1816] 1985, p. 263), in which 'a letter arrived' serves as a reporting clause and 'to urge his nephew's instant return', because it is clausal, is the reported clause.

FIW may contain features of DW and IW and often omits the reporting clause. The effects are similar to that of FIS where the narrator often uses this mode of discourse presentation in an ironic way. An example would be 'Mrs Churchill was unwell' (Austen, [1816] 1985, p. 263) which follows the information that 'A letter arrived from Mr. Churchill to urge his nephew's instant return' (Austen, [1816] 1985, p. 263) so the reader knows that this information must have occurred in the letter that was sent. DW, in line with its counterpart speech category, gives a verbatim account of a written document, but often uses the reporting clause to introduce it. FDW can be equated with genuine writing, as the reporting clause often does not occur.

Thought presentation

The thought presentation scale contains similar categories to those already discussed, but the functions of the parallel modes of thought presentation are critically different. This is due to three factors that differentiate thought from writing and speech presentation. When thought is presented, faithfulness cannot be observed because human beings do not have access to the thoughts of others. Therefore, the summary aspect cannot be applied because we cannot assume that there is an anterior thought act. In addition, it is difficult to determine whether and, if so how, thoughts are construed in linguistic form because, although thoughts are part of cognition, it is not conclusive that 'all cognition is thought' (Short, 2007a, p. 236). Therefore, the different forms of thought presentation should be seen as a series of 'effect scales' (Short, 2007a, p. 231).

In the first of the thought categories, internal narration (NI), the character is displayed to be engaged in a specific act of thinking, but neither the propositional content nor the specific thought act are rendered. It is a report of mental or cognitive states and describes the character's cognitive or emotional experience without real reference to his thoughts. NI can also describe a particular emotional reaction. In Semino and Short (2004), NI encompasses all cases where a narrator reports a character's cognitive and emotional experience but not their perceptions. The verb 'puzzle', for instance, in the following example by Hardy, alludes to the mental state of the character: 'Seeing how puzzled Phillotson seemed, Jude said as cheerfully as he could [. . .]' (Hardy, [1881] 1975, p. 192). Semino and Short (2004) initially established a parallel between NI and NV on the speech presentation scale because, according to them, both occupy some intermediate position between the straightforward narration of actions and events. The classification of this category as thought presentation, however, is a far from settled issue. Other scholars apart from Short and Semino have also discussed NI from different perspectives such as, for instance, Simpson (1993, pp. 24–5) who is dubious regarding the classification of NI as discourse presentation. Cohn (1978), in turn, had previously suggested that this phenomenon should be understood as a form of 'psychonarration' (she adds NRTA and IT into this category). Palmer (2004) has illustrated that the depiction of conscience and consciousness is not always verbal, but depicted in the mode of psychonarration (see also Fludernik, 2009).

While Semino and Short (2004, p. 46) opt against labelling these phenomena under the heading of narration because that would exclude its essential mental activity component, Toolan (2001, pp. 119, 143) describes these presentations as 'reports of mental or verbal activity which do not purport to be a character's articulated speech or thought'. That NI does not actually contain characters' mental or verbal activity leads Toolan to argue for the category of NI to be excluded from the thought presentation scale and be placed within the narration proper instead. This reading – aligning NI towards the narrator – sees NI 'as a statement that the narrator makes about the inner world of his or her characters' (Short, 2007a, p. 236). Instead Short (2007a, p. 236) introduces a new category, Narrator's Presentation of/Reference to Thought (NT), which constitutes more straightforward thought presentation equivalences of NV and NW and also takes the equivalent position to NW and NV on the thought presentation scale (Short, 2007a, p. 237). An example would be 'he began to think' in 'As he left the room, Lord Henry's heavy eyelids drooped, and he began to think' (Wilde, [1890] 1994, p. 68).

If NI is considered as thought presentation it should be positioned next to NT. If it is seen as part of narration, as Leech and Short (1981, pp. 341–2) and Toolan (2001, p. 142) have done, and seen as the narration of internal states or events (parallel to the narration of external events), then it should be placed on the left hand side of NT and included within N. As such, examples of NI would not present thoughts, but rather the narrator's statements of the internal world. Short (2007a) suggests that what is labelled as NI in the corpus analysed for Semino and Short (2004, p. 237) should be re-examined because these examples 'appear to cover a wide range of different kinds of phenomena' (2007a, p. 235).

NRTA expresses the thought act, the topic, but not the exact thoughts. Similar to NRSA, the thoughts appear to be summarized, but it is one of the most inexact categories because a summary cannot really take place within thoughts. After Frank Churchill's departure, Emma's deploring attitude towards this is conveyed in NRTA: 'and foresaw so great a loss to their little society from his absence' (Austen, [1816] 1985, p. 266). Next, IT consists of the thought act, the topic and the propositional content, but not necessarily the precise details of the thought act. When Emma, in Austen's *Emma*, engages in matchmaking between Mr. Elton and Harriet, the narrator presents Emma's thought in IT: 'She thought it would be an excellent match; and only too palpably desirable, natural, and probable, for her to have much merit in planning it' (Austen, [1816] 1985, p. 63). FIT, which, contrary to FIS, is extensively used in the fictional corpus investigated by Semino and Short (2004,

p. 13), is a very open category, because, in terms of the words, grammar, syntactic, orthographic and deictic distinctions used, it contains features from DT and IT. Some other scholars prefer to amalgamate both categories in what is known as free indirect discourse (FID). Jefferson (1981, p. 42), for instance, suggests that FID is a mixture of proper narrative or proper speech and thought. Toolan (2001, p. 135) points out that this amalgamated category can be characterized in multiple ways: as substitutionary narration, as combined discourse, as a contamination, tainting or colouring of the narrative or as a dual voicing.

As previously stated, there are clear functional and effectual differences between the categories of speech and though presentation, despite the fact that the various linguistic strategies that realize each form are parallel in structure, as Leech and Short (1981) pointed out and Short and Semino (2004) verified. These differences in functions result from the different nature of the discourse presentation modes as such, namely that it is impossible for a witness to truthfully report the thoughts of others. Nevertheless, recourse to more direct thought presentation is a more direct way of entering into the character's mind as the narrator is not controlling the thought world of the character. In this end of the scale, DT tends to be construed with a reporting clause and the reported clause presented in inverted commas. The final category, that of FDT, only shows the direct thoughts of the character or thinker and is considered the freest way of reporting the thought process of characters.

Of all the categories described here, free indirect discourse (FID) has been the one studied most frequently for the last 100 years, especially, although not exclusively in narratology. Pascal (1977), McHale (1978) and Bakhtin (1981) have, for example, emphasized the 'dual voice' and the effects of FID. Banfield (1982) analyses the implications of FID for narration which she considers 'unspeakable' because, unlike discourse (which is both communicative and expressive), narrative does not contain a genuine addressee (nor any textual trace of one), nor a genuine speaker (cited in Toolan, 2006c). Stanzel (1984), in turn, stresses that FID typically comes with internal character focalization and defines FID as mimetic diegesis, because it tells aspects of a character's own words.

To sum up, a few issues regarding the different modes of discourse presentation need highlighting. Generally speaking, the modes of discourse presentation can be viewed along reduced or increased character alignment, although effect or function, especially for the different categories of speech and thought presentation, are different. Speech and writing presentation, on the other hand, are considered to be similar in relation to their associated effects (Semino and Short, 2004, p. 50).

See also *corpus stylistics, historical stylistics* (Key Branches).

Ellipsis

See *cohesion* (Key Terms).

Entailment

See *presupposition and entailment* (Key Terms).

Experiential meaning

See *ideational meaning* (Key Terms).

Focalization

The studies devoted to explaining the notion of focalization are not only abundant but also varied as to their informing disciplines and main influences (Herman, 2002, 2009; Toolan, 2001; van Peer and Chatman, 2001). Focalization is a term that emanates from narratology but its impact has been very much felt in stylistic circles too. Although the existing attempts at a definition are, similarly, countless, the origins of such endeavours can be located in the structuralist tradition of which Gerard Genette is one of its most famous proponents. Genette (1972, 1980) coins focalization partly as a reaction to point of view (see *point of view*), for the latter, Genette claims, appears to merge two narrative phenomena that need to be understood separately, the now classical distinction of 'who sees?' versus 'who tells?'. Rimmon-Kenan (1983, 2002) acknowledges Genette's distinction but takes issue with his reasoning as to why the substitution of focalization is necessary:

> The story is presented in the text through the mediation of some 'prism', 'perspective', 'angle of vision', verbalized by the narrator though not necessarily his. Following Genette (1972), I call this mediation 'focalization' [. . .].

> Genette considers 'focalization' to have a degree of abstractness which avoids the specifically visual connotations of 'point of view'. (Rimmon-Kenan, 2002, p. 72)

Genette's preference for the term focalization, thus, originates from, on the one hand, the fact that point of view appears to overlook the 'seer vs. narrator' dichotomy, and, on the other, because point of view may be perceived as semantically overloaded with reference to visual aspects. Other scholars (Rimmon-Kenan, 2002; McIntyre, 2006) have pointed out that focalization is not exactly free from optical references either, so the apparent abstractness that justifies the substitution has not been widely accepted by the academic community. Rimmon-Kenan, nonetheless, incorporates the very useful distinction between 'who sees' and 'who speaks', so her discussion of the term focalization is, in practice, rather close to that of Genette. More recent approaches, however, tend to avoid dwelling too much on this issue and prefer a general definition, as here exemplified by Jahn: 'the submission of (potentially limitless) narrative information to a perspectival filter' (Jahn, 2007, p. 94).

The Genettian model distinguishes three main types of focalization: non-focalization or zero focalization, internal focalization and external focalization. The first type gives the control of the narrative to the 'teller', the narrator, so that filtering of information via any other mediator is virtually discarded; narratives with omniscient narrators would be prototypical examples. In internal focalization the story is viewed through the eyes of some internal participant in the story known as 'reflector character'. This situation constrains the perspective from which the story is presented to that of the reflector. If that reflector's perspective is kept steady throughout the narrative we can talk of fixed focalization; if the original reflector's angle is alternated with the perspective facilitated by further reflectors, then focalization is said to be variable; finally, if the same story is recurrently being told from the viewpoint of many reflectors, that narrative is characteristically displaying multiple focalization. External focalization indicates that mediation is kept to a minimum; so readers (or audiences in the cases of drama or cinema, for instance) are only given information which is externally accessible, that is, information on characters' attitudes, thoughts or emotions are not narratively contemplated. Externally focalized narratives could have simply been captured by a camera or a tape recorder. For instance, instances of dialogue without reporting clauses or stage directions are obvious cases of external focalization.

Genette's classification has been much criticized and reworked although most of the subsequent proposals still acknowledge its value as, at least, the original point of departure. Besides the reservations expressed above by Rimmon-Kenan, Bal (1997) has separately voiced some forceful and convincing criticisms towards the Genettian model; her most important departure concerns the reduction of focalization types to two, internal and external. Bal's critique affects primarily the zero and external categories subsumed under external focalization as, for her, focalizers can either be integral components of the story or external elements without a role in the storyworld (see *narration*, especially intradiegetic and extradiegetic narrators). Bal objects to Genette's vague indications as to 'who is seeing what' in his zero and external groups, but she also calls into question the existence of totally unmediated external or zero focalization as such a level of neutrality is simply impossible to achieve.

Modern narratology enjoys now the advantage granted by temporal perspective on all of these issues, so its practitioners are capable of highlighting flaws and lacks in the original proposals of the past. For instance, narratology considered itself 'a timeless and culture-independent discipline' (Jahn, 2007, p. 94), yet it has nowadays become apparent that 'their seemingly neutral theoretical models may have been shaped by cultural and historical contingencies' (Jahn, 2007, p. 94). To cultural and historical determinants, Jahn (2007, p. 102) adds the role that cognitive sciences are playing in our understanding of narratological concepts. Where more traditional positions rely mainly on the textual components of narratives, cognitive considerations are increasingly incorporating the role of the reader as active participant in the creation of mental worlds to which they are transported in the process of reading (*deictic shift theory*) or which they cognitively project (*text world theory, mental spaces theory*). Finally, it needs to be acknowledged that discussions on the nature of focalization are never too far apart from those on point of view. As a general tendency, point of view seems to have been the term of choice adopted by stylisticians (McIntyre, 2006; Short, 1996; Simpson, 1993) whereas narratologists have opted for the former coinage. It appears that the particularly strong linguistic basis that stylisticians endow their analyses with becomes the main point of divergence between the two camps. Having said this, though, the two groups represent akin disciplines, not discrete and totally dissenting schools of thought.

Rimmon-Kenan seems to be a case in point to illustrate the affinities existing between stylistic and narratological approaches. In her discussion of the various types of focalization, she concurs with Bal in describing an external as well as an internal perspective, but she also claims that these two angles need to be conceptualized in relation to the so-called facets of focalization (2002, p. 78). These facets work on three main planes directly influenced by Uspensky (1973), the spatio-temporal, the psychological and the ideological planes. Fowler (1986) also benefits from the latter's taxonomy although his research has borne fruit in relation to point of view, not focalization types (see *point of view* for a more detailed explanation). Further distinctions are based on the genre primarily chosen by narratologists, narrative fiction, whereas stylisticians have managed to spell out the peculiarities of the use of point of view use as much in prose, poetry or drama (Short, 1996; McIntyre, 2006). Rather than creating a false sense of opposition between these two disciplines, focalization and point of view should be viewed, instead, as sides of the same coin each one capable of bringing to the fore distinctive aspects of textual style. For a detailed analysis on the way stylistics and narratology are interconnected see Fludernik (1993, 1996) and Shen (2005).

See also *narratology* (Key Branches), *deictic shift theory*, *focalization*, *mental spaces*, *point of view*, *text world theory* (Key Terms).

Foregrounding

4grounding is deviation and parallelism, and 4grounding ☺ at u.

This 'sentence' displays multimodal and linguistic elements that go beyond the (linguistic) signs usually expected to be used in a reference book: The cardinal number '4' has replaced the prefix 'fore'. Users of SMSs or chat-rooms will know that this is an abbreviation frequently appearing as a communicative device in new media. To decode the meaning of the cardinal number in this sentence the reader has to utter it. What is exploited here is the homophony between the cardinal number '4' and the prefix 'fore'. Similarly, 'u' is an abbreviation, which stands for the personal pronoun 'you', and the icon '☺' is used as a visual realization of the concept of 'smiling'.

Many scholars draw on visual features to explain foregrounding as elements of a text which stand out somehow or are deviant from (or parallel to) what one would expect or what is conventional. Short (2007c), in his web-based course, for example, uses similar and deviating fonts as well as colours to highlight the concepts and the terms 'parallelism' and 'deviation'. A literary example which illustrates foregrounding is the title of Dylan Thomas's poem 'A Grief Ago' (1936). This is an example of linguistic deviation at the level of lexico-grammar, because the collocation of 'grief' with 'ago' is rare in Standard English. The adverb 'ago' frequently collocates with expressions of time, as in 'a week ago', and not with emotions like 'grief' (see Hoey, 2005). At the phonological level, elements such as rhyme and alliteration are examples of foregrounding.

Foregrounding is closely related to the Russian Formalist concept of 'defamiliarization' (*ostranenie*, i.e., 'estrangement' or 'making strange') which was introduced into literary criticism by Shklovsky (1917). Shklovsky claimed that as things become familiar to us, we stop noticing them. Such 'automation' and 'habituation' mean staticity and conservatism. Therefore, in his view, the function of art is to make people look at the world from a new perspective, to defamiliarize the familiar in order to make them re-perceive what they have stopped noticing because of its familiarity and, ultimately, to make them recognize the artfulness of the expression itself. Foregrounding is a central means of defamiliarization.

The term foregrounding is also used in the arts. The object that is positioned in the foreground is measured against what is portrayed in the background, and it is often assumed that this object is perceptually more salient and hence more important. An object may also be visually foregrounded by means of features such as, for instance, its size or colour, which can make it stand out as salient in contrast to other represented elements.

In stylistics, the theory of foregrounding is essential (also in teaching) because of the central question in stylistics of how a text means. Foregrounding relates to linguistic devices on all levels of language that somehow stand out against the background of the text in which they occur, for example, or against contextual factors such as genre. Foregrounding is a relative concept because it can only be measured if norms and conventions are established and observed and if these are related to complex contextual features. Deviation and parallelism are examples of foregrounding. Deviation refers to moves away from a norm on all linguistic levels (whether language is seen as a system or from a functional point of view). Parallelism, in turn, is characterized by (overuse of) repetitive structures. By these linguistic means, features are promoted into the foreground. The measurement and description of the degree of foregrounding relies on a variety of norms, ranging from linguistic norms over contextual and historical norms to statistical norms which characterize the foregrounding behaviour of a particular item or feature under investigation (see *corpus stylistics* and *historical stylistics*). Rhetoric plays a role here as well because rhetorical language can be seen on a continuum of deviation from standard language, as outlined in Aristotle's *Poetics*.

Foregrounding enhances the meaning potential of the text. At the same time, that meaning potential can be exploited because foregrounding appears to be explicitly addressed at the reader and tends to create a 'poetic effect' which makes for aesthetic experience or for reader progression (Toolan, 2009). As such, foregrounding may also serve as an analytic category to evaluate literary texts, or to situate them historically. Stylistics is interested in styles, in the essence of text, the characteristics of genre, conversational exchange and so on. Foregrounding occurs in and is relevant to the analysis of all genres, text-types and registers (see e.g., Douthwaite, 2000).

The question about the extent to which foregrounding plays a role in the mind of the reader has been addressed by Emmot (1996, 2002a), Gibbs et al. (2002), Miall and Kuiken (1994) and van Peer (1986, 2002, 2007). In his empirical tests, van Peer (2002) confirms, for example, that foregrounding is perceived by readers and that attention is drawn by deviation. When texts are characterized by foregrounding they are processed more slowly and the amount of affective responses by the reader increase. This, it is argued, enhances the aesthetic appreciation and impacts on the reader's perception of the text. The question of whether (and when) readers focus on the way in which something is written rather than on its contents is complex and needs to be further addressed.

See also *corpus stylistics*, *empirical study of literature*, *formalist stylistics*, *historical stylistics*, *pedagogical stylistics* (Key Branches).

Grammatical metaphor

Term coined by the linguist M. A. K. Halliday (1994) to refer to grammatical constructions which are employed to perform grammatically non-typical tasks. Grammatical metaphors can be either ideational (alternatively experiential) or interpersonal. Ideational (grammatical) metaphors are grammatical constructions in which parts of speech are employed to realize functions other than their prototypically assigned ones, as when processes are expressed via nouns instead of verbs. To exemplify this, participants are prototypically realized by (pro-)nominals, processes by verbals and circumstances by adverbials as in 'Susan' (participant) 'is smoking' (process) 'more and more' (circumstance). Here the configuration of participant, process and circumstance corresponds to our perception of how the situation is conceived of in the real world: someone (participant) doing something (smoking) to a certain extent (circumstance). The same information might however be presented in a grammatically different way by means of nominalization of the entire construction into 'Susan's increased smoking' (participant), which can then be predicated by further constituents such as 'worries' (process) 'me' (participant). This phenomenon is called ideational (grammatical) metaphor. Ideational grammatical metaphor in the shape of nominalization is a prevalent stylistic feature of scientific discourse, since it enables interlocutors to talk and write about scientific phenomena as 'things'. Another effect of the grammatical metaphor of nominalization concerns its ability to condense meaning as in the following example provided by Halliday (2004, p. 656): 'The argument to the contrary is basically an appeal to the lack of synonymy in mental language' which may be seen as a nominalized version of something like 'In order to argue that this is not so he simply points out that there are no synonyms in mental language'. Condensing discourse via nominalization would indicate some sort of expectancy as to what receivers would need to be familiar with, that is, not only the topics being discussed but also the prototypical structural traits of that particular discourse variety. Consequently, this kind of grammatical metaphor is typically associated with the discourse of experts. Furthermore, it often has the effect of leaving out the identity of the 'doer' of a process which may be convenient in contexts where the doer is unknown, or where the sender wishes to draw attention away from the doer.

When it comes to the interpersonal, social, function of language, interlocutors may likewise employ grammatical constructions to perform non-typical tasks. The prototypical mood choice for a statement in English is that of a declarative clause, commands are typically imperative and questions interrogative. Nonetheless, interlocutors may well choose to answer a question by means of an interrogative construction ('What is the capital of Chile?' → 'Isn't it Santiago?'), or encode what is really a demand for the window to be closed as a statement ('Gosh, it's cold in here'). Such grammatically non-typical choices are called interpersonal (grammatical) metaphors and have semantic implications. The use of an interrogative construction to answer a question may, for instance, signal uncertainty, while the use of a declarative instead of the prototypical imperative construction 'Close the door' may be seen as a marker of politeness (see entry). Both examples may furthermore be considered to reflect the power relations between the interlocutors involved. In the stylistic analysis of literature, interpersonal grammatical metaphor is thus a useful concept to be employed in the description of relations between characters and the way these relations are constructed by linguistic means.

See also *ideational meaning*, *interpersonal meaning*, *politeness*, *textual meaning* (Key Terms).

Icon, Iconic, Iconicity

An icon is a sign which somehow imitates through its form what it signifies. While the linguistic sign is generally characterized as arbitrary, with no motivated relation between form and meaning, onomatopoeic expressions may be seen as motivated, and hence iconic, by some kind of reflection of meaning in their form. Examples are 'cuckoo' and 'murmur' whose sonic form mirrors (aspects of) the concepts that they signify in a way that is absent with words such as 'book' and 'watch'. Iconicity arguably also exists at a syntactic level (i.e., syntactic iconicity, see De Cuypere, 2008; Willems and De Cuypere, 2008), where word order and the sequencing of events may be seen to reflect the order of real-world events, or where short sentences may create a staccato effect, while very long sentences will be interpreted differently. In multimodal stylistics, attention has furthermore been paid to typographic iconicity (Nørgaard, 2009), where the visual side of written verbal language imitates what it signifies. An example of this is the use of capital letters (i.e., visual prominence) to signify loud sounds (i.e., sonic prominence) as in 'SHUT UP!' and 'VROOM VROOM'. From a multimodal perspective, layout, too, may be seen as iconic. Iconic poetry like George Herbert's 'Easter Wings' ([1633] 1983), composed in the physical shape of wings, is an obvious example of this, but also the use of blank space to signify silence would qualify as iconic.

In his typology of the sign, the American semiotician Peirce (1931–58) divides the sign into three categories, 'icon', 'symbol' and 'index', of which the icon is defined as above; the symbol refers to the arbitrary sign, and the index is used to designate signs which display a physical and/or causal relation between the signifier and the signified, as in the relation between smoke and fire.

See also *arbitrariness*, *signifier*, *signified* (Key Terms).

Ideational meaning

According to the functional linguist M. A. K. Halliday (1994), language has evolved to simultaneously express three different types of meaning: ideational, interpersonal and textual meaning. Different grammatical systems are employed for the analysis of the three types of meaning. Ideational meaning (sometimes referred to as 'experiential meaning') concerns the way experience is represented, or constructed, through language. This is done by means of configurations of participants, processes and circumstances in the linguistic system known as 'transitivity'. Participants are typically realized by nominals, processes by verbals and circumstances by adverbials as exemplified by 'In London' (circumstance) 'Peter' (participant) 'went jogging' (process) 'every day' (circumstance). In the analysis of transitivity patterns, semantic content is given priority over form in the sense that constituents are labelled according to their semantic function. Halliday thus operates with six basic process types (plus associated participants and circumstances) into which it is claimed that all types of experience can be sorted. The process types are material, mental, verbal, relational, behavioural and existential processes. The processes with a higher level of representation in language are material processes (processes of doing in the material world : 'eat', 'run', 'give'); mental processes (processes of cognition, affection and perception: 'know', 'hate', 'see'); verbal processes (processes of verbal action: 'say', 'respond', 'indicate'); and relational processes (processes expressing being in terms of some kind of relation: 'appear', 'become', 'have') (Halliday, 1994).

The many applications of the transitivity model to the analysis of literature (Burton, 1982; Halliday, 1971; Kennedy, 1982; Nørgaard, 2003; Toolan, 1998) have demonstrated that ideational meaning is a useful tool for unravelling how a given text constructs its world, characters and actions in terms of who is doing what to whom, where, when, why and with what. With regard to characterization for example, the choice of many material processes may construct one character as more active and dynamic than a character who is mainly represented as the participant of mental processes. Alternatively, a character may, for instance, be portrayed by means of material processes in one passage of the text and by mental processes in another, thus developing or displaying different aspects of his/her personality in the course of the text. In an analysis of a passage from Conrad's *The Secret Agent* ([1907] 2007), Kennedy (1982) demonstrates how configurations of participants and processes are employed for special effects in the passage where Mrs Verloc kills her husband with a carving knife. Here Mr Verloc is constructed as a passive observer of his own death by means of mental processes of perception ('heard', 'saw', 'take in') and intransitive material processes which do not extend to other participants ('waited', 'was lying', 'expired'). Mrs Verloc, in turn, is constructed as somehow distanced from her own actions, since parts of her body and the murder weapon, rather than Mrs Verloc herself, are represented as the participants (i.e., agents) of her actions. Another famous stylistic analysis of ideational meaning occurs in Halliday's (1971) article on Golding's *The Inheritors* ([1955] 2005), in which he points to the significance of transitivity patterns in Golding's construction of the different worlds and world views of the novel. Golding's novel concerns the extinction of the Neanderthal people by homo sapiens, and Halliday's analysis reveals how one group of characters, the Neanderthals, are construed linguistically as primitive and ineffective by means of transitivity patterns of processes which typically do not extend to and impact on other participants (be they objects or people). 'The inheritors' (i.e., homo sapiens), on the other hand, are defined as more sophisticated by goal-oriented actions through material processes which impact on other participants.

Since ideational, interpersonal and textual meanings are intimately intertwined, the analysis of ideational meaning may well be combined with considerations about the two other types of meaning in the stylistic analysis of a given text.

See also *interpersonal meaning*, *textual meaning*, *transitivity* (Key Terms), *M. A. K. Halliday* (Key Thinker).

Illocution

See *speech act theory* (Key Terms).

Implicature

See *cooperative principle*; *cooperation* (Key Terms).

International Association of Literary Semantics

The *International Association of Literary Semantics* (*IALS*) is an association of scholars researching all aspects of literary meaning, and drawing on a range of theoretical paradigms and academic disciplines, including linguistics, poetics, philosophy, psychology, narratology, formalism, structuralism, cognitivism, pragmatics, stylistics and literary theory. Founded in 1990, the association hosts an international conference approximately every four years. The association was created by the founding editor of the *Journal of Literary Semantics* (Trevor Eaton), and is unofficially linked to that journal by unity of interests.

See also *Journal of Literary Semantics* (Key Terms).

Interpersonal meaning

According to the functional linguist M. A. K. Halliday (1994), language has evolved to simultaneously express three different types of meaning: ideational, interpersonal and textual meaning. Different grammatical systems are employed for the analysis of the three types of meaning. Interpersonal meaning is linked to the relations that are created between interlocutors in communication; so when we use language to interact with one another we are also establishing and indicating the social relationship between the participants in that interaction. According to Halliday, when we embark on human interaction we take on a series of 'speech roles', the first two of which he identifies as 'giving' and 'demanding'. Halliday elaborates and states that we do not simply choose which speech role to use but also which 'commodity' to exchange when either giving or demanding, which results in the second choice between 'exchanging information' or 'exchanging goods and services' (Eggins, 2004, pp. 144–5). These four basic moves of 'statement', 'question', 'offer' and 'command' is what Halliday refers to as 'speech functions' (Eggins, 2004, p. 145). Interpersonal meaning is analysed mainly in terms of 'mood' and 'modality'. A mood analysis brings to the fore the grammatical structures that project the various speech functions; so, it throws light on how speakers or writers use language in relation to other interlocutors and in terms of the four basic speech functions of question, statement, command and offer, as in 'What time is it?', 'It is four o'clock', 'Give me the bread' and 'Would you like some bread?' (Halliday, 1994, pp. 68–85). Central aspects to consider in relation to speech functions are the distribution of speech roles, (i.e., who is speaking and for how long), the speech functions employed (e.g., does a character ask a lot of questions or state things as given facts) and the grammatical realization of speech functions (i.e., the significance of congruent and incongruent grammatical choices; see *grammatical metaphor*). Modality, on the other hand, concerns the interpersonal 'colouring' of utterances in terms of probability, usuality, obligation and inclination, thus encoding the attitude of either the characters or the narrator. Other linguistic elements such as vocatives and naming are also of relevance to the construction of interpersonal relations. Another approach to interpersonal meaning is seen in the field of politeness theory (Brown and Levinson, 1987), which focuses more specifically on the notions of 'face' (Goffmann, 1955), politeness strategies and face-threatening interlocutory acts (see entry). 'Face' is the public self-image that people have of themselves and which may respectively be maintained or threatened by other interlocutors in conversation.

A stylistic analysis of interpersonal meaning reveals how a given text constructs relations between characters and can also project narratorial attitude by linguistic means. In Joyce's short story 'Two Gallants' ([1914] 1992), one character, Lenehan, is constructed by interpersonal linguistic choices as a cooperative, attentive and insecure interlocutor when in the company of his alleged 'friend', Corley, through constant questioning and frequent use of modality. Corley, on the other hand, is constructed interpersonally as self-confident and not particularly attentive or cooperative. Linguistically this interpersonal image is realized by lack of epistemic modality, his overstretched turns holding the floor for too long, and his refusal to answer Lenehan's questions indicating a position of power (Nørgaard, 2003, pp. 91–151). Narratorial attitude, in turn, may be expressed by means of modality markers. This is seen most frequently with first-person narrators like that of Camus's *L'Etranger* (Engl. *The Stranger*) who makes prolific use of epistemic forms such as 'maybe', 'I don't know', 'may have happened': 'Mother died today. Or maybe yesterday, I don't know. I had a telegram from the home: "Mother passed away. Funeral tomorrow. Yours sincerely." That doesn't mean anything. It may have happened yesterday' ([1942] 1989, p. 3).

Since ideational, interpersonal and textual meanings are intimately intertwined, the analysis of interpersonal meaning may well be combined with considerations about the other two types of meaning in the stylistic analysis of a given text.

See also *grammatical metaphor, ideational meaning, modality, textual meaning* (Key Terms), *M. A. K. Halliday* (Key Thinkers).

Journal of Literary Semantics

The *Journal of Literary Semantics* (founded 1972) is an international peer-reviewed journal which publishes two yearly issues. The journal is devoted to research into the relations between linguistics and literature and the intellectual understanding of all aspects of the meaning and value of literary texts. It is of particular interest to theoretical and applied linguists, narratologists, poeticians, philosophers and psychologists, wherever their interests intersect with literature and literary production.

Website: www.degruyter.de/journals/jls

See also *International Association of Literary Semantics* (Key Terms).

Langage

See *langue and parole* (Key Terms).

Language and Literature

Language and Literature is an international peer-reviewed journal on stylistics and the official journal of the *Poetics and Linguistics Association* (*PALA*). It publishes articles on the linguistic analysis of literature and related areas of language and literary studies. The journal covers literary as well as non-literary genres and invites contributions from a wide range of theoretical and methodological perspectives of relevance to the interface of stylistics, linguistics and literary criticism. The journal publishes four issues a year.

Website: lal.sagepub.com

See also *Poetics and Linguistics Association* (Key Terms).

Langue and *parole*

Terms employed by the Swiss linguist Ferdinand de Saussure (1916) to distinguish between any particular use of language (*parole*) and the underlying system of the language (*langue*) such as English, French or German. Speakers of English do not know and use the entire English language, its words, conventions and grammatical rules (i.e., *langue*), but it is nevertheless this underlying *langue* that enables interlocutors to produce and understand utterances (i.e., *parole*) in that language. On the basis of instances of language use (*parole*), general rules and conventions of the underlying language system (*langue*) may be established as we see it for instance in grammar books of the English language. A third term used by Saussure in this connection is that of *langage*, which refers to the universal phenomenon of language that characterizes human beings.

The concepts of *langue* and *parole* do not just apply to national languages, but can be employed to describe other systems of meaning which may likewise be considered in terms of system and instantiation. In the case of literary studies, including stylistics, individual literary texts may hence be seen as *parole* and thereby as instantiations of an underlying system of a literary *langue*, which, in turn, may be extracted from the individual realizations of the system.

See also *Ferdinand de Saussure* (Key Thinkers).

Lexical cohesion

See *cohesion* (Key Terms).

Locution

See *speech act theory* (Key Terms).

Mental spaces theory

Mental spaces theory was originally formulated by Gilles Fauconnier (1994, 1997) and has served, together with conceptual metaphor theory, as basis for the expanded and more sophisticated conceptual blending theory. Mental spaces theory (MS) is concerned with exploring the meaning construction involved in text comprehension and underscores the dynamic aspects of human understanding. This framework metaphorically uses the notion of 'spaces' to refer to the way in which meaning is conceptualized in human understanding and emphasizes that such conceptualization is an 'on-line' procedure, that is, mental spaces are created as a result of, on the one hand, the interaction between textual information and, on the other, the interactants' 'background knowledge, various kinds of reasoning, on-line meaning construction, and negotiation of meaning' (Fauconnier, 1997, pp. 7–8). Fauconnier defines mental spaces as 'partial structures that proliferate when we think and talk, allowing a fine-grained partitioning of our discourse and knowledge structures' (1997, p. 11). Because of the dynamic and unfolding nature of these mental spaces, they are to be understood as temporary configurations which contrast with the more stable characteristics of other conceptual structures such as mental domains (see *conceptual metaphor theory*). Mental spaces can be created only if mappings between those mental spaces are established, that is, if some sort of correlation between those cognitive constructions is allowed. Because of the multileveled nature of meaning creation, the number of possible mappings depends on the current ongoing discourse, that is, grammatical clues alone are not sufficient to project mental spaces.

The fluidity with which mental spaces relate to one another is possible thanks to what Fauconnier calls mental space lattices (1997, p. 38). These cognitive structures are organized in a hierarchical way that permits the constant creation of further partitions should the discourse circumstances so dictate it. At any given moment in the processing of meaning, though, there is one space which acts as 'base space' (Fauconnier, 1997, p. 38) and one that becomes the 'focus space' (Fauconnier, 1997, p. 38), although Fauconnier confirms that very often base and focus spaces coincide. The base space plays a central role at any stage during comprehension; the hierarchical nature of the mental space lattice, consequently, dictates the point of origin for subsequent spaces to be created, such point being the initial base space. Additionally, the various spaces forming the lattice are interrelated by the presence of connectors which establish mappings between counterpart 'elements'. This function is positively assessed by Stockwell who states that MS allows for a 'unified and consistent means of understanding reference, co-reference, and the comprehension of stories and descriptions whether they are currently real, historical, imagined, hypothesized or happening remotely' (2002, p. 96). These connectors, unlike other components of mental spaces, do not require to be introduced by linguistic clues; instead, they are conceptual in nature and serve as facilitators for setting up mappings between the various spaces. For instance, one of the main connectors identified by Fauconnier is the 'identity connector' which comes into play every time the same referent is realized as distinct 'elements' (discussed below) in different mental spaces, as when noun phrases are substituted by pronouns. The mapping between spaces allows discourse interactants to infer that both the antecedent and the anaphor (that is, the noun phrase and the pronoun respectively) are in a relation of co-reference. Fauconnier refers to this particular mapping as the 'Access Principle': 'an expression that names or describes an element in one mental space can be used to access a counterpart of that element in another mental space' (Fauconnier, 1997, p. 41). As far as comprehension is concerned, thus, the Access Principle aids discourse participants to cut down on the cognitive effort they are required to invest in discourse comprehension.

Besides the external structure of the mental space lattice, the cognitive construction of spaces also affects the internal configuration of individual spaces. The initial creation of mental spaces is linguistically marked by space builders which are linguistic units capable of launching the conceptual space. These expressions literally project the creation of a mental space and are typically realized by locative expressions such as prepositional phrases, adverbs, connectives and subject-verb constructions followed by an embedded clause (Evans and Green, 2006, p. 370). This newly created mental space is capable of reflecting the various aspects of the reality invoked by the linguistic markers acting as space builders, including past and future situations, hypothetical eventualities, as well as beliefs and attitudes. Secondly, the internal structure of mental spaces relies on the various 'elements' inhabiting them; these can be constructed either on-line or can precede the current discourse, that is, they can be processed according to the circumstances of the particular discourse or can be part of the background information often also called upon in the creation of spaces. 'Elements' are characteristically realized by noun phrases and can either generate a definite interpretation (NPs with a definite article and names) or an indefinite interpretation (NPs identified by an indefinite article, zero article or plurals). Finally, MS justifies the on-line processing of any given current discourse by accounting for the way in which discourse participants are thoroughly capable of tracking and monitoring the various spaces forming the mental space lattice. The grammatical categories of tense, aspect and epistemic modality are the linguistic units that aid such complex monitoring. Tense and aspect, for instance, facilitate the anchoring of temporal parameters whereas epistemic modality markers clarify the speaker's attitudinal stance, belief system and knowledge concerning the likelihood of the propositions included in the particular discourse.

Despite the sophistication achieved by the MS framework as propounded by Fauconnier, there are concerns among practitioners in relation to the practical applications of this model to longer stretches of discourse. As Stockwell confirms, MS is 'mainly focused on the discussion of simple sentences' (2002,

p. 97; see also Semino, 2003, pp. 91, 97). The fact that MS has now evolved into the more sophisticated conceptual blending theory seems to suggest that the former may have achieved a situation of impasse clearly solved by the latter. For applications of MS to literary texts see Sanders and Redeker (1996), Semino (2003) and Stockwell (2002).

See also *blending theory, conceptual metaphor theory, text world theory* (Key Terms).

Metaphor

In rhetoric and other traditional approaches to figurative language, a metaphor is defined as a figure of speech, or trope, and is often seen as a kind of linguistic embellishment. In metaphor, a comparison of two distinctively different, yet similar, things is established by the claim that 'X is Y', as in 'my love is a rose'. Meaning is thereby transferred from the metaphorical term, 'a rose' to the subject, 'my love', and we may take the metaphor to imply that the speaker finds his/her love as beautiful as a rose (even if a rose also has thorns).

I. A. Richards (1936) introduced the terms 'tenor' and 'vehicle' to refer to respectively the subject and the metaphorical term, while cognitive linguists like Lakoff and Johnson (1980) employ the terms 'target' and 'source'. For a word or expression to be metaphorical, the vehicle (or source) must be set out explicitly, whereas the tenor (or target) may merely be implied. If somebody says 'my rose is crying' while actually referring to a human being, only the vehicle is explicitly expressed which makes this an example of *implicit metaphor*. A *dead metaphor* is a metaphorical expression that has become so ingrained in a given language by extensive popular use that interlocutors do not think of it as metaphorical any longer. Often quoted examples of this phenomenon are 'table leg', 'bottleneck', 'to run for office' and 'to catch somebody's name'.

Another trope which is closely related to metaphor and is likewise based on similarity is the *simile*. In simile, the comparison is made explicit by means of 'as' or 'like', as in 'my love is like a rose'. Due to the shared characteristics of the tropes of metaphor and simile which are both based on a principle of similarity, Jakobson (1956) uses 'metaphor' in a very broad sense to cover both metaphor and simile. In Jakobson's work, metaphor is contrasted with the trope of metonymy (e.g., 'brains' for intelligence: 'she has brains') which, in turn, he regards as being based on a principle of contiguity (i.e., association).

In cognitive linguistics and related approaches such as conceptual metaphor theory and blending theory (see entries), a metaphor is regarded as more than a mere trope. Seen from a cognitive perspective, our understanding of a metaphor is not realized at the level of the utterance, sentence or word, but at a much more fundamental cognitive level. Metaphors are seen as linguistic manifestations of underlying conceptual metaphors which are central to the way humans make sense of the world. One such conceptual metaphor is that of AN ARGUMENT IS WAR (conceptual metaphors in small capitals) which may be realized by means of a number of different linguistic metaphors such as 'Your claims are indefensible', 'He attacked every weak point in my argument', 'His criticisms were right on target', 'He shot down all of my arguments' (Kövecses, 2002, p. 5).

As demonstrated by recent research in visual communication and multimodality, metaphor is not just a linguistic phenomenon but can be realized by different semiotic modes. In *Pictorical Metaphor in Advertising* (1996), for instance, Forceville sets out a theoretical framework for the analysis of pictorial metaphor. A pictorial, or visual, metaphor occurs when one visual element (tenor/target) is compared to another visual element (vehicle/source) which belongs to a different category or frame of meaning. To exemplify this, Forceville (1996, pp. 127–35) provides the example of an advert seen on a British billboard to publicize the use of the London underground. The picture features a parking meter (tenor/target) framed as the head of a dead creature whose body is shaped as the fleshless spinal column of a human being (vehicle/source). In this example, the vehicle visually transfers, or maps, the meaning of 'dying' or 'dead' (because of lack of food) onto the parking meter, resulting in the metaphor PARKING METER IS A DYING CREATURE (Forceville, 1996, p. 131). Considering that the advert wants to promote public transport, having lots of parking meters wasting away in the streets of London can only be a positive thing for underground users and the underground system itself. In addition to visual metaphors, Forceville (1996, pp. 148–61) furthermore detects and describes verbal-visual ('verbo-pictorial') metaphors. In verbal-visual metaphor, the tenor/target consists of verbal text while the vehicle/source is visual, or vice versa.

See also *blending theory, conceptual metaphor, grammatical metaphor, metonymy* (Key Terms), *Charles Forceville, Roman Jakobson* (Key Thinkers).

Metonymy

Metonymy is a figure of speech, or trope, in which a referent is substituted by something with which it is closely associated, and is therefore based on a principle of contiguity (Jakobson, 1956). Examples of metonymy are the representation of the sovereign or monarchy by 'the crown', of newspapers (and other news media) by 'the press' and of drinking alcohol by 'the bottle' ('he has taken to the bottle').

Metonymy resembles and is sometimes confused with the trope of synecdoche. While likewise based on a principle of contiguity, synecdoche occurs when a part is used to represent a whole or a whole to represent a part, as when workers are referred to as 'hands' or when a national football team is signified by reference to the nation to which it belongs: 'England beat Sweden'. As way of example, the saying that 'The hand that rocks the cradle rules the world' illustrates the difference between metonymy and synecdoche. Here, 'the hand' is a synecdochic representation of the mother of whom it is a part, while 'the cradle' represents a child by close association.

See also *metaphor* (Key Terms).

Metre

Metre refers to the organized pattern of stressed and unstressed syllables which brings about a rhythm that is more regular than that of everyday speech. Metre is often seen in poetry, but may also occur in other types of text. The basic unit of metrical analysis is the *foot*, which is a recurring unit of rhythm. The following line from Keats's 'To Autumn' ([1820] 1983) has five feet, each consisting of a weak syllable followed by a stressed syllable (underlined):

To <u>swell</u> | the <u>gourd</u>, | and <u>plump</u> | the <u>ha</u>- | zel <u>shells</u>

As illustrated by the fourth and fifth feet of this example, metrical boundaries do not always correspond with word boundaries.

The standard metrical feet in English are listed below:

Iamb: an unstressed syllable followed by a stressed syllable ('receive')
Trochee: a stressed syllable followed by an unstressed syllable ('bottle')

Anapest: two unstressed syllables followed by a stressed syllable ('anapest')

Dactyl: a stressed syllable followed by two unstressed syllables ('poetry')

Added to these are the spondee (two syllables with strong stress) and the pyrrhic (two syllables with light stress) which are sometimes employed for rhythmic variation.

Verse lines can be classified according to the number of feet that make them up; thus a verse line consisting of one foot is called monometer, a line of two feet is called dimeter, and so forth: trimeter (three feet), tetrameter (four feet), pentameter (five feet), hexameter (six feet), heptameter (seven feet) and octameter (eight feet).

The metre of verse lines is categorized according to the most frequently recurring metrical foot and the number of feet per line. A verse line consisting of five iambs is called iambic pentameter, a line of six trochees is called trochaic hexameter, etc. Iambic pentameter is the most common metre in English poetry and is, among other things, the standard metre of English sonnets.

Blank verse is the name given to unrhymed lines in iambic pentameter, as we see it in much Elizabethan drama as well as in poetry such as Milton's *Paradise Lost* ([1667] 1983) and Wordsworth's 'The Prelude' ([1805] 1983). In much of Shakespeare's drama, noble people speak in blank verse, whereas prose is employed as the natural speaking idiom of characters who belong to the lower classes. In *Hamlet* (1604–5 in Evans, 1997), additional meaning is created by metrical form when it comes to the style of the lines spoken by Hamlet himself. Following the conventions mentioned above, Hamlet's lines are in blank verse at the beginning of the play, as are those of other nobles, but when he changes and appears to be mad later in the play, he starts speaking in prose. Interestingly, however, he only does so when in the company of other people, but switches back to blank verse when alone, which may be seen as a metrical indication that rather than being truly mad, he only pretends to be so.

Free verse is a term employed to refer to poetry consisting of verse lines whose rhythmic pattern is not organized into metrical feet. In addition to this, most poetry in free verse has irregular line length and is not structured by means of end rhyme. Today, much English poetry is written in free verse.

See also *rhyme* (Key Terms).

Mind style

Mind style has been a topic of special interest for stylistics scholars since its original coinage by Fowler in *Linguistics and the Novel* (1977), where he states that mind style 'refer(s) to any distinctive linguistic presentation of an individual mental self' (p. 103). Fowler's subsequent work (1986, 1996) highlights the particular relationship this concept holds with the more general notion of point of view (see *point of view* and *focalization* for a more stylistic and narratological focus respectively). In *Linguistic Criticism* (1986), Fowler distinguishes three main types of point of view, psychological, ideological and spatio-temporal. Briefly, spatio-temporal point of view corresponds to the locative and temporal perspectives imprinted in texts. Ideological point of view encompasses 'the system of beliefs, values, and categories by reference to which a person or a society comprehends the world' (1986, p. 130). The third category comprises those aspects more prototypically associated with a psychological perspective, that is, the consideration as to who 'is presented as the observer of the events of a narrative, whether the author or a participating character' (1986, p. 134). The concept of mind style for Fowler, however, emerges specifically from the way the ideological content (see *ideational meaning*) of texts is linguistically expressed, which evidences the influence of Hallidayan approaches to language:

> Language serves for the expression of content: it has a representational, or as I would prefer to call it, an ideational function [...] the speaker or writer embodies in language his experience of the phenomena of the real world; and this includes his experience of the internal world of his own consciousness: his reactions, cognitions, and perceptions, and also his linguistic acts of speaking and understanding. (Halliday, 1971, p. 327)

Based on the former premises, Fowler originally understood mind style as the linguistic projection of the workings of people's minds and concretized it in the following way:

> I have called it mind-style: the world-view of an author, or a narrator, or a character, constituted by the ideational structure of the text. From now on I shall prefer this term to the cumbersome 'point of view on the ideological plane' which I borrowed from Uspensky. (Fowler, 1996, p. 214)

It is important to clarify that mind style, on the one hand, and the various types of point of view, on the other, function on different narrative planes. Mind style indicators neither underscore the position of a narrator as omniscient teller or focalizer (psychological point of view), nor the possible leaps into the past or future of the story (temporal point of view); instead, they project the beliefs, emotions, attitudes and opinions that singularize a particular character, author or narrator as these materialize linguistically. Leech and Short (1981, 2007) have amply delved into the idiosyncrasies of mind style too, and have expressed a preference for this expression to the sometimes also used 'world-view' (Leech and Short, 2007, p. 151). They emphasize, alongside Fowler, that mind style creation relies heavily on the accumulation of specific forms in the linguistic input of the mind style projectors, be these narrators, authors or characters, so that the more recurrently particular linguistic indicators crop up in texts, the more marked the mind style. For instance, Fowler's initial description of mind style projection looks at 'vocabulary, transitivity, and certain syntactic structures' (Fowler, 1996, p. 214). Semino and Swindlehurst also echo such a position:

> The study of mind style therefore involves the identification of linguistic patterns that account for the perception of a distinct world view during the reading of a text. The notion of 'patterns' is particularly important here. Mind style arises from the frequent and consistent occurrence of particular linguistic choices and structures within a text. (Semino and Swindlehurst, 1996, p. 144)

Despite the above, Leech and Short have also suggested that mind style expressed in a single sentence is also feasible (2007, p. 151), although recent work incorporating corpus linguistic methods has proven that the presence of recurring patterns over a larger amount of text becomes a rather more efficient way of projecting mind styles (Hoover, 1999; Semino, 2007 Archer and McIntyre, 2005). Nevertheless, as Semino says, 'a degree of systematicity is needed for mind style to work although this does not have to be complete' (2007, p. 163). In the same way, Leech and Short defend that mind style indicators do not necessarily have to reflect particularly unconventional world views (see Montoro, 2010a, 2010b, for an alternative stance) but can encapsulate as much 'natural and uncontrived' (2007, p. 151) positions. Yet, Leech and Short's subsequent analyses of psychologically idiosyncratic characters (such as the mentally disabled individual in Faulkner's *The Sound and the Fury*) appear to confirm that the closer to the unorthodox end on a normality-to-unconventionality cline we can place a character, the stronger the force of the mind style being projected. Semino (2002, 2006a, 2006d, 2007) has more recently inherited the mind style baton and has significantly expanded on how fictional mental functioning is generally displayed. To such aim, she investigates not only the ways in which mind styles are projected, but also how cognate disciplines and approaches (narratology in particular, but also corpus and cognitive linguistics, and pragmatics) can enrich our understanding of mind style processes. Furthermore, the concept of mind style is also being analysed in relation to other non-linguistic manifestations, especially in cinematic formats (Montoro, 2010a, 2010b). The sheer volume of stylistic studies investigating mind style in a variety of texts (Boase-Beier, 2003; Black, 1993; Bockting, 1994; Gregoriou, 2003; Hoover, 2004; Leech, 2007; McIntyre, 2005) indicates that the ways in which mind style projection can be studied are far from exhausted, which ultimately underscores the special interest aroused by this narrative notion.

See also *focalization*, *ideational meaning*, *point of view* (Key Terms).

Modality

Modality is a topic primarily discussed in linguistics but its impact on stylistic approaches to language has been enormously felt. However, decisions as to which elements are to be considered under the general notion of modality vary depending on the discipline. In general, modality can be defined as the potential of language to project the speaker's or writer's attitude about the proposition expressed. The term 'attitude' is here amply and loosely defined, so attitudinal stances may refer to a variety of speaker responses ranging from desire to obligation and duty, certainty or uncertainty concerning the likelihood of the propositional content of the utterance. Stylistics has shown particular interest in the concept of modality when coupled with studies on the notion of point of view, focalization and mind style, for this aspect of language has proven especially fruitful to help disambiguate via objective linguistic means some possible fuzziness in the understanding of how the concepts above function. Fowler, for instance, summarizes modality as follows:

> A narrator or a character may directly indicate his or her judgements and beliefs, by the use of a variety of modal structures. Modality [. . .] is the grammar of explicit comment, the means by which people express their

> degree of commitment to the truth of the propositions they utter, and their views on the desirability or otherwise of the states of affairs referred to. (Fowler, 1996, pp. 166–7)

So in a sentence such as 'George must already have received my present', the speaker is exhibiting some degree of confidence on the actuality of what is expressed in the utterance; similarly the speaker can express some wish or desire as in 'I wish George had already received my present'.

In linguistics, the concept of modality is widely used to refer to a very specific, closed class of words called 'modal verbs' whose main features are:

> Modal auxiliaries are normally followed by the infinitive, which is bare [...]. Modal auxiliaries can only occur as the first (operator) element of the verb phrase. They cannot occur in nonfinite functions, i.e. as infinitives or participles, and as a consequence of this can occur only as first verb in the verb phrase [...]. Modal auxiliaries are not inflected in the 3rd person singular of the present tense; i.e. they have no -s form. (Quirk et al., 1985, pp. 127–8)

Yet, linguistics scholars have not reached an agreement with regard to terminological matters and types of modality. Quirk et al. (1985), for example, distinguish between 'intrinsic' and 'extrinsic' modality:

> (a) Those [meanings] such as 'permission', 'obligation', and 'volition' which involve some kind of intrinsic human control over events, and
> (b) Those such as 'possibility', 'necessity', and 'prediction', which do not primarily involve human control of events, but do typically involve human judgement of what is or is not likely to happen.
>
> These two kinds, between which there is a gradient, may be termed INTRINSIC and EXTRINSIC modality respectively. (Quirk et al., 1985, p. 219)

Stylistics, however, would take issue with the above on two fronts. On the one hand, modality seems to be understood as a phenomenon that affects simply modal verbs whereas some authors defend that it may be realized by other grammatical categories too (modal adverbs, modal lexical verbs, modal nominal expressions). Secondly, other logicians and linguists replace the terms intrinsic and extrinsic with further denominations, the most common being 'deontic' (Lyons, 1977; Perkins, 1983; Allan, 2001) or 'root' (Coates, 1983) for the former, and 'epistemic' (Lyons, 1977; Palmer, 1986, 1990, 2001; Perkins, 1983) for the latter. Furthermore, establishing simply a binary opposition between intrinsic and extrinsic modality might be rather reductionist. For instance, Quirk et al.'s intrinsic category includes the meaning of 'volition' (termed 'boulomaic' by others) under the same heading as 'permission' and 'obligation', even though it could be argued that there is just too big a semantic gap for the two to be considered on the same plane (see Nuyts, 2001 and Ziegeler, 2006). Another perspective emerges from the work of Perkins (1983) who furthers the discussion on modality taxonomies by proposing the distinction between 'boulomaic' and 'deontic' categories:

> It is nevertheless clear that, in English at least, there is a clear semantic distinction between expressions such as WANT, DESIRE, HOPE, YEARN FOR, on the one hand, and ORDER, DEMAND, INSIST, OBLIGE, on the other, and therefore boulomaic, as opposed to deontic, modality [. . .] will both have a place [. . .] in this book. (Perkins, 1983, pp. 14–15)

Such distinction has also rung true in most stylistic approaches to the analysis of literature, especially as utilized by Simpson (1993) in his modal grammar of point of view (see *narrator* entry). He delineates four distinctive categories, deontic, boulomaic, epistemic and perception, borrowed and reworked from the two major divisions previously established by Quirk et al., as well as by Perkins. Simpson's emphasis, however, is on understanding how modal meanings actually have some bearing on the linguistic manifestation of point of view. Deontic modality realizes a continuum of commitment from permission (1) through obligation (2) to requirement (3):

(1) You may leave
(2) You must leave
(3) You should leave (Simpson, 1993, p. 47)

Modal verbs are, clearly, major exponents of deontic modality, and for that matter, any other type; yet they are not the only modal markers, as expressions of the type 'be adjective/participle + that' ('it is advisable that. . .') and 'be adjective/participle + to' ('you are allowed to. . .') or 'modal nominal expressions' (Perkins, 1983) such as 'the obligation to...' or 'a prohibition on' can equally convey deontic modality. As Simpson points out, 'the deontic system is of crucial relevance to the strategies of social interaction, especially to tactics of persuasion and politeness' (1993, p. 48) because of the obvious implications and effects on the addressee.

Closely related to the deontic category is that of boulomaic modality, which relates to the notions of 'desire' and 'will', although some scholars (Quirk et al., 1985; Palmer, 1986) prefer to regard boulomaic modality as simply a subcategory of the deontic type mode. Conflating the two categories, though, could result in the loss of clear differing nuances between acts of demand and requirement (deontic), on the one hand, and those of wishing and desiring (boulomaic), on the other. In contrast with the former type, there are no modal verbs that express boulomaic content; instead such information is conveyed through modal lexical verbs, adjectival/participial constructions, modal nominal expressions and related modal adverbs: 'I wish...', 'we hoped...', 'it would be desirable that...'.

The category of epistemic modality is one on which most studies seem to agree, especially as far as the type of meaning conveyed by epistemic markers, which is the speaker's certainty or lack of it concerning the truth value of the proposition expressed in the sentence:

> [Epistemic] is derived from the Greek word meaning 'understanding' or 'knowledge' (rather than 'belief'), and so is to be interpreted as showing the status of the speaker's judgements and the kind of warrant he has for what he says. (Palmer, 1986, p. 51)

Modal verbs are the main carriers of epistemic modality (may, might, could), although not the only ones: adjectival and participial constructions of the type 'be...to' ('he was likely to', 'she was supposed to') are possible too, together with modal lexical verbs ('wonder'), modal adverbs ('possibly') and modal nominal expressions ('the possibility of...').

Simpson's fourth type of modality, perception, is actually considered by Perkins as a subdivision of the former one. As Simpson states:

> It is distinguished by the fact that the degree of commitment to the truth of a proposition is predicated on some reference to human perception, normally visual perception. (Simpson, 1993, p. 50)

The main modalizers conveying this meaning are adjectives in the 'be... that' ('it became plain...') construction, related modal adverbs ('apparently') and lexical modal verbs ('his hands looked...').

Finally, Simpson also highlights the fact that on occasions, there is an obvious lack of attitudinal comment in texts as they appear devoid of modality or totally unqualified. Compare, for example, (a) 'you may have made a mistake' and (b) 'you have made a mistake'. Deprived of its modalizer, sentence (b) conveys not the confidence or lack of it a speaker may have about the truth value of a proposition, but the proposition itself. These instances are known as 'categorical assertions' and can be declared 'epistemically non-modal' due to the absence of modal indicators. Their use instead of their modalized counterparts responds to a decision by the speaker to indicate the strongest commitment possible to the factuality of the proposition. For further linguistic and discourse studies on the notion of modality see Barbiers et al. (2002), Bybee and Feischman (1995), Facchinetti et al. (2003), Frawley (2006), Halliday (1994), Hoye (1997) and Portner (2009). For stylistic applications to textual and multimodal formats see Jeffries (2007), Leech (2008), Leech and Short (2007), Montoro (2010b), Nørgaard (2010a), Papafragou (2002), Quigley (2000) and Toolan (2001).

See also *narrator*, *point of view* (Key Terms).

Multimodality

'Multimodality' is a term used to refer to the object of a field of research, as well as to the actual theorizing about it. When designating the object of a field of research, multimodality refers to the multiplicity of semiotic modes that go into communication. A good example of this is the meaning-making involved in printed advertisements, which typically includes modes such as visual images, wording, colour, layout and typography. Proponents of multimodal theory aim to sketch out frameworks, or 'grammars', of all the different modes involved in communication as well as of their interaction – the claim being that:

> Multimodal texts integrate selections from different semiotic resources to their principles of organisation. [...] These resources are not simply juxtaposed as separate modes of meaning-making but are combined and integrated to form a complex whole which cannot be reduced to,

> or explained in terms of the mere sum of its separate parts. (Baldry and Thibault, 2006, p. 18)

One of the most influential currents of multimodal theorizing is that conducted by proponents of social semiotic multimodal theory such as Baldry and Thibault (2006), Bateman (2008), Kress and van Leeuwen (1996, 2001), O'Halloran (2004), O'Toole (1994) and van Leeuwen (2005a). These scholars build their theoretical and methodological frameworks on Halliday's 'social semiotics' with the aim of exploring the extent to which the principles behind linguistic meaning-making captured by Halliday's theory of language (see *M. A. K. Halliday*) may also apply, if only in part, to semiotic modes other than the verbal. In *Reading Images* (1996), a seminal work in the field (which while multimodal in scope, was not actually proclaimed to be so), Kress and van Leeuwen, for example, examine whether and to what extent visual images may be seen to construct ideational, interpersonal and textual meaning (see entries) in ways similar to those uncovered by Halliday for verbal language in his *Introduction to Functional Grammar* (1994). Soon followed work on other modes: colour (Kress and van Leeuwen, 2002), typography (van Leeuwen, 2005b, 2006), speech, music, sound (van Leeuwen, 1999), layout (Bateman, 2008); as well as work which more explicitly addresses the *interaction* of different modes, rather than focusing on individual modes in relative isolation (Baldry and Thibault, 2006; Boeriis, 2008; Kress and van Leeuwen, 2001; van Leeuwen, 2005a).

Another current in multimodal thinking is that which is informed by cognitive theory and is put forward by proponents such as Forceville (1996). One area in which a cognitive approach to multimodality has been particularly well developed is that of conceptual metaphor theory (see entry). Scholars working on the multimodal realizations of conceptual metaphors argue that new developments on multimodality can actually underscore and positively redress the initial flaws of the original theoretical tenets as initially put forward by Lakoff and Johnson (1980, 2003).

Being a new field of research, multimodal theorizing faces a number of challenges. One example of this is the obvious need to clarify what exactly constitutes a mode. While verbal language is sometimes referred to as a mode, for instance, further scrutiny will reveal that this definition is inaccurate, since written verbal language differs from spoken verbal language to an extent that makes it necessary to distinguish between the two as separate semiotic modes. Both of these, in turn, consist of a number of (sub-)modes: spoken verbal language is made out of wording and sound; written verbal language of wording, typography, colour and arguably also layout. Another challenge faced by proponents of multimodal theory is the question of how to theoretically and methodologically capture all the semiotic modes – and their interaction – which go into a given text or act of communication. As indicated above, the field initially faced a tendency to investigate multimodal meaning-making mode by mode, while academics in the field today increasingly consider the meanings created when modes interact (Boeriis, 2008). Nevertheless, a comprehensive 'grammar of multimodality' capturing all modes and their interaction will probably remain an intriguing, ideal, yet unreachable, goal. While these challenges and more have to be faced by future work in multimodality, much is obviously to be gained by acknowledging the significance of the great variety of semiotic modes involved in meaning-making, and by aiming to describe these as systematically as we do verbal language.

Multimodal stylistics is a very recent branch of stylistics which makes a point of acknowledging that *all* texts are multimodal (including those which may at a first glance seem mono-modal), and which consequently aims to extend the stylistic tool kit to better accommodate the multimodal aspect of meaning-making. When reading poetry, most readers sense that in addition to wording, the visual, too, is significant – especially so, perhaps, in iconic poetry like Herbert's 'Easter Wings' ([1633] 1983), which looks like that which it signifies by being shaped as wings by its layout. Other literary texts such as Sterne's *The Life and Opinions of Tristram Shandy* ([1759–67] 1978) and Foer's *Extremely Loud and Incredibly Close* (2005) experiment explicitly with the multisemiotic potential of the novel by making use of special typography, layout, images and other visual effects, thereby inviting a multimodal stylistic approach for their analysis. The multimodality of conventional prose texts is arguably not as immediately obvious as that of poetry and visually more experimental prose, yet such texts are nevertheless also multimodal, consisting as they inevitably do of the modes of wording, typography and layout, and can therefore be approached from a multimodal stylistic perspective, too. Finally, the multimodal take on stylistics opens up for an extension of the concept of the literary text to encompass also the meaning potential of elements such as the book cover and the paper quality, for instance, if the text put up for analysis is a novel. Added to this, multimodal stylistics also displays descriptive potential in the analysis of drama and film where modes other than the verbal clearly need to be considered.

Since multimodal stylistics is a very recent branch of stylistics, the critical output in the field is sparse but growing. Simpson and Montgomery (1995) and Montoro (2010a, 2010b), for instance, consider the multimodal stylistics of film, McIntyre (2008) is concerned with the multimodal stylistics of (filmed) drama, Nørgaard (2009, 2010a, 2010b, 2010c) explores the multimodal potential of literary prose from a social semiotic perspective, while Gibbons (2010) devotes herself to the cognitive take on multisemiotic literary texts.

See also *multimodal stylistics* (Key Branches), *ideational meaning, interpersonal meaning, textual meaning*, (Key Terms), *Charles Forceville, M. A. K. Halliday, Theo van Leeuwen* (Key Thinkers).

Narrative

Establishing exactly what constitutes a narrative is not an easy enterprise. We can start by considering the following definitions:

> One will define narrative without difficulty as the representation of an event or a sequence of events. (Genette, 1982, p. 127)
>
> The representation [. . .] of one or more real or fictive events communicated by one, two or several [. . .] narrators [. . .] to one, two or several narratees. (Prince, 2003a, p. 58)
>
> Simply put, narrative is the representation of an event or a series of events. 'Event' is the key word here, though some people prefer the word 'action.' Without an event or an action, you may have a 'description,' an 'exposition,' an 'argument,' a 'lyric,' some combination of these or something else altogether, but you won't have a narrative. (Abbott, 2008, p. 13)

These are but three of the many attempts by scholars to come up with a comprehensive description of narrative. Besides the above, Toolan (2001, p. 1) also suggests that the layman's understanding of narratives as processes requiring a 'teller', something to tell (a 'tale'), and someone to tell it to (the 'addressee') leaves out some of the traits that should be integral to this notion. For instance, should narratives be reduced to these three elements, then, it would be hard to distinguish narratives from other communicative events such as conversations with friends, phone calls or celebratory speeches. For Toolan, one aspect in which narratives differ from the latter three is in the salient role played by the teller of the story, so that processing the narrative is as much to learn about the occurrences in the tale as it is about experiencing how the telling entity presents it. Thus, Toolan's contribution to a definition states:

> A narrative is a perceived sequence of non-randomly connected events, typically involving, as the experiencing agonist, humans or quasi-humans, or other sentient beings, from whose experience we humans can 'learn'. (Toolan, 2001, p. 8)

Not only does this new proposal refer to the necessary presence of 'events' as Genette, Prince and Abbott do above too, but also, the purposeful sequentiality of such events is emphasized. Therefore, narratives presuppose that something needs to happen in a particular order, irrespective of whether the order in which events occur and the actual presentation (textual or otherwise) of those occurrences coincide; moreover, those happenings need to involve some cognizant beings from whose experiencing humans can learn. Here 'learn' appears to be used in the very broad sense of the type of benefit gained by recipients of that narrative (emotional, psychological, informative or cognitive). According to this definition, a ballet performance, as much as novels, short stories, oral narratives, folk tales, pantomime, films or comic strips can be categorized as different types of narrative. Definition endeavours, consequently, are not particularly scarce. In an attempt to tackle this issue, Mary-Laure Ryan (2007) has resorted to list a series of basic characteristics which determine the prototypical or marginal nature of a particular text as narrative, rather than its inclusion or not in the category since, as she explains herself, narratives are, by definition, 'fuzzy':

> Rather than regarding narrativity as a strictly binary feature, that is, as a property that a given text either has or doesn't have, the definition proposed below presents narrative texts as a fuzzy set allowing variable degrees of membership, but centered on prototypical cases that everybody recognizes as stories. (2007, p. 28)

Her list of conditions for narrative prototypicality includes:

> **Spatial dimension**: 1) Narrative must be about a world populated by individual existents.

> **Temporal dimension**: 2) This world must be situated in time and undergo significant transformations. 3) The transformations must be caused by non-habitual physical events.
> **Mental dimension**: 4) Some of the participants in the events must be intelligent agents who have a mental life and react emotionally to the states of the world. 5) Some of the events must be purposeful actions by these agents.
> **Formal and pragmatic dimension**: 6) The sequence of events must form a unified causal chain and lead to closure. 7) The occurrence of at least some of the events must be asserted as fact for the storyworld. 8) The story must communicate something meaningful to the audience. (Ryan, 2007, p. 29)

In relation to this set, a ballet performance could, at least for some, be acknowledged as a more unorthodox member of the category of narrative under condition 6. The kind of causality generally experienced in the more traditional forms of narrative fiction could be said to be missing in particularly experimental performances of ballet more concerned with emotional reactions from the audience than with the sequentiality of the various acts and scenes. As Ryan states, we might still have enough components to include dance formats as narratives although we might need to situate them at the more marginal end of the cline.

Traditionally, narratologists have drawn a basic distinction between two aspects of narratives, differently termed by the various theorists, but which essentially encompass similar (if not totally equivalent) features. An initial differentiation was made between 'fabula' and 'sjuzhet' by the Russian Formalists (Propp, [1928] 1968; Tomashevsky, 1965). The French structuralists preferred to use 'histoire' and 'discours' respectively, whereas more contemporary narratologists have opted for 'story' and 'discourse' (Chatman, 1978). The dichotomy, thus, is established between fabula/histoire/story on the one hand, and sjuzhet/discours/discourse on the other. The first set conveys the sense of the chronological sequence of events as these would have logically occurred, whereas the second refers to the actual manifestation of those events, not necessarily (in fact, hardly ever) in the same order in which they took place. Wales makes a distinction between the 'deep structure' of a narrative versus the 'surface structure' (2001, p. 367). The terms here mentioned are not free from controversy either (see McIntyre, 2006 and Toolan, 2001 for a review on this issue) so, as analysts we need to be aware of the variation in terminology and choose the most appropriate to serve our interests.

The work on narrative issues undertaken by the Russian Formalists can be illustrated by reference to Propp's ([1928] 1968) structuralist morphology. Based on his analysis of 115 Russian fairy tales, Propp suggests a framework of events (functions) as they occur in those fairy tales. Similar to a corpus linguist his main aim is to identify recurrent patterns and features (constants) against the background of deviating, random or unpredictable elements, which he calls variables (Toolan, 2006a, p. 461). He identified 31 recurrent functions, which are manifested in a fixed sequence, although some of those can also be seen as pairs. Therefore, the functions of characters in a story remain constant. Some examples of those functions are, for instance, the first one which identifies that 'one of the members of a family absents himself from home (an extreme exponent of this function represented by the death of one of the parents)', or function sixteen which stresses that 'the hero and villain join in direct combat' (Toolan, 2006a, p. 460). Among the seven basic character roles also singled out as constants in fairy tales are the following: villain, donor/provider, helper, princess (+father), dispatcher, hero (seeker or victim) and false hero. Characters may take on more than one role and one role may also be represented by more than one character. Propp's framework has been used especially in anthropological studies, and, strikingly, applied to genres as diverse as children's stories and crime series, although it has also been criticized for being too reductionist and for ignoring the various levels of detail that are part of a story. Yet, there exists a substantial degree of agreement on what readers (intuitively) regard as essential to a narrative, which suggests that some structure based on common sense does indeed exist. Although what could be called 'narrative competence' and 'culture-specific abilities' or 'intuitive knowledge' remain highly debatable notions, Propp's model can also be read as an example of how readers are able to rely on intuitions and to deduce or summarize the plot.

Barthes's ([1966] 1977) functional characterization of narratives illustrates the French structuralist take on issues relating to the concept of narrative. He distinguishes between three major levels of narrative structure: (a) functions (as in Propp); (b) actions (roughly, equivalent to characters – cf. Greimas's (1966) actants) and (c) narration (equivalent to *discours* or discourse). In Barthes's framework, functions create coherence in narratives and can be further subdivided into functions proper and indices. Indices give the reader information about the characters' state of mind and the general atmosphere.

Finally, it is also worth mentioning that the analysis of narratives has not been circumscribed to the fictional variety. The most famous take on natural narratives is that of Labov and Waletzky (1967) and Labov (1972) in what has come to be known as the sociolinguistic approach. In his investigation of the narratives of ordinary people and of personal experience, Labov (1972, pp. 359–60) sees narratives as 'one method of recapitulating past experience by matching a verbal sequence of clauses to the sequence of events which [. . .] actually occurred'. One of Labov's ultimate aims in describing narratives from a sociological perspective was to relate the narrator's social characteristics – class, gender, age, ethnicity, geography – to the structure of the narrative. Labov and Waletzky (1967, p. 12) suggest an analytical framework which isolates 'the invariant structural units which are represented by a variety of superficial forms'. The clause is seen as the fundamental grammatical unit, which is accompanied by semantic functions. Clauses are combined with one another and grouped into sections with different functions. They answer, for example, questions, such as 'What happened next?' or 'What's the point?'.

Therefore, narratives can be said to follow a specific pattern perfectly encapsulated by Labov's famous 'diamond' picture which describes the progression of an oral narrative. Oral narratives are said to be built around the following six concepts: 'evaluation', 'resolution', 'coda', 'abstract', 'orientation' and 'complication action' (see Toolan, 2001, p. 149). The orientation, for instance, provides information about the setting or the context. The abstract 'is an initial clause that reports the entire sequence of events of the narrative' (Labov, 1997, p. 402). The coda is 'a functional device for returning the verbal perspective to the present moment' (Labov and Waletzky, 1967, p. 39). There may also be the 'climax', and the 'denouement', which convey the resolution of the action. Clauses which are not chronologically ordered would illustrate the complicating action and provide the referential function which reports a next event. The relevant question is that of 'What happened?'. The evaluative function of the narrative which answers the question 'What's the point?' is realized through clauses which tell the readers what to think about a person, place, etc.

Narrative is crucial to a stylistic investigation. Yet, because the production, reception and use of narrative is seen as a meta-code or a human universal (and a feature which distinguishes human beings from animals in an even more pronounced way than creative language usage as such), narrative has been explored from other linguistic angles as well, e.g., within the areas of sociolinguistic investigation and psycholinguistics, as well as cognitive linguistic approaches (see Fludernik, 1993, 1996).

See also *narratology* (Key Branches), *focalization*, *narrator*, *point of view* (Key Terms).

Narrator

A narrator is typically the entity or agent that tells the story. Some scholars (Toolan, 2001) suggest that it is precisely the prominent role of the telling voice that singularizes narratives as a distinctive type of communicative event. As is the case with the concept of narrative, there is no lack of attempts at establishing a typology of narrators, both from narratological and stylistic circles, the more often quoted being that of Genette (1980). Genette draws on the Aristotelian distinction of mimesis and diegesis, roughly understood as ways of 'showing' and 'telling' respectively. He then identifies various narrative levels at which narrators can work and establishes a preliminary distinction between extradiegetic and intradiegetic narrators, here summarized by Herman et al.:

> [Extradiegetic] A narrator who is not part of any surrounding diegetic frame. Extradiegetic narrators are to be distinguished from intradiegetic narrators (i.e., character-narrators) who occupy a place in a storyworld and tell narratives evoking another embedded storyworld. (Herman et al., 2005, p. 156)

An extradiegetic narrator does not take part in the story being told in any way. The opposite type would be an intradiegetic narrator which generally refers to a figure that actually belongs in the general narrative despite the fact that the narrative being told involves other people's circumstances. One of the most famous examples of an intradiegetic narrator is Scherezade, the narrator of the tales in *Arabian Nights* (1954), who does belong in the general narrative frame despite that not involving her own but other people's stories.

These two terms are used in tandem with a second classification of narrators, the so-called homodiegetic and heterodiegetic types, defined as:

> Both extradiegetic and intradiegetic narrators can be either absent from or present in the story they narrate. (A narrator who does not participate in the story is called 'heterodiegetic' (Genette, 1972, pp. 255–6), whereas the one who takes part in it, at least in some manifestation of his 'self', is 'homodiegetic' (pp. 255–6)). (Rimmon-Kenan, 2002, p. 96)

Scherezade needs to be seen as heterodiegetic and intradiegetic for her tales do not involve her as character. Extradiegetic narrators providing accounts of former versions of themselves, for instance, are typically considered extradiegetic homodiegetic; Rimmon-Kennan (2002) suggests that Pip in *Great Expectations* is an example of this type. In practice, though, distinguishing all these levels might not always be totally realistic or even useful. To simplify, third-person tellers tend to be known as heterodiegetic despite their optionality in belonging to the main story (intradiegetic) or not (extradiegetic), the latter corresponding to classic omniscience. Likewise, first-person voices are generally referred to as homodiegetic. Based on the concept of point of view, Fowler (1986, 1996) proposes an alternative classification. His typology is much more grounded on the linguistic features displayed by the telling voice on each occasion and is directly connected to how psychological point of view (see entry) is projected in texts. Fowler presents two initial types, in turn also subcategorized further: internal and external narration on the one hand, and narration types A, B, C, and D, on the other. Internal narration presents the perspective of an element from within the story, be it a character's consciousness (type A narration) or an omniscient narrator with access to characters' feelings, attitudes and emotions (type B). External narration avoids claiming access to the characters' thoughts or feelings, nor does it make the narrator's thoughts and feelings explicit either (type C narration); the narrator's persona, however, might be underscored in relation to his/her knowledge of the actions and events of the story (type D), although still avoiding any evaluation or thought presentation.

Linguistically, the four types can be clearly identified; for instance, Fowler claims that type A, by being the most subjective, 'consists of either first-person narration by a participating character, or third-person narration which is strongly coloured with personal markers of the character's world-view, or which includes free indirect discourse or internal monologue' (1996, pp. 170–1). Instances of modality and *verba sentiendi* ('words of feeling') are also typical of this type. Type B is consistently characterized by third-person narration of the omniscient kind, with total access to the characters' consciousness: 'to a greater or lesser degree, the author gives an account of the mental processes, feelings, and perceptions of the characters, so the chief linguistic marker of this variant of internal narration is the presence of *verba sentiendi* detailing intentions, emotion, and thoughts' (Fowler, 1996, p. 173). Type C is associated with the most impersonal and detached form of narration so *verba sentiendi* or any type of moral judgement would be suppressed. Type D, despite emerging from an external perspective, allows the narrator's persona to have some kind of saying about the actions and events of the story, if not about their feelings, emotions and thoughts. That persona might be highlighted by first-person pronouns and perhaps some modality but the impossibility of accessing the inner consciousness of the characters is marked by the presence of 'words of estrangement' ('as if', 'evidently'), metaphors and comparisons: 'These expressions pretend that the author – or often one character observing another – does not have access to the feelings or thoughts of the characters' (Fowler, 1996, p. 178). Fowler's model, nonetheless, has been recently much improved in the framework proposed by Simpson (1993) who combines narratological aspects and linguistic indicators in his 'modal grammar of point of view in narrative fiction'. Simpson proposes two broad categories of narration ('Category A' and 'Category B') decided on the basis of who the teller of the story is, thus, very close in nature to Fowler's internal and external perspectives. 'Category A' corresponds to first-person narratives in which a participating character in the story is also the one who tells. 'Category B' is primarily characterized by a non-participating third-person teller, but a crucial further subdivision is established: 'Category B narratives in Narratorial Mode' and 'Category B narratives in Reflector Mode'. If the teller of the story is totally disembodied in as much as he/she does not intrude in the characters' consciousness, but narrates from a floating position instead, then the story is using a Category B in the Narratorial mode. If the story is narrated in the third person but from the point of view of one of the participants made focalizer or reflector, then that narrative falls within Category B in the Reflector mode. Although Simpson's model owes a lot to its immediate predecessor, Fowler's, the dual nature of his Category B also acknowledges the classical narratological dichotomy of the 'seer' versus the 'teller'. Furthermore, Simpson expands the linguistic indicators identified by Fowler in what he calls 'shadings', distinguished as positive, negative and neutral shading. Each narration type can, consequently, be coloured further depending on the most prevalent linguistic indicators. For instance, Category A positive (+ve) narratives will most likely display a concentration of *verba sentiendi*, evaluative adjectives and adverbs, deontic and boulomaic modalities (see *modality*) and, sometimes, also some instances of generic sentences. Category A with negative shading (–ve), on the other hand, will highlight epistemic and perception modalities, epistemic modal auxiliaries, modal adverbs and modal lexical verbs, as well as perception adverbs. The effect of such shift is one of bewilderment, uncertainty or self-questioning in the negative category. The neutral shading allows texts to be free from narratorial modality as the story is told through categorical assertions alone; sequences of straightforward physical description with little attempt at psychological development are also characteristic. Category B in both modes is also capable of displaying the three kinds of shading although the effects are, naturally, different. For instance, category B (N) neutral achieves the highest level of impersonality by underscoring an absence of direct description or analysis of thoughts and feelings of characters, so it feels virtually journalistic in style. Conversely, B(R)+ve can contain not only occurrences of deontic and boulomaic modality and evaluative adjectives and adverbs, but also free indirect discourse. If the free indirect discourse particularly emphasizes the inner working of the reflector's mind via thought presentation, then stream of consciousness is used. In sum, Simpson's classification seems, up to date, the most thorough attempt at establishing a definitive linguistic basis for the classification of narratives without neglecting narratological concerns. As Simpson himself declares, though, more work is needed on the subject as second-person narratives, for instance, seem to have been neglected in the current framework.

See also *focalization*, *modality*, *narrative*, *point of view* (Key Terms).

Negation

See *negative polarity* (Key Terms).

Negative polarity

Polarity is a term employed in linguistics to refer to the choice in language between positive and negative as in 'is'/'isn't', 'mature'/'immature'. Positive and negative polarity may be expressed morphologically ('friendly' vs. 'unfriendly'), syntactically ('friendly' vs. 'not friendly') as well as lexically ('friendly' vs. 'hostile'). In the case of morphologically and syntactically realized polarity, negative polarity is regarded as marked, since its construction involves the addition of linguistic material to its positive counterpart (the prefix 'un' and the negative adverb 'not' above). With lexically realized polarity, categorization is slightly more difficult since it can be hard to determine whether a word like 'bald', for instance, should be regarded as negative, and whether 'loud' and 'heavy' are really the positive, unmarked, members of the antonymic pairs 'loud'/'quiet' and 'heavy'/'light' as suggested by Givón (1979, p. 133). In their treatment of negation, linguists like Jespersen (1917, p. 42) and Givón (1979, p. 133) nevertheless operate with a lexical category of 'inherent negation' which consists of words that are positive in form but arguably negative in meaning.

In stylistics, the use of negative polarity as a meaning-making device is of particular interest. According to psycholinguistic research (Clark and Clark, 1977), the decoding of negative constructions is more difficult and takes more mental operations than the decoding of positive constructions, since this process involves the cognitive establishment of the positive construction *as well as* its negation. The decoding of the proposition 'The dress is not white' thus involves the establishment of the positive 'The dress is white' as well as its negation. Pragmatic linguists, in turn, have proved that negative constructions tend to flout Grice's (1975) maxims of quantity and manner. Negative constructions, therefore, ignore the premises by which speakers are expected to provide enough information in their contributions (quantity) and do so unambiguously (manner). By way of example, the negative proposition about the dress above only tells us what the dress is not, but not what it is (Beige? Blue? Or perhaps dirty?). In Leech's view 'a negative sentence will be avoided if a positive one can be used in its place. Moreover, [. . .] when negative sentences ARE used, it will be for a special purpose' (Leech, 1983, p. 101).

This 'special purpose' referred to by Leech would seem of interest from a stylistic perspective. A key to understanding the 'special' meaning-making potential of negative polarity can be found in cognitive linguistics, where it is claimed (in line with psycholinguistic research) that the linguistic negation of a frame evokes the frame (Lakoff, 2004). The following passage from James Joyce's short story 'Two Gallants' ([1914] 1992, p. 49) is a good example of this. In this story it is said about a character, Corley, on his way to a rendezvous that 'He approached the young woman and, without saluting, began at once to converse with her'. Here, the decoding of the negative construction involves the establishment of the word or concept which is negated ('saluting') as well as of its negation ('without saluting'). By mentioning the fact that Corley does not salute the girl, the construction simultaneously activates the reader's awareness that he could have done so, thereby foregrounding the rudeness and intimacy of his behaviour towards the woman which, when considered in its historical context, is rather pronounced (cf. Nørgaard, 2007).

The idea that the negation of the frame evokes the frame is developed further in Werth's text world theory (1999) about the ability of discourse to construct mental images – so-called text worlds – in our minds. According to Werth (1999, pp. 253–4), negatives have world-building properties in the sense that in a given text world, a negative construction may construct a textual sub-world. A good example of this is provided by Hidalgo-Downing (2002) who argues that the negations in the following lines from a poem by Szymborska (1999) create a textual sub-world within the text world of the sister's life which is described by the poem: 'My sister's desk drawers don't hold old poems/and her handbag doesn't hold new ones' and 'Her coffee doesn't spill on manuscripts'. By means of negation, these lines simultaneously establish the text world of the sister's life and a sub-world in which drawers and handbag do hold poems and where coffee spills on manuscripts – a sub-world we take to be that of the lyric persona. In line with the above, Nahajec (2009) examines the implicit meaning created by negation in poetry from a pragmatic-cognitive perspective. A slightly different approach to negative polarity is taken by proponents of the linguistic theory of polyphony known as ScaPoLine (Nølke, 2006) who investigate the ability of negatives to encode different voices or viewpoints in discourse. According to this linguistic paradigm, the proposition about the dress above involves two voices, or viewpoints: The negative construction (viewpoint 2), 'The dress is not white', negates and thereby entails its positive counterpart (viewpoint 1), 'The dress is white'. The choice of the negative construction is not a random choice out of the blue but a way of coding (and responding to) the view that somebody expects/hopes/believes that the dress is white. The responsibility for the viewpoints can usually be determined by the narrative context of the sentences, and the voices may belong to different characters, the narrator, 'public opinion', earlier 'versions' of the current speaker, etc. The negative polarity of the speaker's proposition above about the colour of the dress (viewpoint 2) may, for instance, be a reaction to, and hence entail, somebody else's belief that the dress is (or should or would be) white (viewpoint 1). The proposition could, for example, be a reaction to – and encoding the viewpoint of – the 'public opinion' that wedding dresses should be white. Alternatively, the speaker may have bought a dress she thought was white, but later realize that it is actually bright yellow. In that case, the responsibility for viewpoints 1 and 2 can both be ascribed to the same speaker. From a polyphonic perspective, Nørgaard (2007) demonstrates how Joyce in 'Two Gallants' ([1914] 1992) employs negative polarity as a subtle means of encoding the voices of different characters, the different voices of the same character, and even the voice, or viewpoint, of the reader.

See also *cooperative principle*, *text world theory* (Key Terms).

Parallelism

See *foregrounding* (Key Terms).

Perlocution

See *speech act theory* (Key Terms).

Poetics and Linguistics Association

The *Poetics and Linguistics Association, PALA*, is an international association for people with an interest in stylistics, poetics and associated fields of language and linguistics. The association hosts an annual international conference and sponsors a number of smaller events which are typically organized by some of the members' special interest groups such as the narrative group, the corpus stylistics group and the rhetoric and pedagogy group. The association's journal, *Language and Literature* (see entry), is a peer-reviewed journal of international scope which is published four times a year. In addition to this, the association also publishes *PALA Occasional Papers* and *PALA Proceedings*, both of which are online publications. The PALA website is found at: www.pala.ac.uk

See also *Language and Literature* (Key Terms).

Point of view

As is the case with focalization (see entry), much has been written on the notion of point of view (Bray, 2007; Fowler, 1986, 1996; Jeffries, 2000; Leech and Short, 2007; McIntyre, 2004, 2006; Sotirova, 2004, 2005). These two concepts have been discussed and analysed in parallel ways in narratology and stylistics respectively (see *focalization*). 'Point of view' appears to have won the battle for stylisticians, especially as it has traditionally been the term of choice for some of the founding and most famous practitioners of the discipline: Fowler, Leech, Short, Simpson and Wales. The latter (Wales, 2001), for instance, underscores the variety of meanings this notion encompasses:

> 1. Point of view in the basic aesthetic sense refers to 'angle of vision' [. . .].
> 2. Even in ordinary speech we use point of view in the figurative sense of the way of looking at a matter, rather than a scene, through someone's eyes, or thoughts [. . .].
> 3. Point of view in the figurative sense entails not only the presence of a conceptualizing character or focalizer, but also a particular way of conceptualizing: a world-view or ideology [. . .].
> 4. An aspect that has been particularly developed relates point of view to the larger discourse situation of narrator-text-reader. (Wales, 2001, pp. 306–7)

In practice, a very general definition of the term understood as the perspective or filter through which events are perceived would need to incorporate much of the content present in the four senses described by Wales. Practitioners of stylistics have traditionally used the point of view typology suggested by Fowler (1977, 1986, 1996) who borrowed it, in turn, from that of Uspensky (1973). Fowler (1996, p. 162) distinguishes three types, spatio-temporal, ideological and psychological point of view. The first type refers to how readers position the story in space and time. In relation to the former, for instance, readers need to get a sense of the various locations of the storyline and deictic markers (see *deixis*) such as adverbs ('here', 'there'), demonstrative determiners and pronouns ('this' and 'that'), deictic verbs ('bring', 'take') and locative expressions (prepositional phrases) help to anchor the narrative spatially. Similarly, temporal parameters allow us to place the story alongside a timeline, despite the fact that events can and very often do appear temporally scrambled in the form of flashbacks or flashforwards.

Temporal representation, in particular, has been of special interest to narratologists (Genette, 1980; Rimmon-Kenan, 2002) who generally approach the relationship between textual time and story time via three notions: order, duration and frequency. Order considers the possible asynchronisms between the storyline and its textual presentation. Asynchronous textual manifestations, called 'anachronies' by Genette (1980), can introduce events that happened prior to the current moment of the story (analepses or flashbacks) or anticipate situations that will occur later on (prolepses or flashforwards). Duration refers to the ratio of textual space to temporal length. For instance, the pace of a story may appear rushed or quickened if certain temporal gaps are noticeable because they have not been given any textual space whatsoever; these instances of temporal vacuum are known as 'ellipsis'. The opposite effect is achieved when events that would not logically stretch in time are awarded considerable textual presence, what is known as 'descriptive pause'. 'Summary' is achieved by condensing a lengthy period of time in a relatively small textual space. Finally, by means of the 'scene' technique, story and text duration are presented as very similar, as in dialogue or in plays.

The final way of dealing with the ratio textual versus story time is via the notion of frequency. Frequency refers to the number of times that a particular incident in the story is textually represented: singulative frequency is the default parameter so events would be made textually manifest as often as they occur in the story, that is, we are told once what happens once, twice what happens twice and so on. Repetitive frequency, on the other hand, emphasizes a particular event by textually representing it more than once, as when various characters convey the same circumstance from their own perspective, with as many recountings as there are characters. Iterative frequency, finally, spares us the need to unnecessarily encounter situations that would happen routinely on more than one occasion (for instance, narrators do not inform their readers of the number of times characters presumably wake up, have showers, or eat lunch, unless these happen to have some special significance for the story). Linguistically, temporal point of view is indicated via deictic adverbs ('now', 'then'), tense (present, past) and temporal expressions (prepositional phrases). Fowler's spatio-temporal point of view seems rather close, although not totally equivalent because the temporal component is not so clearly established there, to sense number one in Wales's definition above.

The second type of point of view suggested by Fowler is ideological point of view defined as 'the system of beliefs, values, and categories by reference to which a person or a society comprehends the world' (1986, p. 130); it is sense number three in Wales's classification that appears evoked now. Fowler subsequently considers who might be behind the transmission of a particular ideology in texts, whether the author via the figure of the implied author, the narrator, the author surreptitiously speaking through the narrator or simply the characters. Such considerations would place ideological point of view on a similar plane to sense four in Wales's definition. Fowler (1996, p. 166) highlights two ways in which ideological point of view is linguistically indicated, one explicit and a second more indirect. Modality (see entry) is one of the ways in which ideology is explicitly projected in texts and can be realized in the form of the prototypical modal verbs or via modal adverbs or sentence adverbs, evaluative adjectives and adverbs, verbs of knowledge, prediction and evaluation and generic sentences. The second, less conspicuous, way in which ideological point if view is manifested has actually developed into a well-known way of describing the linguistic (verbal and otherwise) realizations of narrators', authors' and characters' consciousness, the so-called mind style (see entry):

> The world-view of an author, or a narrator, or a character, constituted by the ideational structure of the text. From now I shall prefer this term to the cumbersome 'point of view on the ideological plane'. (Fowler, 1996, p. 214)

There has been plenty of work on the way mind style functions and the markers that point to individual manifestations in texts. Some of the linguistic indicators that have been named as mind style projectors include transitivity patterns, metaphor use, under- and over-lexicalization and certain syntactic structures. Psychological point of view, finally, 'concerns the question of who is presented as the observer of the events of a narrative, whether the author or a participating character; and the various kinds of discourse associated with different relationships between narrator and character' (Fowler, 1996, pp. 169–70). This final take on point of view is more clearly reminiscent of the distinction 'who sees' vs. 'who tells' traditionally discussed in narratology in relation to focalization (see entry) and, as a matter of fact, Fowler does liken the two terms (1996, p. 169).

As stated above, stylisticians seem to have preferred 'point of view,' although they have not discarded 'focalization' totally, especially as it relates to the role of characters as 'focalizers' or 'mediators'. One important factor that seems to clearly differentiate the two main disciplines dealing with issues of point of view and focalization is the primarily linguistic slant of stylistics in relation to its sister discipline, narratology. A particularly illuminating example of how linguistics can help practitioners decide on the various types of point of view is provided by Short (1996) who, instead of proposing a further taxonomy, gathers a list of likely viewpoint indicators comprising of schema-oriented language, value-laden language, given versus new information, deixis, representations of thought and perception and psychological sequencing. Short (2000) and others (McIntyre, 2004, 2006) have extended the list to also include graphology, presupposition and Grice's co-operative principle. Simpson (1993), in turn, has attempted to combine narratological aspects and linguistic indicators in his 'modal grammar of point of view in narrative fiction' (see *narrator*). It seems clear, nonetheless, that more work on point of view is still needed; it also ensues that, as formats other than the written are incorporated in stylistic analyses (Gibbons, 2010; Montoro, 2010a, 2010b; Nørgaard, 2010a), point of view indicators will extend to include multimodal aspects too.

See also *narratology* (Key Branches), *cooperative principle*, *focalization*, *mind style*, *modality*, *narrator*, (Key Terms).

Polarity

See *negative polarity* (Key Terms).

Politeness

One of the main fields of research that pragmaticians have been involved with for some time is the issue of politeness. There is a mass of publications in this area (see, for instance, the *Journal of Pragmatics* and the *Journal of Politeness Research*) as linguistic politeness has been scrutinized from a variety of perspectives. Stylistics has not been immune to the influence of politeness proposals and the application of some politeness tenets has resulted in very interesting insights into the nature of literary language. When pragmaticians discuss politeness, though, they tend to make a distinction between the layman's understanding of the term and the scholarly definition. For the non-specialists, politeness simply refers to the way individuals are expected to conduct themselves in a given society, abiding by the social norms that characterize that group or culture. Linguistic politeness, on the other hand, deals with the linguistic forms used to express social balance and social appropriateness, although politeness researchers certainly include social and cultural norms that influence what is labelled 'polite linguistic behaviour'.

The most famous, commented upon and reworked model of linguistic politeness is, undoubtedly, that proposed by Brown and Levinson (1987). Despite the fact that not everybody agrees wholeheartedly with this framework (Watts, 2003; Werkhofer, 2005), it still offers a comprehensive way to understand how social interaction is reflected in language. This model has been amply exploited in the analyses of literary texts too (Busse, 2006b; Culpeper, 1998; Ermida, 2006; Fitzmaurice, 2000; Gross, 2000; Simpson, 1989), especially, albeit not exclusively, in relation to drama. This model is known as the 'face management view' because the whole apparatus is structured around the notion of 'face', a term that Brown and Levinson borrow from Goffman (1967):

> The term face may be defined as the positive social value a person effectively claims for himself by the line others assume he has taken during a particular contact. Face is an image of self delineated in terms of approved social attributes – albeit an image that others may share, as when a person makes a good showing for his profession or religion by making a good showing for himself. (Goffman, 1967, p. 5)

In Goffman's definition, face refers to the self-image every individual projects when they enter into some kind of interaction with others, which also reveals how much there is at stake in human social relations: for instance, the individual's reputation in relation to their profession, their religion, their family or their social connections. Brown and Levinson (1987) elaborate on Goffman's term and build their model on two notions called 'negative' and 'positive' face:

> Negative face: the want of every 'competent adult member' that his/her actions be unimpeded by others.
>
> Positive face: the want of every member that his/her wants be desirable to at least some others. (Brown and Levinson, 1987, p. 62)

If we compare Brown and Levinson's concept of positive and negative face to the non-specialist's understanding of politeness as 'social norms', we can see that the former have substituted wants and needs for the layman's social rules. They also underscore that speakers are aware of, not only their own wants, but also their interlocutors', so the concept of face in interaction is bidirectional. Brown and Levinson go on to consider that in normal circumstances (there are some exceptions to this rule, such as emergencies when the values embodied in the concept of face are suspended), speakers' and hearers' wants are often 'interfered with' or cannot be 'attended to'. Linguistically, this inability to see to the other interactant's wants needs to be met by the so-called Face Threatening Acts (FTAs). So, every time we need to ask for a favour from somebody, for instance, we are impinging upon the negative face of our addressee, for their freedom to act is being compromised by our needs and, consequently, a FTA is implemented.

As FTAs are not only unavoidable, but common occurrences in social interaction, Brown and Levinson's describe five linguistic superstrategies which aim at mitigating the impositions created by the FTAs. These are: 'Bald on record politeness', 'positive politeness', 'negative politeness', 'off-record politeness' and 'don't perform the FTA' (Brown and Levinson, 1987). The superstrategy 'Don't perform the FTA' clearly avoids troubling the social harmony that Brown and Levinson's framework is built upon. So, if a speaker considers that performing a particular FTA might disturb social balance, it might be in everybody's interest that such action is simply avoided. For instance, you might be in desperate need of some spare change to buy a ticket for the last train home but might find yourself surrounded by strangers in the middle of an isolated train station. It is up to you, the speaker, to weigh up the risk of actually performing the FTA and asking some of those strangers for some cash or simply eschewing the task and spend the night at the station.

At the opposite end of the scale we find the 'bald on record politeness' option which describes those situations in which FTAs are performed 'in the most direct, clear, unambiguous and concise way possible' (Brown and Levinson, 1987, p. 69). Linguistically, directives are the clearest instances of bald on record politeness. Such an upfront option, however, tends to be avoided in the interest of amenity among interactants. Speakers can, instead, opt for the use of 'positive politeness': 'Positive politeness is redress directed to the addresse's positive face, his perennial desire that his wants [...] should be thought of as desirable' (Brown and Levinson, 1987, p. 101). This superstrategy is linguistically realized in a variety of ways such as 'by claiming common ground' (if we notice and attend to the hearer's interests, wants and needs or use in-group identity markers, such as in-group language or dialect), by 'conveying that the speaker and hearer are cooperators' (if we make offers, promises or are optimistic) or by 'fulfilling the hearer's wants' via the offer of some gifts, sympathy or understanding.

The fourth superstrategy is 'negative politeness' which refers to those cases which redress the threat to the negative face of the hearer; there are, as with positive politeness, quite a few possible linguistic realizations for this superstrategy, such as 'be indirect', that is, do not straightforwardly state your aims; 'do not presume or assume', which can be achieved by the use of questions or hedges; 'do not coerce your hearer' by being pessimistic about the expectations of the FTA being successful ('I don't suppose you could do me a favour'); and 'communicate your wants to not impinge upon the hearer's' by apologizing ('I'm so sorry for troubling you...') or stating your needs in an impersonal way (with passive forms, for example). Finally, the speaker can also make use of the 'off-record' suprastrategy which aims for contextually ambiguous indirectness so that the speaker can deny that the FTA is actually being performed or intended if the hearer somehow takes offence. The 'off-record' option can be linguistically expressed through conversational implicature (see *cooperative principle*) as conveyed by hints or irony, for instance, or by being vague and ambiguous.

In stylistics, politeness models, especially Brown and Levinson's (1987), have been used to illustrate characters' social relations. Because of the conversational nature of drama, politeness frameworks appear to be specially suited to this genre. Also, it is important to note that Brown and Levinson's framework is designed under the assumption that interactants always work towards social cooperation and the maintenance of social harmony which, however, is not always the case as impoliteness models have successfully proved (Bousfield, 2008; Culpeper, 1996; Culpeper et al., 2003). In fact, investigations on linguistic politeness have evolved to incorporate the articulation of linguistic impoliteness too. The manifestation of linguistic impoliteness, understood as the intentional creation of utterances not conceived to maintain but to disturb social harmony, has also found its way into stylistic analyses as Bousfield (2007), Culpeper (2001) and Rudanko (2006) demonstrate.

See also *pragmatic stylistics* (Key Branches), *cooperative principle* (Key Terms).

Possible worlds theory

The origins of the theoretical framework known as possible worlds theory are firmly grounded on the formal semantics principles defended by philosophers such as Kripke (1972), Lewis (1973), Plantinga (1979) and Rescher (1979). It is the adaptation and application by narratologists, though, that has brought this model closer to stylistic concerns. In the latter group, the work of Ryan has been especially influential (1991a, 1991b, 1992, 1998, 2006) although much is also due to literary theorists Doležel (1988, 1989, 1998a, 1998b) and Pavel (1986). Initially, philosophers of language were concerned with investigating the truth value of sentences; subsequent adaptations have retained some of those interests but have amply reformulated the framework to incorporate specifically literary aspects. The basic premises of the framework have proven to be particularly advantageous for a diversity of studies on narrative issues ranging from the differentiation and definition of narrative genres (Ryan, 1991a, 1991b), to the analysis of hypertext fiction (Bell, 2007, 2010, fc) or the description of the narrative structure of role-playing games (Punday, 2005).

The foundation principle of possible worlds theory, as it is primarily understood in narratology, is the idea that the reality evoked in texts is made up of a series of worlds. Texts project a series of domains representing a plurality of worlds which are different from the world we inhabit, the so-called Actual World (AW). The text itself creates its own world, the 'Textual Actual World' (TAW) lying at the centre of many other 'Alternate Possible Worlds' (APWs), as explained by Ryan (1991a). Ryan (2006) also emphasizes that the way we relate to fictional texts is based on our understanding their non-actuality but still engaging with the TAWs as if they were real. She compares our engagement with fictional discourses to other non-factual constructions of the type 'if...then' (2006, p. 646) and stresses that whereas the latter underscore the hypothetical and illusory nature of the propositions they contain, fictional discourses appear particularly 'factual' to readers; as Ryan says 'fiction is overwhelmingly told in the indicative mode' (2006, p. 646). The reason why we are capable of relating to TAWs as part of a complete modal system with their own pseudo-factual reality is because of what is known as the 're-centering' of the reader. It seems that by reading fiction we immerse ourselves in a transference process into the TAW resulting in a recognition and acceptance of the rules, norms and circumstances of that reality as actual in the realm of that particular world. Although emerging from different schools of thought, theories of emotion (see *emotion: stylistic approaches*) have also tapped into how humans process fiction emotionally as they would reality, hence engaging in similar displays of affection in the form of laughter, sadness or anger. Also, as explained below, new approaches to possible worlds theory are adding a firmer cognitive slant to the framework so that the re-centring or transference into the TAW can be explained more accurately.

A further tenet of possible worlds theory lies in the way in which the various worlds are accessed. For a world to be considered possible, it needs to show a certain degree of accessibility, measured against the so-called Principle of Minimal Departure. According to this principle, unless otherwise stated, the physical and logical principles that govern our AW are still in place in any of the APWs evoked in texts. Hence if the TAW refers to the existence of reptilians we should assume that those creatures belong to the same biological category as those we have in the AW. The way to measure the closeness of any world to the AW is by considering its accessibility, that is, by contemplating how easy it is for a non-inhabitant of that world to learn of its circumstances. Such measuring is implemented in relation to a series of 'accessibility conditions' which are the circumstances that will allow us to gain entry into any of the possible worlds. These conditions include (summarized from Ryan, 1991b, pp. 558–9):

(a) Identity of properties: TAW is accessible from AW if the objects common to TAW and AW have the same properties.
(b) Identity of inventory: TAW is accessible from AW if TAW and AW are furnished by the same objects.
(c) Compatibility of inventory: TAW is accessible from AW if TAW's inventory includes all the members of AW, as well as some native members.
(d) Chronological compatibility: TAW is accessible from AW if it takes no temporal relocation for a member of AW to contemplate the entire history of TAW.
(e) Physical compatibility: TAW is accessible from AW if they share natural laws.
(f) Taxonomic compatibility: TAW is accessible from AW if both worlds contain the same species, and the species are characterized by the same properties.

(g) Logical compatibility: TAW is accessible from AW if both worlds respect the principles of noncontradiction and of excluded middle.
(h) Analytical compatibility: TAW is accessible from AW if they share analytic truths, i.e., if objects designated by the same words have the same essential properties.
(i) Linguistic compatibility: TAW is accessible from AW if the language by which TAW is described can be understood in AW.

So, the more compatible a TAW is with the AW, the more accessible it becomes. That compatibility is helped by the objects in that world also existing as objects in the AW with the same properties (condition A); by those objects being part of some category which also exists in the AW (condition C); or by the temporality of the TAW being compatible with the time constraints of the AW (condition D); according to this last condition, thus, reading a particular text spanning 250 years in the TAW would not actually 'take up' that length of time. Possible worlds theory also considers the creation of APWs as constructed through the various points of view of the characters of a story. Based on their distinctive attitudes, general situation and circumstances, characters are capable of giving rise to their own private APWs. So the realm of worlds would be populated in accordance with the character's wishes ('Desire World'), duties ('Obligation World'), fantasies ('Fantasy World'), knowledge ('Knowledge or Epistemic World'), objectives and aims ('Goals and Plans World').

Stylistic applications of possible worlds theory to the analysis of literature have highlighted that this framework is not to be likened to other models clearly construed with a specific cognitive perspective in mind. Bell (2007, p. 46) underscores that the focus of possible worlds theory does not lie in explaining the cognitive mechanisms by which narrative comprehension occurs in readers' minds but in establishing the ontological status of the worlds evoked in texts. Similarly, Semino (2003) points out that possible worlds theory has so far neglected establishing clearly what the reader's role is. For instance she states that original versions of the framework do not engage with the way in which linguistic features can cue in world creation (see also Semino, 2006b). Recently, though, this lack has been satisfactorily addressed as Bell (2007) is quick to point out the usefulness of employing traditional linguistic analyses to clarify the prompts that readers are provided with so that they can enter the various worlds. Today there is a tendency to acknowledge that contemplating cognitive aspects of narrative comprehension can be advantageous to marry traditional views on possible worlds theory and cognitive linguistic positions. Stockwell in his analysis of literary reading considers that 'the approach can be adapted so that we can speak of discourse worlds that can be understood as dynamic readerly interactions with possible worlds: possible worlds with a narratological and cognitive dimension' (2002, p. 93). Even one of the first proponents of narratological perspectives on possible worlds theory is acknowledging the need for further cognitive work. As Ryan states 'The importance of PW theory is not limited to providing a logical and phenomenological account of fictionality. I believe that its most significant – and still largely unrecognized – contribution to narrative theory is to offer a cognitive model of narrativity that transcends the boundary between fiction and nonfiction' (2006, p. 647).

See also *cognitive stylistics/poetics, emotion: stylistic approaches* (Key Branches), *text world theory* (Key Terms).

Presupposition and entailment

Presupposition and entailment are two issues generally discussed in pragmatics to illustrate language in use. Pragmatics looks into how these two notions are realized because they underscore, respectively, instances of the so-called 'pragmatic inferencing' versus 'semantic inferencing'. Yule defines both terms as: 'A presupposition is something the speaker assumes to be the case prior to making an utterance. Speakers, not sentences, have presuppositions. An entailment is something that logically follows from what is asserted in the utterance. Sentences, not speakers, have entailments' (Yule, 1996, p. 25). Consider, for instance, the following sentences:

a1) The Queen of Sheba killed her servant.
a2) Her servant died.

By virtue of the semantic characteristics of the verb 'killed', sentence 'a1' entails sentence 'a2'. The verb 'kill', therefore, always entails the same sense of 'murdering' or 'slaying'. In contrast, see the following:

b1) I resent spending so much money at Christmas time.
b2) I spend lots of money at Christmas time.

'b1' is context-dependent and relies on the presupposed 'b2' to be true, i.e., if I utter 'b1' is simply because I assume 'b2' to be true. Presupposition and entailment can be distinguished by applying the so-called negation test. According to Saeed: 'A sentence (p) entails a sentence (q) when the truth of the first (p) guarantees the truth of the second (q), and the falsity of the second (q) guarantees the falsity of the first (p)' (Saeed, 1997, p. 90); this means that negating our initial 'a1' should completely invalidate the entailment:

a3) The Queen of Sheba did not kill her servant.
a4) *Her servant died.

The falsity of the first sentence has cancelled out the previous entailment. If the negation test is applied to presuppositions, there is a different set of correlations established between the initial and the presupposed sentence:

b3) I don't resent spending so much money at Christmas time.
b4) I spend lots of money at Christmas time.

Despite its negative status, 'b3' still presupposes 'b4' which proves that the connection between these two sentences is one of presupposition and not entailment.

Although presupposition and entailment are concepts primarily discussed in pragmatics, they can also be used for the stylistic analysis of characters' relationship and social connections. Using presupposing sentences implies that interactants in the communicative act share a certain amount of knowledge. If this communicative act is a conversation between characters, then such exchanges can reveal a lot about the type of social connections existing between them. If, on the other hand, the communicative act includes a narrator who uses lots of presupposing sentences, then, it is the reader who is assumed to share a certain amount of knowledge for them to be able to infer the intended meaning. One of the clearest ways in which presupposition is exploited in fiction is through the use of the definite article 'the': whenever a fictional entity is introduced by the definite determiner as opposed to its indefinite counterpart 'a/an', the narrator is deliberately creating a false sense of commonality with their readers. This use also implies more deductive and referential work from the reader.

See *pragmatic stylistics* (Key Branches), *cooperative principle*; *cooperation* (Key Terms).

Reference

See *cohesion* (Key Terms).

Referent

In one sense of the word, the referent is the extra-linguistic entity to which a linguistic expression, as well as other types of sign, refers. The referent may be imaginary as well as real. While the referent of the lexical item 'book' is thus the object of a book in the external world, the referent of 'unicorn' is the object of this particular fantasy creature in an imagined external (i.e., extra-linguistic) world. When describing the meaning of a given word or expression, the referent must be distinguished from the signified, which is the abstract notion, rather than the object, to which a signifier refers.

Secondly, in the study of cohesion, reference is a linguistic phenomenon which involves a referring item such as a pronoun and a linguistic item referred to, that is, the referent. In the utterance 'I know a good photographer. He works in Manchester', 'he' is the referring item and 'a good photographer' is the referent. Alternatively, it might be argued that 'he' and 'a good photographer' are a case of 'co-reference', that is, of two referring items which both refer to the same real-world (or fictional) referent. Text-internal reference may either be anaphoric or cataphoric. In anaphoric reference, the referent precedes the referring expression as in the example above. In cataphoric reference, the referent follows the referring expression as in the first line of Ian McEwan's novel *Black Dogs* (1992) 'Ever since I lost mine in a road accident when I was eight, I have had my eyes on other people's parents', where 'mine' refers forwards in the text to 'parents'. This extract illustrates well the process of referent-tracking that readers engage in when reading in order to make sense of the text. In the search for a cataphoric referent of the pronoun 'mine', readers may first tend to wrongly assume that 'mine' refers to 'eyes', since the nominal nature of the latter makes it qualify as the first possible referent in the text succeeding the referring item. As we read along, however, we realize that our capacity for referent-tracking has fooled us, as probably intended by the author. In this grammatical sense of the concept, reference is a cohesive device which plays a significant role in the tying together of sentences for the creation of text.

See also *cohesion, signifier and signified* (Key Terms).

Rhyme

Rhyme is a stylistic device which is employed in poetry in particular, but may also be encountered in drama as well as outside literature in advertising and other types of text. Rhyme is the repetition of the last stressed vowel and the following speech sounds in two or more words, most typically positioned at the end of verse-lines. Rhyme is closely related to other types of sound similarity such as alliteration, assonance and consonance (see entries).

The different types of rhyme are classified by their position as well as by the phonological make-up of the rhyming words. In terms of position, the most frequent type of rhyme is *end rhyme*, which consists of rhyming words at the end of two or more verse-lines as in Keats's 'To Autumn' ([1820] 1983), of which the first four lines follow here:

> Season of mists and mellow fruitfulness,
> Close bosom-friend of the maturing sun;
> Conspiring with him how to load and bless
> With fruit the vines that round the thatch-eves run;

Sometimes rhyme occurs within a single verse-line as in the first line of Shelley's 'The Cloud' ([1820] 1983). This is called *internal rhyme*:

> I bring fresh <u>showers</u> for the thirsting <u>flowers</u>.

When classified in terms of the phonological make-up of the rhyming words, a distinction is made between several types of rhyme: *Masculine rhyme* is rhyme consisting of a single stressed syllable ('hat'/'cat'). *Feminine rhyme*, or *double rhyme*, is found in two rhyming syllables, of which the first is stressed and the second unstressed ('stranger'/'danger'). *Triple rhyme*, in turn, involves three rhyming syllables ('mystery'/'history'). *Pararhyme* or *half rhyme* is used by some to refer to rhyming words where the final consonant sound is the same ('ill'/'shell'), and by others to refer to instances where respectively the initial and the final consonant sounds are the same while the intervening vowel sound is different ('hall'/'hell'). *Imperfect rhyme* occurs when the rhyme is forced or somehow distorted ('tomb'/'worm'; 'wing'/'caring'). The use of imperfect rhyme makes for variation in patterns of otherwise perfect rhyme and is furthermore sometimes used for comic effect.

Basically, rhyme is a largely phonological and hence sonic phenomenon, but there are also instances of rhyme where the similarity is not in sound, but in spelling. Such rhyme is said to 'rhyme to the eye' and is consequently called *eye rhyme* ('daughter'/'laughter'). Sometimes eye rhyme can be explained by reference to historical changes in pronunciation, which means that something that looks like eye rhyme to a contemporary reader may have been an example of perfect rhyme at the time of composition.

In poetry, regular patterns of rhyming lines are referred to as *rhyme schemes*. In the analysis of such patterns, the different end rhymes are given an alphabetical letter, beginning with 'a'. Different rhyme schemes have different names and some are characteristic of particular types of poetry. Thus, for instance, lines which rhyme 'abab' are called *alternating rhyme* or *cross rhyme*, 'abba' is called *enclosed rhyme*, and 'aa' and 'bb' are *couplets*. While the traditional (Italian) Petrachan sonnet is characterized by the following rhyme scheme: 'abba abba cde cde' or 'abba abba cdc dcd', the typical rhyme scheme of the later (English) Shakespearian sonnet is 'abab cdcd efef gg'.

Since language users rarely rhyme in their everyday written or spoken prose, rhyme tends to highlight the poetic nature of the text in which it occurs. But rhyme is more than mere poetic decoration. By means of sound similarity (and/or visual similarity), it is a cohesive device which creates links between words and helps tie verse-lines together into stanzas. It furthermore makes for a certain foregrounding of the words which rhyme with possible interpretive consequences. Outside poetry, rhyme is also found in drama. In Shakespeare's plays, for instance, rhyming couplets are often employed to signal the end of scenes, thus functioning as a cue to actors to leave the stage as well as helping the audience to catch a change of scene in theatre where no curtains would signal such changes. Rhyme is also frequently used as a stylistic device in advertising, as exemplified by the slogan of Haig Scotch whisky: 'Don't be vague. Ask for Haig.'

In multimodal stylistics, the concept of rhyme is employed in a broader sense of the word to refer to different types of similar elements which 'rhyme to the eye' and thereby create cohesion. One example of this is colour-rhyme, where e.g., the colour red at one point in a layout may 'rhyme' with the colour red somewhere else in the same layout and thus create cohesion. In the multimodal sense of the word, rhyme may also occur across semiotic modes. An example of cross-modal rhyme, and hence of cross-modal cohesion, is seen in Jonathan Safran Foer's novel *Extremely Loud and Incredibly Close* (2005), where a black page appears to rhyme with verbal references nearby to the grave of the protagonist's deceased father.

See also *alliteration*, *assonance*, *cohesion*, *consonance* (Key Terms).

Rhythm

See *metre* (Key Terms).

Schema

See *schema theory* (Key Terms).

Schema theory

The origins of modern schema theory as it has been used for the analysis of literature lie in last century's Gestalt psychology of the 1920s and 1930s. Some scholars (Semino, 1997; Stockwell, 2006) go much further back in time and name Kant's *Critique of Pure Reason* ([1787] 1963) as the work where the organization of knowledge as the mental structures that are schemata is first described. Among the work of Gestalt psychologists, Bartlett's *Remembering: A Study in Experimental and Social Psychology* (1932) is accepted as the most influential formulation of the theory. Later reworkings are those of Abelson (1987), Rumelhart (1975, 1980, 1984), Rumelhart and Norman (1978), Schank (1982a, 1982b, 1984, 1986) and Schank and Abelson (1977). Whereas Rumelhart's and his collaborators' background is in cognitive psychology, Schank and Abelson are concerned with human and Artificial Intelligence (AI). They all propose that cognition is based on a series of knowledge structures that determine how mental activity takes place, the so-called schema (plural 'schemata'). Stockwell summarizes the functioning of these configurations as follows:

> Essentially, the context that someone needs to make sense of individual experiences, events, parts of situations or elements of language is stored in background memory as an associative network of knowledge. In the

> course of experiencing an event or making sense of a situation, a schema is dynamically produced, which can be modelled as a sort of script based on similar situations encountered previously. New experiences and new incoming information are understood by matching them to existing schematic knowledge. (Stockwell, 2003, p. 255)

Therefore schemata help us make sense of the world by allowing the retrieval of the exact type of stored information pertaining to each particular situation. The now classic example, virtually always quoted, is that of the 'restaurant' schema: we understand that going for a meal involves elements such as choosing a particular place, sitting down and ordering from a set menu, having the food brought to our table, eating it and finally paying for this service before leaving. Sequentiality is particularly important in our understanding of the classical view of the restaurant schema as we do not tend to pay before eating; however, new components may need to be incorporated to the existing pockets of knowledge as circumstances change. Thus, deciding to eat out in a fast-food restaurant will totally alter the original sequentiality as we are asked to pay for our order in advance. Similarly, self-service places are characterized for the lack of people waiting tables, and take-away establishments by the fact that the food will be consumed outside the premises. In *Scripts, Plans, Goals and Understanding* (1977), Schank and Abelson present a model of human knowledge that would cater for the functioning of schemata. Their more general intention was also to come up with a framework that could be applicable to Artificial Intelligence. The more dynamic aspects of schema formation are later described in Schank (1982). For Schank and Abelson a 'script' (term that replaces schema but which essentially refers to the same configuration of knowledge) is:

> A structure that describes appropriate sequences of events in a particular context [. . .]. Scripts handle stylized everyday situations [. . .]. [A] script is a predetermined, stereotyped sequence of actions that defines a well-known situation. (Schank and Abelson, 1977, p. 141)

So arranging to go out for a meal with your friends is possible because everybody roughly shares the same restaurant schema/script. Scripts can be classified as 'situational', 'personal' and 'instrumental' and also contain a number of elements that prompt each particular script, the so-called 'slots'. These slots can be realized by 'props' (for instance, the menu card in a restaurant), the 'roles of participants' (us as consumers, the waiter as worker), the 'entry conditions' (such as the fact that the establishment needs permission to serve food), the 'results' (being fed), the 'scenes and their sequence' (sitting down, being given the menu, ordering). But scripts are not, in Schank and Abelson's framework, the only way of organizing knowledge. They suggest a cline based on specificity, from those configurations that refer to the more specialized level of knowledge to those that convey the more general. Scripts are considered examples of specific rather than general knowledge but at higher levels we can find 'plans', 'sub-goals', 'goals' and 'themes'. The higher up in the hierarchy we need to go, the more indisputably individualized the knowledge structure becomes. This particular aspect highlights the socio-cultural idiosyncrasy of schemata that vary not only from individual to individual but are also dictated by social and cultural parameters.

The framework as postulated by Schank and Abelson is later reformulated by Schank in *Dynamic Memory: A Theory of Reminding and Learning in Computers and People* (1982a) because of his dissatisfaction with some aspects of the original one. As the title itself suggests, Schank defends the changing potential of schemata, an issue decidedly neglected in Schank and Abelson (1977). Also, Schank discusses how understanding is largely based on the notion of reminding, as in why it is that certain situations are suggestive of some other situations and how we use this capability in general mental processing. Schank considers 'Memory Organization Packets' (MOPs) to be the systematizing frames overseeing the functioning of other lower-level schemata. But more importantly, Schank also reflects on how schemata are not only pockets for the storage of knowledge but also structures necessarily subjected to change.

This dynamic component of schemata is taken on by Cook (1994) especially as it refers to literary language. Cook is particularly concerned with establishing an alternative to the exclusively textual analyses of literature that characterized some of the most conventional formalist work on literary language. Cook argues that literariness is not simply based on the linguistic manifestations that give way to 'deviation' or 'foregrounding', but that it is the potential for 'schema disruption' and subsequent 'schema refreshment' that essentially defines literariness. When compared to literary texts, for instance, Cook (see also Rumelhart, 1980) considers that advertisements lack an ability for disruption and that their main function is, instead, either preserving the existing schemata ('schema preserving'), strengthening them ('schema reinforcing') or simply increasing their number ('schema adding'). Literariness, on the other hand, appears to challenge the reader's schemata ('schema disruption') to such an extent that novel cognitive connections need to be established ('schema refreshment'). Such a definition of literariness, however, has become quite contentious as it seems to suggest that deviation is only possible in literature (compare to everyday creativity or foregrounding techniques in humorous discourse), and that literary texts which, somehow appear to confirm existing mainstream assumptions (political, social, cultural, religious), cannot aspire to claims of literariness. More modern takes on schema theory have pointed out a series of controversial flaws in its formulation:

> Schema theory remains difficult to test empirically. It is not predictive, not verifiable because not falsifiable, and the event that is processed by a dynamically updating schema is not repeatable. The defence that the theory was developed to facilitate computer programming applies only to early versions; Schank's later work draws stronger connections with human cognition and learning. All of this means that the conclusions it is possible to draw from a schema theoretic analysis are not entirely objective and rely on subjective interpretation. (Stockwell, 2003, p. 261)

Despite the above, schema theory has been amply invoked in stylistic analyses of literary language; for instance see Cockcroft (2004), Culpeper (2000), Jeffries (2001), Semino (1995, 1997), Stockwell (2000, 2003, 2006), Verdonk (1999) and Weber (1992) for further takes on this framework and its practical applications.

See also *cognitive stylistics/cognitive poetics* (Key Branches).

Script

See *schema theory* (Key Terms).

Signified

See *signifier and signified* (Key Terms).

Signifier and signified

Terms coined by the Swiss linguist, Ferdinand de Saussure, for his description of the sign. According to Saussure, signs do not correspond directly to real-world objects. Instead, the sign is seen to consist of two components which are as inseparable as the two sides of a sheet of paper: the signifier (*signifiant*) and the signified (*signifié*). The signifier is the written or spoken word – or, more broadly, the image, the sound, the gesture, etc. – while the signified is the concept that the signifier expresses. The word 'book' is thus a sign which consists of the speech sounds or lettering that make up the word (the signifier) as well as of the concept of a book (the signified).

Having thus nuanced the traditional view of the sign, Saussure further argues that the relation between the signifier and the signified is arbitrary, meaning that there is no natural relationship between the two. There is nothing 'bookish' about the word 'book' or the sound /bʊk/. This is also revealed by the fact that the signifier of the concept of a book is 'book' in English, but 'libro' in Spanish and 'książka' in Polish. The relation between the signifier and the signified is determined by convention rather than motivated by a natural connection between the two. That meaning is determined by convention means that a speech community has agreed on labelling a concept in a particular way.

An exception to the above is the onomatopoeic word, like 'cuckoo' and 'rattle', whose written or spoken form, i.e., the signifier, imitates what it signifies. Since onomatopoeic words are relatively few, Saussure argues that such words are a rather marginal phenomenon and do therefore not undermine the claim that signs, and thereby also language, are arbitrary.

See also *arbitrariness*, *icon*, *iconic*, *iconicity* (Key Terms).

Speech act theory

Speech act theory falls within the broader discipline of pragmatics whose focus lies in describing the characteristics of language in use. Speech act theory has traditionally provided stylisticians with a sound set of principles and models to explicate the contextualized use of language which stylisticians have also benefited from. The basic tenet of speech act theory as devised by Austin (1962) is the realization that when humans use language, they actually 'do' something more than simply uttering those words. According to Austin, there is more to language than just the meaning of individual words and phrases, hence the title of his collection, *How to Do Things with Words* (1962).

Speech act theory was later elaborated on by Austin's pupil John R. Searle (1969, 1976, 1979). Because the exchange of words or statements cannot only be evaluated in terms of truth and certainty, truth and certainty are often not very useful if an addressee attempts to understand the intentions and goals of what is said by an addresser. Consider such examples as (a) 'Merry Christmas!', (b) 'I hereby declare the meeting closed', or (c) 'It's cold in here!'. What is more important in these examples is to understand the context in which these utterances occurred, whether they are appropriate and therefore achieve their goals and convey the intended message to the hearer. For example, conventionally speaking, example (a) can only function as a seasonal greeting; example (b) needs to be uttered by somebody who has the power to close a meeting and example (c) may function as a description of the temperature in a room but it may also be intended as a request to somebody to shut the door. From a speech act theoretical point of view communication is therefore contextual, dynamic and goal-oriented because the speaker usually has an intention when communicating. Communication can only be successful if the hearer grasps that goal and replies compliantly. To communicate means to act.

In speech act theory, the basic verbal unit is the speech act, which is 'an utterance made by a certain speaker/author to a hearer/reader in a certain context' (Kortmann, 2005, p. 231). A speech act consists of three parts: (a) the locution, (b) the illocution and (c) the perlocution. The locution or the locutionary force refers to the phonological/syntactic and semantic properties (proposition) of the sentence (that is, the content). The illocution or the illocutionary force, which is often seen as the most important aspect of a speech act, refers to the speaker's/author's communicative intentions and goals. The perlocution or the perlocutionary force describes the effect on the addressee. For example, in the utterance 'It's cold in here!', the locutionary force is made up by the words themselves, their syntactic and semantic properties that shape that utterance as a statement. The illocutionary force would be that of an indirect request in which the speaker asks the hearer to close a door, although he/she does not use the prototypical question 'Could you please shut the door? It's cold in here!'. The perlocutionary effect of this utterance would be the subsequent result of the indirect request in that somebody actually performs the action of shutting the door or window.

Proponents of speech act theory are particularly interested in identifying the communicative intentions that can be construed by utterances, and in the linguistic devices that mark and help identify the illocutionary force of a speech act. Also, the conditions that have to be fulfilled for a successful speech act are of crucial importance.

Austin's classification of speech acts and his focus on so-called performative verbs was later revised and extended by John R. Searle. Searle (1969, 1976, 1979) distinguishes between five basic types of speech acts (Kortmann, 2005, p. 231):

(a) Assertives and representatives, which are used to describe the world (to state, to express, to claim, to tell, to describe).
(b) Directives, which aim at getting people to do something, that is, usually a change of the world is involved that is specified by the speaker (e.g., to give an order, to ask something or to request something).
(c) Commissives, which are used by the speaker to commit himself/herself to some future action which will also change the world in some way (here often to the advantage or disadvantage of the hearer; e.g., to promise, to threat or to commit oneself to something).
(d) Expressives, which are used to express the speaker's feelings and opinions; (e.g., to thank, to greet, to congratulate, to apologise or to complain).
(e) Declarations, which function to change the external situation because these speech acts illustrate that the world can be changed through language (baptism, marriage, divorce).

There are certain linguistic devices which have the potential for explicitly conveying the intended speech act. The 'speech act verbs', such as 'congratulate', 'urge', 'warn' or 'ask', may indicate which speech act is used. When occurring in a construction like 'I promise' or 'I forgive you', these verbs indicate the illocutionary force actually performed by the speaker (see also Wierzbicka, 1987). As such, they are called 'performative utterances' because they occur in the first-person singular, declarative, present tense, indicative, active. Often the adverb 'hereby' can be inserted. Additionally, so-called illocutionary force indicating devices can also be used. For example, particles like 'please' to reinforce a request fulfil this function as well as the three major sentence types – declarative, interrogative and imperative.

For a speech act to be successful certain 'felicity conditions' have to be fulfilled. Searle presents four types:

(a) Propositional content conditions, which 'represent restrictions on what can be said about the world by means of a certain speech act' (Kortmann, 2005, p. 233).
(b) Preparatory conditions, which refer to the obligatory real-world conditions under which a speech act is uttered.
(c) Sincerity conditions, which refer to the speaker's attitude towards the content expressed.
(d) Essential conditions, which is the most important criterion for classification.

Adhering to all these rules and conditions represents an 'ideal' communicative situation. A speech act may be successful although one of these conditions is not fulfilled, because it is common for speakers to avoid complying with all communicative conditions (see *cooperative principle*; *cooperation*).

Speech acts may also be indirect, as in the example 'It's cold in here!' mentioned above. Speech acts that look like statements may function as requests and speech acts that look like announcements may have the function of a warning or a threat. In indirect speech acts, speakers perform the speech act (the primary act) by another speech act (the secondary act). Both speech acts have to be assessed and evaluated and can only be understood when seen as mutually dependent upon one another. Again, these indirect speech acts may also be highly conventionalized and are reliant on principles of cooperation (see *cooperative principle/cooperation*) and play a crucial role in assessing linguistic politeness (see *politeness*). An obvious example would be a simple request like 'Could you please pass me the salt?'. It functions to make the hearer pass the salt to the speaker rather than simply to make the hearer give the answer 'yes'.

The development of speech act theory also has played a significant role in the development of pragmatics. The initial focus on language usage and of pragmatics as the study of meaning in context was not originally supported by linguists, but developed from a branch of philosophy. This branch criticized attempts in formal logic in which natural language was described by principles of formal logic, such as truth conditions and truth values. Language philosophers, such as John L. Austin, John R. Searle or

Herbert P. Grice advocated a countermovement to traditional logic and tried to explain the central features of natural language and ordinary communication.

Speech acts have been extensively investigated cross-culturally (Bloom-Kulka et. al., 1989) and from a diachronic point of view (Jucker and Taavitsainen, 2008) as well as synchronically (Wierzbicka, 1987). For stylistics, the analysis of speech acts is especially important for fictional dialogue and characterization (Burton, 1980; Culpeper, Short and Verdonk, 1998; Short, 1996).

See also *pragmatic stylistics* (Key Branches).

Speech presentation

See *discourse presentation* (Key Terms).

Style

If 'style' is defined as variation of language usage, then this definition may be difficult to grasp and to support because we would have to ask, for example, what this stylistic variation is measured against, for what purpose, in which context and by whom. A definition of style is also further complicated by the different uses and the variety of senses that the notion of 'style' has been credited with in the different branches of stylistics. For example, socio-pragmatically speaking, 'style' may be related to the degree of formality of the text in question. From a variationist-sociolinguistic perspective, 'style' may be seen as a social variable correlated with gender, for example. And anthropologists, in turn, would define style differently because they engage with style in the contextual domain. The difficulty of defining what style is has also been exploited as an excuse to criticize and even belittle stylistics; a criticism that is based on the (wrongly assumed) simple identification of style/stylistics and the style of an author.

Leech and Short (1981, p. 11) define style as 'the way in which language is used in a given context, by a given person, for a given purpose, and so on'. In other words, style is by no means restricted to the style of a particular author, but can be characteristic of a situation, a character, a particular text, a particular linguistic expression that is investigated over time and so on. Hence, style may be seen as a particular way of writing or speaking. This is where the points of intersection between style, stylistics and rhetoric are most pervasive.

Also, the linguistic term 'register' bears resemblance with the term 'style', because register refers to the particular linguistic features that mark text-types or situations like an interview, a political speech or legal language. As such, it is obvious that style may also vary with regard to medium and degree of formality, which, as mentioned, is particularly important for socio-pragmatic investigations of style.

Wales (2001, p. 371) stresses that style 'is distinctive: in essence, the set or sum of linguistic features that seem to be characteristic: whether of register, genre or period, etc.'. This textual notion, that is, a reference to the language used, is what may lead the stylistician to talk about the style of Shakespeare's (1604–5) *Hamlet* or the style of Paul Auster's (2006) *The Brooklyn Follies*. However, this is only one side of the coin. There can be no doubt about the fact that each speaker or writer makes use of the language which is at his disposal at the time of writing or speaking. Style therefore cannot be seen as 'an ornamentation of the sense of an utterance' (Carter and Stockwell, 2008, p. 295), because it is always motivated, for example, by the speaker's personal choices and belief systems and socio-cultural factors at every level.

Style is also motivated choice from the set of language or register conventions or other social, political, cultural and contextual parameters. The inference of meaning from the choices made is then an equally difficult task because it has to move between a continuum of seeing each choice as stylistic and meaningful and potentially innovative, on the one hand, and of embracing complex conventions and norms, on the other. All utterances may be characterized by a particular structure or style, even if that is a relatively unmarked or plain style. Yet what becomes obvious is that in order to describe the stylistic choices made in a text, a base of comparison or reference (i.e., a reference corpus) is useful. Stylistics has therefore given up wanting to discern a compulsory univocal equation between form and meaning, because language usage always needs to be contextualized, and style may also be seen as an interpersonal feature which involves psychologically and socially motivated choices. For a description and identification of the characteristic linguistic features in literary texts, the stylistic tool kit represents an apt means of investigation, which interacts with notions such as norm and deviation, stability and change, the conventional and the innovative or foreground and background.

See *introduction*, *critique of stylistics* (Key Terms).

Style (journal)

Style is an international peer-reviewed journal devoted to research in style, stylistics and poetics. The journal invites contributions from a diverse range of theoretical and methodological perspectives such as discourse analysis, rhetoric, computational linguistics, literary criticism, cognitive linguistics and pedagogical stylistics and welcomes research into literary as well as non-literary genres. The journal is published in four issues per year.

Website: www.style.niu.edu

Substitution

See *cohesion* (Key Terms).

Synchronic

See *Ferdinand de Saussure* (Key Thinkers), *historical stylistics* (Key Terms).

Synecdoche

See *metonymy* (Key Terms).

Syntactic iconicity

See *icon, iconic, iconicity* (Key Terms).

Text and texture

In linguistics, a text is traditionally seen as a stretch of sentences which are linked together by various means to form a unified whole, reflected also by the etymology of 'text' from Latin 'textus': 'that which is woven, web' (*OED*). In this sense of the word, a text can be either written or spoken. For analysis, spoken texts such as conversations, political speeches or classroom interaction can be recorded and transcribed. Although utterances such as 'Stop!', 'No eating', and 'Mind the gap' may be seen as complete texts in their own right, most texts consist of more than one word, phrase or sentence. From a broader semiotic perspective, the concept of 'text' has been extended beyond the verbal to comprise a larger range of collections of signs which form a unified whole. In this extended sense of the word, phenomena as diverse as a film, a building and a mobile phone may be regarded as texts.

'Texture', in turn, refers to the way language is 'weaved' together to form text. In the case of verbal texts, texture is created by means of various cohesive devices such as reference, conjunction, ellipsis and lexical cohesion, and by means of the coherence in context of the linguistic choices which make up the text. In an examination of texture, Eggins (1994, pp. 85–95) experiments with the construction of 'non-text' by removing and manipulating elements which usually make a text cohesive and coherent. Although the resulting texts may well be seen as textually problematic and nonsensical, it might however be argued that in the particular context of illustrating 'non-text', Eggins's experimental texts must, in fact, be seen as 'text' rather than 'non-text'. Generally, the texture of most literary texts is straightforward. While this is especially the case with literary realism, where the textuality of the text is typically backgrounded and not much noticed, the texture of modernist literature is often of a more complex nature as is the case, for instance, with the stream-of-consciousness passages of Faulkner's *The Sound and the Fury* ([1929] 1978) and Virginia Woolf's *To the Lighthouse* ([1927] 1996), not to mention the texture of Joyce's *Finnegans Wake* ([1939] 1992), which may to some seem bordering on non-text. In multimodal novels like Jonathan Safran Foer's *Extremely Loud and Incredibly Close* (2005), texture is not just a matter of verbal cohesion and coherence, but is also created by cross-modal cohesive links between verbal text and visual images, for instance, and by the coherence in context of the multimodal choices of which the novel consists.

See also *cohesion*, *coherence*, *textual meaning* (Key Terms).

Texture

See *text and texture* (Key Terms).

Text world theory

Text world theory is a relatively recent framework associated with cognitive linguistic perspectives applied to the analysis of discourse. It is primarily based on the research of the discourse linguist Paul Werth (1994, 1995a, 1995b) but due to his untimely death a considerable portion of his work has had to be published posthumously (1999). Text world theory differs from other cognitive-based models in its attempts to provide a fully comprehensive account on how to analyse any piece of discourse. Werth's understanding of what exactly constitutes a piece of discourse is rather broad; as he says, discourse is 'actual stretches of language [. . .]. A discourse is a complete language event, i.e., one with a perceived beginning and end' (Werth, 1999, p. 1). Further developments have pointed out that such an ambitious aim can hardly ever be achieved by any one framework (Gavins, 2007, pp. 6–7). In spite of its inevitable limitations, text world theory is increasingly being used, for instance, to look into the idiosyncratic features of a variety of discourse types, as well as in relation to other stylistic and narratological concerns (Gavins 2003; Montoro 2006a; Whiteley 2008).

The way in which text world theory accounts for the processing of discourse is through mental 'world creation'. Other cognitive linguistic approaches have also used metaphorical mental worlds as the basis for discourse comprehension with the obvious variation in terminology, namely 'schemas' and 'scripts' (see *schema theory*), 'mental spaces' (see *mental spaces theory*) or 'contextual frames' (see *contextual frame theory*).

Werth proposed a three-layered model in which to structure the various worlds, namely the discourse world, the text world and sub-worlds. The discourse world appears at the highest level of the model and typically refers to the most immediate situation surrounding the language event, including the text itself and the participants. The role of the participants in the whole process is of utmost relevance for their background knowledge, memories, attitudes, feelings and emotions come into play in the creation of mental worlds. Clearly, the participants will vary depending on the type of communicative event, that is, writer and reader in the case of written communication, speaker and hearer for spoken communication, film director and audience in the case of cinematic discourse, etc.

The second level of text comprehension is the text world which basically corresponds to the mental representation humans are able to construct when processing different types of discourse. One clear example of the comprehensive nature of text world theory is its interest in emphasizing the top-down as well as the bottom-up nature of discourse comprehension. Text worlds are created when the cognitive capability of humans is combined with the bottom-up input provided by the discourse itself, in the case of written communication, typically supplied by the linguistic clues of the text itself.

Other types of discourse, such as filmic forms, would incorporate additional clues such as the aural and visual aspects. In either case, the presence of those elements cueing the creation of text worlds is essential as they act as the orientational markers that allow participants to anchor texts spatially, temporally and personally. They are the so-called world-building elements as they project a mental image of the communicative event by establishing the time, place and objects inhabiting the text world. Werth named those components 'time', 'place', 'objects' and 'characters' although the latter category has recently been renamed 'enactors' by Gavins (2007) to prevent a possible exclusive association with literary discourses. Linguistically speaking, these world-building elements are easily identified as the time (t) is marked by the tense of verbs, temporal adverbs or adverbial clauses; the location (l) is indicated by adverbials of place, adverbial clauses and locative expressions; the enactors (e) are typically realized by noun phrases and pronouns, as are the objects (o). The world-building elements on their own are still not enough to allow humans to build mental worlds. They situate the world but do not provide any sense of development or movement; such tasks are fulfilled by the function-advancing propositions which are expressions that propel the story forward and facilitate the development of the argument. In a nutshell, they tell us who is doing what, where the enactors are going, or what is happening, for instance; it is not surprising, thus, that their primary linguistic markers are verbs.

Text world theorists have generally resorted to terminology used in systemic functional grammar to classify the various types of processes created by the various verbs, that is, material, relational, mental and verbalization processes, depending on whether verbs indicate actions and events ('eat', 'fall', 'glow'), states of being ('be', 'become', 'have'), states of mind ('see', 'enjoy', 'know') or acts of speaking respectively ('say', 'utter', 'ask'). Once the text world, that is, the mental representation of the discourse world, is on its way, Werth describes how it is habitual to witness different kinds of branching out from that initial text world. He terms these subdivisions 'sub-worlds' and categorizes them as deictic, attitudinal and epistemic. Gavins's more recent reformulation of the model (2007) dispenses with the notion of sub-worlds and proposes, instead, the categories of 'world switch' and 'modal world' as possible departures in relation to the starting text world. Her research into a variety of discourse types has led Gavins to conclude that the term 'sub-world' is slightly misleading as it presupposes some kind of subordination of these formations to a previously existing text world. There are some discourse types capable of creating text worlds alongside world switches and other cases, such as focalized narratives, that do not appear to even necessitate an initial text world. World switches result from spatial alternation, flash-backs, flash-forwards and direct speech. Modal worlds appear in modalized propositions, focalized narratives, hypothetical and conditional constructions, all forms of thought presentation and indirect speech. Finally, text world theory underscores that bearing in mind the accessibility of the propositions enabling the formation of text worlds is crucial for discourse comprehension. Some of the propositions in the language event show some content which is directly verifiable by the participants, hence known as participant-accessible information. On other occasions, there are certain details, thoughts, conversations or knowledge which only the enactors in the text-world can have direct access to, with the participants having to rely on their account to process those propositions. This is called enactor-accessible information. Most language events will include propositions whose content displays a mixture of participant-accessible and enactor-accessible information. This distinction is particularly useful in relation to the type of discourse we are processing: factual texts relating to external elements that form part of the discourse world of the participants are easily classified as participant-accessible; fictional texts, on the other hand, include components pertaining exclusively to the story world to which the participants can only gain indirect access via the enactors, hence enactor-accessible information. As in some other frameworks (*possible worlds theory*, *blending theory*), text world theorists represent the various levels of worlds diagrammatically so that the complex process of discourse comprehension can be more easily understood.

See also *cognitive stylistics/cognitive poetics* (Key Branches), *blending theory*, *mental spaces theory*, *possible worlds theory* (Key Terms).

Textual meaning

According to the functional linguist M. A. K. Halliday, language has evolved to simultaneously express three different types of meaning: ideational, interpersonal and textual meaning. Different grammatical systems are employed for the analysis of the three types of meaning. Textual meaning concerns the organization of text, and the two main resources for the creation of textual meaning are 'Theme' structures and 'cohesion'.

An analysis of Theme structures focuses on the organization of constituents within the sentence with particular emphasis given to the first constituent, Theme, which is a textually prominent position. The rest of the sentence is called 'Rheme'. As illustrated by the following examples, the textual organization of sentences and the placement of lexical material in Theme position (underlined) have semantic implications, since the lexical material placed in the Theme slot is given special prominence:

- <u>The Chinese government</u> launched a security clampdown in Beijing before the Summer Olympics
- <u>A security clampdown</u> was launched in Beijing by the Chinese government before the Summer Olympics
- <u>Before the Summer Olympics</u> the Chinese government launched a security clampdown in Beijing
- <u>In Beijing</u> a security clampdown was launched by the Chinese government before the Summer Olympics

Cohesion, in turn, refers to the linguistic means of tying sentences together to form text, which is done by means of conjunction, reference, ellipsis, substitution and lexical cohesion. The amount and nature of cohesive ties in a text impact on the ease with which the text can be decoded. Some texts display a high number of cohesive ties which are relatively easy to decode, whereas the cohesive nature of other texts may be more complex. In the introductory page of James Joyce's *Ulysses* ([1922] 1993), cohesion is employed as an important meaning-making resource. In the first line of the novel, lexical cohesion is created by the lexical items 'bowl of lather', 'mirror' and 'razor' which clearly belong to the same field of meaning and indicate that someone may be about to shave: 'Stately, plump Buck Mulligan came from the stairhead, bearing a bowl of lather on which a mirror and a razor lay crossed.' Rather than shaving, however, Mulligan 'held the bowl aloft and intoned: *Introibo ad altare Dei*' which clashes with the expectations set up by the lexical set just mentioned. The Latin opening of the Catholic mass, in turn, forms a different collocational pattern of a religious nature with the lexical items 'jesuit', 'solemly', 'blessed' and 'made rapid crosses in the air' in nearby sentences. In a subsequent line the discrepancy of the two lexical sets springs to the eye when they are tied closely together in a paratactic construction stating that Mulligan 'made rapid crosses in the air, gurgling in his throat and shaking his head'. By, thus, coupling the meaning of two lexical sets which are usually semantically far apart, Joyce constructs an image of Mulligan as a character who makes fun of religious ceremony.

Since ideational, interpersonal and textual meanings are intimately intertwined, the analysis of textual meaning may well be combined with considerations about the two other types of meaning in the stylistic analysis of a given text.

See also *cohesion and coherence*, *ideational meaning*, *interpersonal meaning* (Key Terms), *M. A. K. Halliday* (Key Thinkers).

Thought presentation

See *discourse presentation* (Key Terms).

Transitivity

In traditional grammars, transitivity refers to the relation between a verb and dependent constituents in the clause such as direct and indirect objects (Bache and Davidsen-Nielsen, 1997; Greenbaum and Quirk, 1990). A verb which takes an object is transitive ('Janet has bought a new house'), while a verb which does no do so is intransitive ('John is sleeping'). Transitive constructions may be either (a) mono-transitive, consisting of a verb and a direct object ('She drank a cappuccino') , (b) di-transitive, consisting of a verb, an indirect object and a direct object ('She bought him a cappuccino') and (c) complex transitive, consisting of a verb, an object and an object complement: 'She called her dog Cappuccino'. Some verbs can be both transitive and intransitive, depending on the context in which they occur. An example of this is the verb 'read' which is transitive in 'James was reading a novel' but intransitive in 'James read all night'. The study of transitivity is sometimes referred to as the study of valency (Bache and Davidsen-Nielsen, 1997). Valency concerns the number and types of participants, or 'arguments', a given verb takes. An intransitive verb has one argument, the subject, whereas a di-transitive verb has three, a subject, a direct object and an indirect object.

In Systemic Functional Grammar, transitivity is a central concept employed in the description of ideational meaning. Ideational meaning concerns the linguistic representation of the experiential world, which in Halliday's view is constructed as configurations of participants (nominals), processes (verbals) and circumstances (adverbials). Halliday refers to these configurations of constituents as transitivity, thus employing the term in a broader sense than most other grammarians. The systemic functional categorization of transitivity patterns is based on semantic as well as grammatical criteria and the processes types are material, mental, behavioural, verbal, relational and existential processes. The most important of these are material processes (processes of doing in the material world: 'eat', 'run', 'give'); mental processes (processes of cognition, affection and perception: 'know', 'hate', 'see'); verbal processes (processes of verbal action: 'say', 'respond', 'indicate'); and relational processes (processes expressing being in terms of some kind of relation: 'appear', 'become', 'have') (see Halliday, 1994).

In stylistics, the analysis of transitivity has mainly been employed for the analysis of the mind styles (see entry) of different characters (Halliday, 1971, on Golding's *The Inheritors*, 1955) as well as for analysing how different fictional characters are constructed linguistically by means of the configurations of processes of which they are represented as participants (Kennedy, 1982 on Conrad's *The Secret Agent*, 1907; Nørgaard, 2003 on Joyce's 'Two Gallants' ([1914] 1992).

See also *ideational meaning* (Key Terms).

Turn-taking

The 'turn' is one of the central concepts of conversational interaction described by practitioners of the discipline known as conversation analysis. Conversation analysis (CA) studies the structure of conversation which, contrary to what one might think at first sight, follows a very specific set of organizing rules. In CA, the various interventions that speakers have when maintaining a conversation are known as 'turns'. The now well-established CA owes its existence to the work of the sociologists Sacks, Schegloff and Jefferson (1978).

Sacks et al. (1978) suggest that conversations actually follow a system of talk regulation which consists of (a) a turn-allocational and (b) a turn-constructional component. The turn-allocational component regulates the changeover of turns (by selecting the next speaker or regulating the order of turns), while the turn-constructional component embraces the size or length and linguistic texture of turns. The order of speech in drama lends itself very well to an analysis of the turn-taking management. Important questions to be asked are then (a) who speaks to whom, (b) who is not addressed and who is silent (c) who listens, (d) who is responsive, (e) who interrupts, (f) who has the longest/shortest turns, or (g) what is the texture/style of a character's speech (Burton, 1980; Short, 2007).

Sinclair and Coulthard revolutionized the analysis of spoken discourse in *Towards an Analysis of Discourse* (1975) because they developed a model for describing teacher and pupil talk in the classroom. The Discourse Analysis (DA) model (also the 'Birmingham Model') sees conversation as exchange and elaborates on an 'initiation-response-follow-up' (IRF) structure. From their investigation of classroom discourse, Sinclair and Coulthard (1975) have illustrated that language in the classroom is rigidly structured and that the speech acts used can be categorized according to their function. The ranking scale consists of four components: 'transaction', 'exchange', 'move' and 'act'. The stylistic analysis of drama and fictional dialogue has profited immensely from this approach (Short, 1989, 1996; Culpeper, Short and Verdonk, 1998).

See also *pragmatic stylistics* (Key Branches), *John Sinclair* (Key Thinkers).

Unresolved cohesion

See *cohesion* (Key Terms).

Vocatives and naming

The etymology of vocative is based on the Latin verb *vocare* 'to call' (*OED*). In Bühler's (1934) *Organonmodel*, vocatives may be seen as one linguistic means of fulfilling the function of addressing the hearer, as they can be used to address a speaker. The vocative is therefore often associated with speaker identification alone, both in real and fictional conversational discourse. Realized as a nominal group or head alone, vocatives can take on a variety of realizations, their presence is optional, and, they may occur in initial, middle or final position in the clause. Shakespeare's plays (*Riverside Shakespeare* edition, Evans, 1997) abound with instances of vocatives: 'O thou weed' (*Othello* 4.2.66), 'O, you wonder' (*The Tempest* 1.2.427), 'O my lord' (*Hamlet* 3.2.348), 'O Romeo' (*Romeo and Juliet* 3.2. 33) or 'Ah, you kite' (*Antony and Cleopatra* 3.13.88). In Present-day English vocatives may also be realized as personal names, as in 'Sally, you are very cute!' where the personal name 'Sally' functions as a nominal form of address. They may also include a title plus a last name, as in 'Would you please continue with your presentation, my dear Mr Smith!' or they may also contain terms that frequently function as endearments as with the use of 'sweetheart' in 'Sweetheart, I would love to go for a walk'.

When compared with more classical taxonomies of vocatives, Quirk et al. (1985) stress that the modern English vocative cannot be considered a case due to its optionality and freedom of position. They state that vocatives are more 'like an adverbial or, more precisely, like a disjunct'. According to Quirk et al. (1985, p. 612), disjuncts 'have a superior role as compared with the sentence elements. They are syntactically more detached and in some respect superordinate in that they seem to have a scope that extends over the sentence as a whole'. For Bache and Davidsen-Nielsen (1997, p. 107), a vocative is pronounced as a separate tone unit in initial position, while a vocative as the tail or part of the tail of the clause does not receive prosodic prominence at all.

So far only few attempts have been made to define vocatives from a morpho-syntactic point of view, or to incorporate the vocative within a grammatical system that is broad enough to include various functional dimensions of the variety of semantic, lexical and pragmatic variation both in the past and present. Just reconsider the examples 'Would you please continue with your presentation, my dear Mr Smith' and 'Sweetheart, I would love to go for a walk' and try to imagine some of the situations in which these sentences could be uttered and what the functions of the alleged endearments 'my dear Mr Smith' and 'sweetheart' could be in a variety of situations. One reason for the tardiness of incorporating the functional dimension of vocatives in a broad system is that, for a long time, the investigation of nominal forms of address or vocative constructions has been influenced by established models of social structure. These have been used to explain pronoun usage of what is conventionally called the *Tu* and *Vous* distinction, which is also visible in the Early Modern English difference between the use of 'you' and 'thou' forms. Within this tradition, the dominance and exercising influence of the two sociolinguistic classics on the use of forms of address and second-person personal pronouns by Brown and Ford (1961) and Brown and Gilman (1960) have to be mentioned. Brown and Ford's study (1961) represents pioneering research on nominal forms of address in American English using as corpora some American plays, instances of vocatives as employed by members of a Boston business firm and the use of forms of address by business executives. Brown and Ford employ the power and solidarity scale to explain *first name* reciprocation, as in 'Sally' mentioned above, or *title* plus last name reciprocation, as in 'my dear Mr Smith'. Apart from the fact that they limit their analysis to the binary contrast between first names and titles, they apply the social factors of intimacy and distance on the horizontal line, and those of gender and status on the vertical line to their name paradigm. Brown and Ford's (1961) study is laudable because they are among the first to hint at the social relevance of the linguistic phenomena of address and personal pronouns. Also, the study introduces the basic terminology, but their *power* and *solidarity* paradigm cannot comprehensively explain why there may be such a variety of vocative forms in Present-day English and why a nobleman in Shakespeare, for example, addresses his servant condescendingly with the vocative sirrah. Nor can the model be used to explain dramatic meaning.

Vocatives go beyond the strategy of selecting or naming a speaker because they are also direct attitudinal adjunct-like forms of address (Busse, 2006b). For Present-day English, Leech (1999) uses a corpus-based approach to enhance a more focused treatment of what he calls a 'neglected field' (Leech, 1999, p. 107) within English grammar. He differentiates between vocatives and forms of address, and incorporates the former in a formal, functional and semantic concept. Formally, Leech (1999, p. 107) focuses on the vocatives' realization pattern as a nominal group, as in 'my dear Mr Smith' where the name 'Smith' functions as the head of the nominal group and the other elements 'Mr' and 'my dear' further modify it. Leech (1999, p. 108) points out that it is appropriate to see the vocative as part of a speech or a communicative unit (Leech, 1999, p. 108). The semantic functions of vocatives are to gain attention, to identify the addressee and to maintain a social relationship. The categories which Leech (1999, pp. 110–2) establishes range from the most familiar to the most distant. Functions of vocatives are explained in terms of the parameters of gender, the degree of familiarity between interactants and their social status. So, if 'Would you please continue with your presentation, my dear Mr Smith' is uttered by an interviewer in an interview situation, the use of 'my dear Mr Smith' might probably not be sincere in function but rather ironic, and a linguistic sign indicating that the interviewee is not a valuable candidate. Addressing an applicant with the epithet 'my dear' in an interview situation is deviating from a certain norm, because it shows an overuse of linguistic politeness (see *politeness*).

Leech's (1999) results show a progressive familiarization of addressing and naming habits, as first-name address occurs most frequently. In addition, most vocatives by far occur in final position. Leech also says something about the function of vocative positions, for example, initial vocatives serve mostly to attract attention and identify the addressee; final positioning of vocatives serves to identify and to secure or establish social positions (Leech, 1999, p.113).

Busse (2006b) investigates the functions, meanings and variety of forms of address in a corpus of seventeen Shakespeare plays, which are selected according to editorial, thematic, generic, synchronic and diachronic considerations. Contrary to Brown and Gilman's (1960) and Brown and Ford's (1961) parameters of power and solidarity and the rigid social structure allegedly existent in Shakespeare's time, Busse (2006b) claims that nominal forms of address in Shakespeare are experiential, interpersonal and textual markers which reflect and create relationships, identity and attitude as well as messages and habitus. They also structure the discourse, and are meaning-making within a performative context. Drawing on a new categorization of vocative forms, which includes labels like *conventional terms* or *terms referring to natural phenomena*, Busse (2006b) establishes the functional potential of vocative forms also from a quantitative perspective, according to synchronic, diachronic and generic parameters and with regard to the use of vocative forms by the characters of the plays.

See also *historical stylistics* (Key Branches).

Writing presentation

See *discourse presentation* (Key Terms).

Key Thinkers in Stylistics

Deirdre Burton

Deirdre Burton was a lecturer in English at the University of Birmingham where she also studied for her MA (1973) and PhD (1978a) degrees. Her research and teaching interests are in discourse analysis, stylistics and the philosophy of language, but she has also published on linguistic theory, child language and the stylistics of modern drama. Her research output is, in fact, renowned and is still being referred to by stylistics practitioners to this day; for instance, Simpson (2004) briefly discusses her article 'Through glass darkly: Through dark glasses', originally published in 1982; references to her investigation into the nature of discourse can be found in innumerable examples of scholarly work (Edwards and Westgate, 1994; Eggins and Slade, 2005) and her interest in the interface between naturally-occurring and literary dialogue is also used as the basis for discussion by many drama scholars (Culpeper et al., 1998; Herman, 1995; Mandala, 2007).

Among her publications, two seem to have especially attracted the academic attention of language analysts. On the one hand, her monograph *Dialogue and Discourse: A Sociolinguistic Approach to Modern Drama Dialogue and Naturally Occurring Conversation* (1980) has been singled out as one of the few studies that has concerned itself with the role of drama, in general, and the structural features of dramatic dialogue, in particular. As Mandala points out:

> In her ground-breaking work on drama-dialogue and discourse published in 1980, Deirdre Burton claimed that stylisticians typically did not deal with drama texts (1980, p. 3). Apparently, very little has changed since then. (Mandala, 2007, p. ix)

Burton's monograph (1980) is organized in two distinctive parts called 'Dialogue' and 'Discourse' respectively. The first incorporates models borrowed from discourse studies and conversation analysis to explicate the way dramatic dialogue functions. The influence of the Birmingham school can be clearly seen in that tools typically used in discourse studies are applied to the analysis of literature. Burton is adamant in defending that 'a rigorous and comprehensive analysis of dialogue style must be able to draw on a rigorous and coherent theoretical and descriptive framework for the analysis of all naturally occurring conversation' (Burton, 1980, p. ix). So, for instance, she looks into the features of the adult-child style of conversation held between two characters in Harold Pinter's *The Dumb Waiter* (1957). She describes the power relationship established between Ben and Gus and concludes that the seemingly child-like interventions of the latter succeed in gaining the audience's sympathy, in sharp contrast to the dominant role of Ben who inevitably ends up as the villain in the play. Burton strives for accurate analytical methods in literary studies, which has left a significant mark in subsequent approaches to the study of drama and literature in general. The second part of her monograph attempts to develop more extensively the linguistic theory of naturally-occurring talk devised by Sinclair and Coulthard (1975). Further work on the nature of discourse appeared in Burton (1981a, 1981b) and Burton and Stubbs (1976).

The second major influence emerging from Burton's research is illustrated by her analysis of Sylvia Plath's *The Bell Jar* (1963). Burton (1982) convincingly discusses the linguistic representation of power relations via a transitivity model based on the systemic-functional tradition of Halliday and his collaborators. Burton's tripartite treatment of the semantic components of sentences as processes, participants and circumstances highlights the powerless position of the novel's protagonist as she is given electric shock treatment when admitted into a mental-health hospital. Burton underscores a feminist stylistic reading by demonstrating that the main character is not made an active participant in any of the processes (that is, the verbal forms) of the text. Instead, she is made the physical recipient of the electric current administered to her as apparent cure for her depression. Although Burton closely follows Halliday's now classic analysis (1971) of *The Inheritors* ([1955] 2005), she is nowadays acknowledged as having also successfully incorporated a feminist perspective missing from the original by Halliday. The transitivity model used in Burton (1982), however, has been amply reformulated and reworked (see Simpson, 1993, 2004).

Further reading

Burton, D. (1978b), 'Towards an analysis of casual conversation'. *Nottingham Linguistic Circular*, 17, (2), 131–59.

Burton, D. (1984), 'A feminist reading of Lewis Grassic Gibbon's *A Scots Quair*', in J. Hawthorn (ed.), *The British Working-Class Novel in the Twentieth Century*. London: Edward Arnold, pp. 35–46.

Burton, D. and Stubbs, M. W. (1976), 'On speaking terms: Analysing conversational data'. *Midland Association of Linguistic Studies*, 2, (2), 22–44.

Carter, R. and Burton, D. (1982), *Literary Text and Language Study*. London: Edward Arnold.

Ronald Carter

Ronald Carter is Professor of Modern English Language at the School of English Studies at Nottingham University. He studied English and Russian, Comparative Literature and German, and received a PhD in Applied Linguistics from Birmingham University. He was a Visiting Fellow and Visiting Professor at the National University of Singapore, the University of Kyoto, Japan, and Macquarie University, Sydney. Carter was also a member of the English panel for the 2008 RAE (Research Assessment Exercise), with particular responsibility for English language and applied linguistics. Recently, he was elected a fellow of the British Academy for Social Sciences. He was also awarded a 'Member of the Order of the British Empire' (MBE) in the 2009 New Year's Honours List. The MBE is one of several different types of honours bestowed each year by the Queen of Great Britain in recognition of outstanding service to the local and/or national community in a variety of fields. Carter's MBE recognizes his services to local and national higher education.

Carter's groundbreaking research within the field of applied linguistics, corpus and computational linguistics, and discourse-based grammar has had a landmark impact on the interface between language and literature and the teaching of (English) language. Carter has written, co-authored, edited and co-edited over 40 books and 100 articles. One of his most recent publications is the *Cambridge Grammar of English: A Comprehensive Guide. Spoken and Written Grammar and Usage* (2006, co-written with McCarthy). This outstanding grammar is based on a 10-year research programme involving the development of extensive computer-readable corpora of spoken and written

English. The book won the 2007 British Council English Language Innovation Award. Most recently Carter has become interested in the multimodal interplay between language and gesture and in the application of research in the humanities to business contexts as well as in interdisciplinary research in language and health communication.

In stylistics, one of Carter's main interests is in the relationship between language, creativity and pedagogical stylistics, but he has also performed classic stylistic investigations (see, for example, Carter, 1982; Carter, 1993; Adolphs and Carter, 2002). Most recently, he edited the *Language and Literature Reader* (Carter and Stockwell, 2008). One of his claims is that attention to language and language use is crucial for the identification of creativity. Creativity can be associated with both writing and speaking (Carter, 2004, p. 57). Carter (2004, p. 66) does away with the distinction between literary and non-literary language and suggests that literature should be seen as a continuum on a cline of literariness:

> It may be more instructive to see literary and creative uses of language as existing along a cline or continuum rather than as discrete sets of features or as a language-intrinsic or unique 'poetical' register. (Carter, 2004, p. 66)

Depending on genre, consequently, some genres are characterized more prominently for literariness than others (see *corpus stylistics*). Carter's (2004) *Language and Creativity. The Art of Common Talk* uses data from the CANCODE corpus, which consists of a range of speech genres. Based on this material, Carter addresses the issue of creativity, the reasons for its association with written language, the spoken-written continuum and why it is useful to discuss whether 'there is such a thing as literary language' or whether 'all language is literary' (Carter, 2004, p. 53). That all (literary) language is culturally and historically situated and therefore also variable cannot be underestimated because creativity and what counts as creative may be judged differently in various cultures and historical periods. Also, as pointed out by Carter and Nash (1990), it is important to differentiate between 'creativity' and 'composition' because everybody possesses the ability of composition, understood as the ability to do something with language and texts. As such, the question of whether a reader chooses to 'respond to a text (spoken or written) in a literary way – as a poetic text as it were – is one crucial determinant of its literariness'

(Carter, 2004, p. 69). Also, the relationship between creative language use and power, gender or social class needs to be explored.

The concept of a 'language play' (Carter, 2004, p. 72) is a deeply rooted human endowment and exists on all levels of language, within all registers, situations and so on (see also Cook, 2000). That these considerations similarly have a severe impact on the language classroom in both first- and second-language as well as foreign-language teaching (see Brumfit and Carter, 1986; Carter and McRae, 1996) is obvious. Carter (2004, p. 213) stresses the need

> to establish continuities between literary and everyday languages and establish stronger bridges between language and literary teaching. The idea that creativity exists in a remote world of literary 'genius' can be demotivating to the apprentice student of literature, especially in contexts where a second or foreign language literature is taught. (Carter, 2004, p. 213)

Further reading

Carter, R. A. (1982), 'Style and interpretation in Hemingway's "Cat in the Rain"', in R. A. Carter, (ed.), *Language and Literature. An Introductory Reader in Stylistics*. London: Unwin Hyman, pp. 64–80.

Carter, R. A. (2004), *Language and Creativity. The Art of Common Talk*. London: Routledge.

Carter, R. A. and Nash, W. (1990), *Seeing through Language: A Guide to Styles of English Writing*. Oxford: Basil Blackwell.

McCarthy, M. and Carter, R. A. (2006), *Cambridge Grammar of English. A Comprehensive Guide Spoken and Written English Grammar and Usage*. Cambridge: Cambridge University Press.

Noam Chomsky

Avram Noam Chomsky is an American linguist, philosopher and left-wing intellectual whose generativist approach to language had an immense impact in linguistics and beyond in the latter half of the twentieth century. After studies at the University of Pennsylvania and Harvard, he published his famous first monograph, *Syntactic Structures* (1957), based on his doctoral work which was supervised by Zellig Harris. This book caused a major shift in linguistic thinking. He is Emeritus Professor of Linguistics at the Department of Linguistics and Philosophy, Massachusetts Institute of Technology. Over the years, he has received honorary degrees from more than 30 universities around the world, among them Cambridge University, Harvard University, the University of Delhi, Uppsala University and the University of Bologna. He is, in addition, a celebrated but controversial critic of American foreign policy, known in particular for his opposition to the US military involvement in Vietnam, Afghanistan and Iraq.

Central to Chomsky's linguistic theory is the assumption of innateness, given the rapidity with which we acquire our native language. In Chomsky's view the normal human infant is genetically endowed with a language faculty, by which it can rapidly and naturally advance to native-language fluency in ways that we do not rapidly and automatically advance, by age 6 or 7, to proficiency in mathematics or playing a musical instrument. We naturally become fluent because of our linguistic genetic endowment – our language competence – just as our genes enable us, around the age of 12 or 13, to become sexually reproductive. This faculty is commonly called the 'language acquisition device' (LAD). The generativist modelling of this innate linguistic faculty has changed over the years, but one still-influential account argues that a small number of crucial principles and parameters are part of our mental hard-wiring, and explain our rapid comprehension and production of various kinds of anaphora and complex-clause construction, because all natural languages deploy the same principles and parameters, with slightly different settings for different languages. Language 'competence', rather than language 'performance' (i.e., usage), is thus the overriding focus of Chomskyan linguistics, which can consequently be characterized as a predictive – and perhaps even normative – approach to language rather than a purely descriptive one. While non-prototypical and ungrammatical sentences feature frequently in everyday language use, Chomskyan linguists are not interested in such sentences, as they do not tell us anything about the language competence that enables individuals to produce grammatically correct sentences. Nor are scholars from this linguistic school interested in genre and register variation or other types of variation due to the context in which a given utterance occurs. Creativity in language, on the other hand, has their attention, since new sentences which are grammatically correct may tell us something about the underlying grammatical principles by which they have been generated. It should be noted that grammaticality in Chomsky's sense of the word refers to grammatically well-formed sentences with no view to meaning (hence the grammatically correct, but semantically dodgy 'colourless green ideas sleep furiously'); and that creativity is seen as the ability of human beings to produce an infinite set of sentences on the basis of a finite set of rules.

Over the years, the generativist paradigm has grown considerably and gone through repeated major revisions in response to ongoing research in the field, with Chomsky himself as one of the main proponents of such revisions. In addition to *Syntactic Structures* (1957), Chomsky's major publications include *Aspects of the Theory of Syntax* (1965), *Language and Mind* (1972a), *Studies on Semantics in Generative Grammar* (1972b), *Knowledge of Language* (1986) and *The Minimalist Program* (1995). With Morris Halle, he published the much famed *The Sound Pattern of English* (1968). Altogether, Chomsky's approach to language has had a huge impact on different academic fields such as cognitive linguistics, language acquisition, philosophy and psychology. It has also inspired academics working in the field of stylistics, though the heyday of Chomskyan stylistics was rather brief. In 'Generative grammars and the concept of literary style' (1964) and 'Literature as sentences' (1966), for instance, Ohmann employs Chomskyan linguistics to argue and demonstrate that the styles of different authors can be characterized by the transformations involved in their writing. In *Unspeakable Sentences* (1982), Banfield argues for the relevance of Chomskyan linguistics to stylistics in an application of the generative approach to narrative fiction with particular emphasis on narrative perspective (see also Fludernik, 1993, 1996). Attridge's *The Rhythms of English Poetry* (1982) follows Chomsky and Halle (1968) in an investigation of metrics. Thorne (1965), Hayes (1966), the early Fowler (1972) and Dillon (1978) are other examples of work done in stylistics from a transformational-generative perspective, but altogether the Chomskyan take on stylistics has not had a lot of followers.

Further reading

Collins, J. (2008), *Chomsky: A Guide for the Perplexed*. London: Continuum.

McGilvray, J. (1999), *Chomsky: Language, Mind, and Politics*. Cambridge: Polity Press.

Smith, N. (2004), *Chomsky: Ideas and Ideals*. Cambridge, New York, Melbourne, Madrid: Cambridge University Press.

Catherine Emmott

Catherine Emmott is a Senior Lecturer at the University of Glasgow where she has worked since 1989. She has also been a Visiting Fellow at several other universities around the world (the University of California, Santa Barbara, the University of Amsterdam and the University of Utrecht). Her international status is supported by her many other academic and professional commitments such as being assistant editor of the journal *Language and Literature*, being a member of several editorial boards (*Encyclopaedia of Language and Linguistics* (Brown, 2006); de Gruyter's book series *Narratologia*; the journals *Storyworlds: A Journal of Narrative Studies* and *English Text Construction*), forming part of the governing body of *IGEL* (*International Society for the Empirical Study of Literature and Media*) as well as being a consultant and generally helping with editorial matters for the publication of various dictionaries and handbooks.

Her main lines of research are related to the mental processing of text, discourse anaphora and stylistics. Emmott's main contribution to the study of text analysis to this date is her monograph *Narrative Comprehension: A Discourse Perspective* (1997). In this volume, Emmott develops her contextual frame theory (see entry) which tries to explain the cognitive mechanisms that take place during reading. Her framework is structured around the notion of 'frame' defined as the 'mental store of information about the current context, built up from the text itself and from inferences made from the text' (Emmott, 1997, p. 121). Emmott introduces the notions of 'priming' and 'binding' (see *contextual frame theory*) and also deals with the issue of how readers are capable of assigning reference to pronouns whose antecedents are not part of the immediate co-text. All these notions have turned this monograph into one of the founding texts for what is now known as cognitive stylistics or cognitive poetics. Her ample contributions to books published in this area attest to this (Emmott, 1992, 1994, 1995, 2002a, 2002b, 2003a, 2003b).

The interdisciplinary nature of Emmott's work is a further characteristic of this scholar's publications. For the past 8 years, Emmott has collaborated closely with colleagues from the Psychology Department and Centre for Cognitive Neuroimaging at the University of Glasgow in what is now known as the *STACS* project (*Stylistics, Text Analysis and Cognitive Science: Interdisciplinary Perspectives on the Nature of Reading*), formerly the *LINCS* project (*Literature, Narrative and Cognitive Science*). This close collaboration began in

2002 as a way to amalgamate the perspectives of cognate but distinct disciplines from the social sciences and textual studies areas, that is, psychology and stylistics. The other main co-investigator is Professor Sanford, also of the University of Glasgow. The project relies on Emmott's stylistic and linguistic input which is then incorporated into the type of experiments typically characterizing psychological lines of research. Therefore, the project's methodology has the linguistic and stylistic analysis of the textual samples employed for the subsequent psychological experiments at its core, which separates it from other psychological investigative enterprises that have traditionally paid less attention to the features of the texts themselves. For instance, one of the aspects they have looked into is the functioning of 'double perspectives' in fiction which they define as:

> Cases where a reader might be supposed to be thinking two things at once. We will draw on the core narratological notion of 'unreliable focalization' [. . .] to examine examples where readers view events through the eyes of a character who is fundamentally mistaken. In such cases, it may be necessary for readers to override the message of a text. This observation should provide new insights into the relation between language and mind, since it challenges propositional and 'accessibility' theories in Psychology and Linguistics. (Emmott and Sanford, 2002)

Other stylistic aspects this project has investigated are the effect of foregrounding in readers' attentiveness to texts, discourse features such as direct speech and thought, first and second person narratives, as well as a variety of literary texts, popular fiction and autobiography.

Further reading

The *STACS* project webpage: Emmott, C. and Sanford, A. J. (2002), *STACS project*. http://www.gla.ac.uk/departments/englishlanguage/research/researchprojects/stacsproject/#d.en.53663

Emmott, C. (1997), *Narrative Comprehension: A Discourse Perspective*. Oxford: Oxford University Press.

Emmott, C., Sanford, A. J. and Dawydiak, E. (2007), 'Stylistics meets cognitive science: Style in fiction from an interdisciplinary perspective'. *Style*, 41, (2), 204–26.

Emmott, C., Sanford, A. J. and Morrow, L. I. (2006), 'Capturing the attention of readers? Stylistic and psychological perspectives on the use and effect of text fragmentation in narratives'. *Journal of Literary Semantics*, 35, (1), 1–30.

Sanford, A. J. S, Sanford, A. J., Molle, J. and Emmott, C. (2006), 'Shallow processing and attention capture in written and spoken discourse'. *Discourse Processes*, 42, (2), 109–30.

Monika Fludernik

Monika Fludernik is Professor of English at the English Department of the University of Freiburg (Germany). She studied English language and literature, Indo-European Philology, Mathematics, History and French at the University of Graz (Austria), where she also received her PhD with a thesis on 'Narrator's and Characters' Voices in James Joyce's *Ulysses*'. She completed her 'Habilitation' in the area of English and American Literature and Text Linguistics at the University of Vienna in 1992. Fludernik has received a variety of scholarships; among them is the Humboldt Fellowship for her project on the historical present tense and narrative structure in Early Modern English. She is also a Fellow at the Freiburg Institute for Advanced Studies (FRIAS). Monika Fludernik was awarded the Perkins Prize of the Society for the Study of Narrative Literature in 1996 for her book *Towards a 'Natural' Narratology* (1996), and received the 'Landesforschungspreis des Landes Baden-Württemberg' in 2001. She is a corresponding Member of the Austrian Academy of Sciences and a Member of the Academia Europaea, London.

Fludernik is a versatile scholar who has crossed boundaries between linguistics and literary criticism and written on a variety of authors, novels, genres, periods and theoretical issues in literature, literary criticism and linguistics. First and foremost she is a narratologist. But her fields of research include many more areas, among which are stylistics and cognitive poetics, literature and metaphor, historical linguistics and pragmatics as well as identity or alterity in postcolonial narrative fiction.

Fludernik's work in (historical) and (transdisciplinary) narratology is considered to be a landmark for narratological studies. Her influence on stylistic approaches to the language of fiction in a variety of genres from the past and present is important in terms of the analyses she provides as well as theoretically and methodologically. She has illustrated complex points of intersection between literary criticism, narratology and stylistics and illuminated our understanding of such issues as, for example, natural narratology, narrative voice, narrator and teller, narrativity, narrativization, mimesis and diegesis, the role of the reader and so on. It is beyond the scope of this entry to describe all of her research on the respective topics. Instead, her two works *The Fictions of Language and the Languages of Fiction* (Fludernik, 1993) and *Towards a 'Natural' Narratology* (Fludernik, 1996) will be mentioned as well as one article (Fludernik, 1998) in which she outlines the interplay and the challenges affecting literary criticism and linguistics.

From both a linguistic and a literary perspective, Fludernik (1993) investigates free indirect discourse, that is, the variety of free indirect forms of speech and thought presentation in narrative texts. She critically discusses the claim that 'narrative mimetics provides the very framework within which one has to locate even a predominantly linguistic discussion of speech and thought presentation' (Fludernik, 1993, p. 3). Fludernik (1993) rejects the

> traditional presupposition of an 'original' verbatim direct discourse subsequently adulterated by mediation in (free) indirect speech and speech report. [...] even direct speech representation in a real-life context cannot be identified with verbatim recreation of original discourse. (Fludernik, 1993, p. 435)

Another goal of her study (Fludernik, 1993) is to describe the linguistic properties of free indirect forms (and to test the existent linguistic theories attempting to account for the formation of free indirect forms), and to make available to the international academic community the wealth of German criticism that has been published on this topic. In this connection, she also rejects a corpus-based approach because she does not want to restrict herself to, for example, one period, one author or one genre. Her rejection of corpus-based work stems from her belief that the type of annotation necessary to work with a corpus of texts is still arbitrary. According to her, the categories of free indirect discourse labelled in a corpus are necessarily too broad to be meaningful or too delicate to allow firm conclusions (Fludernik, 1993, p. 9).

Fludernik (1993, p. 439) situates the dual voices of the character and the narrator within a cognitive framework, which is also reliant on interpretation work between the wording of the text and the cultural and textual norms.

The narrative process can be based on a frame-theoretical analysis (Fludernik, 1993, 1996).

Fludernik (1996) provides a theory of narrative which focuses on natural narratives, that is, 'narratives of spontaneous conversational story-telling' (Fludernik, 1996, p. 12). She stresses that 'oral narratives [. . .] cognitively correlate with perceptual parameters of human experience and that these parameters remain the force even in more sophisticated written narratives' (Fludernik, 1993, p. 13). Early written narrative reflects a substrate of oral narrative, discernible in their essentially episodic pattern which is, then, gradually superseded by more complex forms of narrative as written composition becomes the standard. She has shown that the substrates of oral story-telling can be diachronically traced back to medieval story patterns and structure.

Fludernik (1998) discusses the potential of a linguistic investigation of literature as well as its advantages and disadvantages from the point of view of a literary critic. At the same time, she outlines potential methodological points of intersection and compares the two disciplines in terms of results. In this connection, she stresses that both disciplines have to clarify which kind of linguistic investigation as well as literary criticism should be pursued (Fludernik, 1998, p. 125). For the linguistic investigation of literature, she doubts whether the analysis of (a) deviation in literature or (b) regularities in language and (c) the identification of the general paradigmatic potential of language in general account for a comprehensive characterization of 'style', the poetic potential of literature and the intentions of literary dialogue, for example. In turn, she stresses that the application of linguistic methods to literature also demands that analysts define the specific form of literary criticism which is practised. The literary theoretical orientation is goal-oriented and correlates with the text under investigation (text, genre). It is this informed application which enhances both disciplines and their interplay and invalidates the frequently uttered criticism levelled at linguistic applications to literature in general and at stylistics in particular (see *critique of stylistics*).

Further reading

Fludernik, M. (1993), *The Fictions of Language and the Languages of Fiction: The Linguistic Representation of Speech and Consciousness*. London: Routledge.

Fludernik, M. (1996), *Towards a 'Natural' Narratology*. London: Routledge.

Fludernik, M. (1998), 'Sprachwissenschaft und Literaturwissenschaft: Paradigmen, Methoden, Funktionen und Anwendungsmöglichkeiten', in A. Nünning (ed.), *Literaturwissenschaftliche Theorien, Modelle und Methoden*. Trier: WVT, pp. 119–36.
Fludernik, M. (2009), *An Introduction to Narratology*. London: Routledge.

Charles Forceville

Charles Forceville started his academic training at the Vrije Universiteit Amsterdam where he ended up teaching in the English department for a short period. He is currently Associate Professor in the Media Studies department of the Universiteit van Amsterdam as well as member of the advisory editorial boards for the journals *Metaphor and Symbol*, *Journal of Pragmatics*, *Public Journal of Semiotics* and *Atlantis*. He is involved in several research projects and has also published non-academic work in several Dutch publications.

Forceville is primarily a cognitivist scholar (2005b, 2006a), a term that needs to be understood in its broadest sense. His work on pictorial metaphor, for instance, resulted in the publication of *Pictorial Metaphor in Advertising* (1996). Originating in the conceptual metaphor theory propounded by Lakoff and Johnson (1980) according to which metaphors are a matter of thought rather than language, Forceville's work demonstrates that pictorial forms are as capable of representing metaphorical meanings as language might be. Forceville (1996) is particularly concerned with printed advertisements and billboards and proposes a model that can equally account for the verbal and pictorial manifestations in these two media. Faithful to a rigorous and critical stance in his investigation, this monograph incorporates not only the analyst's considerations of a series of adverts but also a small experiment conveying the responses reported by a number of informants on the metaphorical nature of static images on billboards. Forceville defends that any theoretical proposal needs to be submitted to a falsifiability principle, which also seems in tandem with the work of scholars investigating linguistic and literary issues from an empirical perspective (see *empirical study of literature*). He has subsequently investigated further manifestations of metaphorical content, especially the moving image. This move away from static forms on printed texts has materialized in the study of multimodal realizations of metaphor as his latest publication, *Multimodal Metaphor* (2009), so proves.

The newly-found interest of stylisticians in the interface between literature and film is particularly well served by the research output of this scholar. As part of his enquiry into the metaphorical nature of the moving image, Forceville has published on the multimodal filmic realization of some aspects traditionally associated with stylistic research. Of special relevance is his work on the non-verbal possibilities of free indirect speech and thought in the cinematic adaptation of Ian McEwan's *The Comfort of Strangers* (1981). Forceville (2002a) demonstrates that the confusion deliberately created by McEwan in the printed version of the novel is similarly achieved in Schrader's filmic version (1990) via cross-cuts and snapshots, the position and movement of the camera, the particular use of the *mise en scène*, the music chosen and, finally, the sound effects. Prior to this particular analysis, Forceville had already worked on the same novel to identify the metaphor COLIN IS A CHILD both in the original and the adapted versions (1999).

Further reading

Forceville, C. (1996), *Pictorial Metaphor in Advertising*. London and New York: Routledge.

Forceville, C. (2002b), 'The identification of target and source in pictorial metaphors'. *Journal of Pragmatics*, 34, (1), 1–14.

Forceville, C. (2005b), 'Cognitive linguistics and multimodal metaphor', in K. Sachs-Hombach (ed.), *Bildwissenschaft: zwischen Reflektion und Anwendung*. Cologne: von Halem, pp. 264–84.

Forceville, C. (2007), 'Multimodal metaphor in ten Dutch TV commercials'. *The Public Journal of Semiotics*, 1, (1), 19–51.

Forceville, C. and Urios-Aparisi, E. (eds) (2009), *Multimodal Metaphor*. Berlin: Walter de Gruyter.

Roger Fowler (1938–99)

Roger Fowler was a British linguist who was known in particular for his work on stylistics. Fowler was Professor of English and Linguistics at the University of East Anglia. He was the first Chair of the *Poetics and Linguistics Association* (*PALA*; see entry) (1981–84) and a member of the editorial board of the association's journal, *Language and Literature*.

In the course of his long career, Fowler covered a lot of ground within the field of stylistics. In the late 1960s and early 1970s he was known in particular for his debate with the Oxford literary critic F. W. Bateson which took place in the literary journal *Essays in Criticism* and was later published in Fowler's *The Languages of Literature* (1971). The Bateson-Fowler controversy, as the debate was called, was basically a confrontation between the then new discipline of stylistics and the well-established field of traditional literary criticism, spurred by an unfavourable review of Fowler's 1966 collection of essays on literary style, *Essays on Style and Language*. While Bateson dismissed the idea that linguistics may have anything to offer to the literary critic beyond mere description, Fowler argued for the potential fruitfulness of interdisciplinary work between the two fields of research and called for what he termed 'linguistic criticism'. For a short while, Fowler subscribed to the linguistic paradigm of Chomsky's transformational grammar which resulted in an introduction to transformational syntax in 1971 as well as stylistic pieces from a transformational perspective (Fowler, 1972, 1975). In the late 1970s, however, he moved on to functional linguistics, analysing literature from a Hallidayan perspective, which came to inform much of his later work. In addition to this, Fowler was one of the first stylisticians to embrace Bakhtinian ideas in his writings (Fowler, 1979, 1983). In the late 1970s and early 1980s, Fowler and his colleagues Robert Hodge, Gunther Kress and Tony Trew turned their attention more intensively to the relations between language and social meaning. In *Language and Control* (1979), they proposed a new kind of linguistics, 'critical linguistics', which aimed to examine and uncover the role played by language in the mediation of reality, with particular focus on the ways in which language may be seen to reflect power and social injustice. According to the authors, the book was designed 'not as yet another academic study in sociolinguistics so much as a contribution to the unveiling of linguistic practices which are instruments in social inequality and the concealment of truth' (Fowler et al., 1979, p. 2). Fowler continued his investigation on language, ideology, power and control in *Language in the News* (1991), one of his most popular books.

Further reading

Fowler, R. (1971), *The Languages of Literature*. London: Routledge and Kegan Paul.

Fowler, R. (1977), *Linguistics and the Novel*. London: Methuen.

Fowler, R. (1986), *Linguistic Criticism*. Oxford and New York: Oxford University Press.

Fowler, R. (1991), *Language in the News: Discourse and Ideology in the Press*. London: Routledge.

M. A. K. Halliday

Michael Alexander Kirkwood Halliday is the founder of the functional branch of linguistics known as Systemic Functional Linguistics as well as of the broader field of social semiotics. Halliday grew up and studied in England, where he took a B.A. Honours degree in Chinese language and literature at the University of London and a PhD in Chinese linguistics at Cambridge. In 1965, he became Professor of Linguistics at the University of London, and, in 1976, he moved to Australia to take up the position of Foundation Professor of Linguistics at the University of Sydney. Halliday remained in Australia and, after his retirement in 1987, he was awarded the status of Professor Emeritus at the University of Sydney and Macquarie University, Sydney.

Influenced by B. K. Malinowski and J. R. Firth, Halliday views language as a social phenomenon. Rather than focusing on an abstract concept of language competence, for example, as do more formal theories of language, Systemic Functional Linguistics is a descriptive theory of language which focuses on language in use. One of the main ideas of Hallidayan thinking is the claim that language is purposeful behaviour and that the most basic function of language is to create meaning in different contexts. According to Halliday, language has developed to express, or construct, three major types of meaning simultaneously: ideational (alternatively experiential), interpersonal and textual meaning – referred to as the three metafunctions of language. This is to say that whenever we use language, we make not just one, but three kinds of meaning at the same time: ideational meaning (i.e., meaning relating to how we represent experience), interpersonal meaning (i.e., meaning to do with the relations between interlocutors) and textual meaning (i.e., meaning relating to our organization of texts). For the description and analysis of the three types of meaning, different grammatical systems are employed. Ideational meaning (see entry) is mainly analysed in terms of transitivity, interpersonal meaning (see entry) is explained via mood and modality and textual meaning (see entry) can be investigated by looking into Theme structures and cohesion.

It is central to Hallidayan thinking that meaning is always made in context. Not only should the text be analysed with a view to the context in which it occurs; the context itself is in the text, it is claimed. The contexts of a given text are several: the context of the immediate situation in which the text is uttered as well as the larger cultural contexts of genre and ideology – contexts which are all likely to be realized by the lexico-grammar (i.e., the lexis and the grammar) of the text. This focus on meaning in context has made Halliday's theory foundational in critical linguistics, critical discourse analysis and critical stylistics (see entries).

While not disregarding the significance of language change over time (diachrony), Hallidayan linguistics shows a particular interest in paradigmatic relations, that is, the choices involved in language use at a given point in time and the relations between these choices (synchrony). All choices are seen as functional in the context in which they occur and are considered against the backdrop of that which could have been chosen instead. In this way, the non-chosen is seen to play a role in the construction of meaning along with the chosen wording.

A central concept in Hallidayan thinking is the concept of construal. According to Halliday, it is essential to understand that language does not represent meaning, but constructs – or, in Hallidayan terms, 'construes' – meaning. This is to say that the choices made within the three metafunctions of language do not *represent* ideational, interpersonal and textual meanings which pre-exist these linguistic choices. Instead, the linguistic choices themselves actively *construe* these meanings.

Reflecting his broad interest in language use, Halliday has published in many areas and on many aspects of linguistics such as the theory of intonation, educational linguistics, scientific discourse, Chinese, language and computational linguistics. His oeuvre also contains a number of articles on the stylistics of literature. Without doubt, the most famous of these is 'Linguistic function and literary style: An inquiry into the language of William Golding's *The Inheritors*' (1971). In this article, Halliday takes a closer look at the style of Golding's prose, with a particular focus on the different grammatical choices employed to construe the different worlds and world views that the novel comprises. Golding's novel concerns the extinction of the Neanderthal people by homo sapiens. Through an analysis of transitivity patterns, Halliday reveals how one group of characters, the Neanderthals, are construed linguistically as primitive and ineffective by means of transitivity patterns of processes which do typically not extend to and impact on other participants (be they objects or people), while 'the inheritors', i.e., homo sapiens, are characterized as more sophisticated beings because of their goal-oriented actions, linguistically embodied in action processes which do impact on other participants.

Altogether, Halliday's Systemic Functional Linguistics has left a huge imprint on stylistics. While some stylisticians set out to make explicitly Hallidayan stylistic analyses of text – with Halliday's model of language as the governing principle of their analysis – many others regularly draw on Halliday's ideas, concepts and lexico-grammatical categories, without necessarily being avowed Hallidayan stylisticians.

Further reading

Halliday, M. A. K. (1971), 'Linguistic function and literary style: An inquiry into the language of William Golding's *The Inheritors*', in D. C. Freeman (ed.) (1981), *Essays in Modern Stylistics*. London and New York: Methuen, pp. 325–60.

Halliday, M. A. K. (1994), *An Introduction to Functional Grammar*. London, New York, Sydney, Auckland: Arnold.

Nørgaard, N. (2003), *Systemic Functional Linguistics and Literary Analysis. A Hallidayan Approach to Joyce – a Joycean Approach to Halliday*. Denmark: University Press of Southern Denmark.

Thompson, G. (1996a), *Introducing Functional Grammar*. Great Britain: Arnold.

Toolan, M. (1998), *Language in Literature. An Introduction to Stylistics*. London: Arnold.

Roman Jakobson (1896–1982)

Roman Osipovich Jakobson was a Russian-born linguist whose work had far-reaching impact on linguistics in the twentieth century. When still a student, Jakobson was a key figure of the Moscow Linguistic Circle, which played an important role in the development of Russian Formalism. Due to political upheaval in Russia in 1920, Jakobson moved to Czechoslovakia, where he was one of the founders of the Prague Linguistic Circle, later known as the Prague School, which made significant contributions to the development of structuralist thinking. With the Nazi invasion of Czechoslovakia at the beginning of World War II, Jakobson left Prague for Scandinavia (Sweden and Denmark), where he was associated with Louis Hjelmslev and the Copenhagen Linguistic Circle. In 1941 he fled to the United States, where he founded the Linguistic Circle of New York. From 1949 and until his retirement, Jakobson held a university chair at Harvard University, and later also at the Massachusetts Institute of Technology where he became an honorary Professor Emeritus.

While academically active in several fields, including linguistics, mathematics, physics and biology, the main impacts of Jakobson's work on twentieth-century thinking concern the development of structuralism, semiotics and stylistics. A central contribution of Jakobson's is his attempt to describe the elements that go into any act of verbal communication by reworking Bühler's (1934) tripartite model of communication. Where Bühler's model comprised three factors – the addresser, the addressee and the message – Jakobson (1960) added three additional factors, resulting in a model which consists of the addresser, the addressee, the contact between the two, the code employed for the utterance, the context referred to and the message itself (i.e., the words of the specific utterance):

	CONTEXT	
ADDRESSER	MESSAGE	ADDRESSEE
	CONTACT	
	CODE	

In Jakobson's reworking of Bühler's model, each component of the model characteristically has a particular function of language associated with it. The aspect of communication which focuses on the addresser is called the emotive function, the conative function is language use oriented towards the addressee, the phatic function concerns the contact between the interlocutors, the metalingual function is language use that is oriented towards the code, the referential function is oriented towards the context of the message and the poetic function is language use which focuses on the message itself.

	REFERENTIAL	
EMOTIVE	POETIC	CONATIVE
	PHATIC	
	METALINGUAL	

Although one of the functions is typically dominant, others can also be present in a given verbal expression which means that the expression will either be focused on the addresser, the addressee, the contact between the two, the code employed for the utterance, the context referred to or on the message itself. The dominant function of much verbal art is seen to be that centred on the message itself, that is, the poetic function, whereas more factual texts, such as history books and encyclopaedias, are arguably oriented towards context and must therefore be characterized as predominantly referential in nature. Jakobson himself was particularly interested in the poetic function of language and the elements which are central to the 'literariness' of a given text, though he strongly emphasized that the poetic function can also be dominant outside literature, just as some literary texts may be characterized by functions other than the poetic. One of Jakobson's most quoted examples to illustrate this is the political slogan for presidential candidate Dwight D. Eisenhower: 'I like Ike' (Jakobson, 1960).

Another central idea in Jakobson's work of interest to stylistics is expressed in 'Two Aspects of Language and Two Types of Aphasic Disturbances' (1956). Based on studies of the language deficiencies of people suffering from aphasia, Jakobson's model argues that discourse is basically built upon two fundamental principles: similarity and contiguity. He ties up these principles with the rhetorical figures of metaphor and metonymy, since similarity lies at the heart of metaphor ('my love is a rose') and contiguity – that is, association, or close relation – lies at the heart of metonymy ('crown and sceptre' for 'monarch'). It should be noted that 'metaphor' and 'metonymy' are employed in a fairly broad sense with the former covering both metaphor and simile and the latter comprising metonymy as well as synecdoche. In discourse, it is argued, one topic may lead to another either because of their similarity (the metaphoric principle) or because of their contiguity (the metonymic principle). In Jakobson's view, metaphor is related to the paradigmatic axis of language, the 'axis of selection', which consists of a set of equivalent lexical and grammatical elements from which a selection can be made in the formation of sentences and texts. Metonymy, on the other hand, belongs to the syntagmatic axis of language, the 'axis of combination', where choices from various paradigms are combined into syntagmatic chains, i.e., sentences and text. This is illustrated well by the following example from Fowler (1986, pp. 98–9):

	S Y N T A G M		
P	The	child	Sleeps
A	A	Kid	Dozes
R	Some	youngster	Nods
A	*etc.*	tot	Naps
D		infant	Wakes
I		boy	Dreams
G		woman	*etc.*
M		*etc.*	

Metaphor and metonymy, similarity and contiguity, are furthermore seen as basic principles informing different modes of literature:

> The primacy of the metaphoric process in the literary schools of romanticism and symbolism has been repeatedly acknowledged, but it is still insufficiently realized that it is the predominance of metonymy which underlies and actually predetermines the so-called 'realistic' trend, which belongs to an intermediary stage between the decline of romanticism and the rise of symbolism and is opposed to both. Following the path of contiguous relationships, the realist author metonymically digresses from the plot to the atmosphere and from the characters to the setting in space and time. He is fond of synecdochic details. In the scene of Anna Karenina's suicide Tolstoy's artistic attention is focused on the heroine's handbag; and in *War and Peace* the synecdoches 'hair on the upper lip' and 'bare shoulders' are used by the same writer to stand for the female characters to whom these features belong. (Jakobson, 1956, pp. 77–8)

The metaphoric principle is closely associated with the poetic function of language and the metonymic principle is characteristic of the referential function of language. In *The Modes of Modern Writing* (1977), Lodge pursues these ideas about metaphor and metonymy in a study of the narrative technique of a number of modern writers such as Orwell, Joyce, Hemingway, Larkin and Burroughs.

In the course of his career, Jakobson wrote widely on formal linguistic aspects of literary texts. While praised for his insights concerning the form and structure of the texts put up for investigation, he was sometimes criticized for ignoring the pragmatic, social and historical dimensions of language in his analyses. An illustrative example of this is Jakobson and Lévi-Strauss's (1962) extensive, and rather technical, analysis of lexical, syntactic and metrical features of Baudelaire's poem 'Les Chats' (1847) which caused severe criticism by Riffaterre (1966). Riffaterre accused Jakobson and Lévi-Strauss of disregarding the function of the formal features unearthed by their analysis and of bringing structures to light which were of no consequence to the poetic effect of the text:

> The authors' method is based on the assumption that any structural system they are able to define in the poem is necessarily a poetic structure. Can we not suppose, on the contrary, that the poem may contain certain structures that play no part in its function and effect as a literary work of art, and that there may be no way for structural linguists to distinguish between these unmarked structures and those that are literarily active? (Riffaterre, 1966, p. 191)

Notwithstanding such criticism, the impact of Jakobson's foundational work on the development of modern stylistics should not be underestimated.

Further reading

Bradford, R. (1994), *Roman Jakobson. Life, Language, Art*. London and New York: Routledge.

Jakobson, R. (1987), *Language in Literature*. Edited by K. Pomorska and S. Rudy. Cambridge, Mass.: Belknap Press.

Geoffrey N. Leech

Geoffrey N. Leech is Emeritus Professor of Linguistics and Modern English Language at Lancaster University. In March 2009, he was awarded an Honorary Fellowship of Lancaster University which honoured his long service and lasting contribution to the University. He is the editor of the Longman series *Studies in Language* and a member of various editorial boards. Leech has written, co-authored and co-edited 29 books and over a hundred articles and papers in the areas of English grammar, stylistics, semantics, computational linguistics and pragmatics.

In his 2008 book *Language in Literature. Style and Foregrounding*, Leech points out:

> From the 1970s, I went through a period of being distracted, and sometimes overwhelmed, with other non-literary interests and preoccupations. In particular, I was engaged in the swiftly developing field of pragmatics [. . .] and in the equally swiftly developing field of corpus linguistics. These took me away from literary studies, but I never lost my interest and joy in examining literary texts closely [. . .]. When I look back on more than forty years of research and publication, it is working on language in English literature that has given me most enduring pleasure. (Leech, 2008, p. viii)

This quotation not only testifies to the outstanding versatility of Geoffrey Leech's research profile, but also illustrates the extent to which the stylistic analysis of literature is rewarding to the linguist and influential in other linguistic areas.

Leech's (1969) *A Linguistic Guide to English Poetry* is a landmark in early stylistic approaches to poetry. Going beyond the framework that was used in literary criticism, Leech shows the need for a more detailed, systematic and rigorous tool kit for the analysis of metrics in poetry. He advances stylistic issues in phonetics and phonology and interlinks his analysis with pragmatic aspects of performance and 'an ear open for readerly matters of interpretation and affect' (Carter and Stockwell, 2008, p. 60).

Leech has furthered the theory of foregrounding and its application to stylistics. His book *Language in Literature: Style and Foregrounding* (2008) represents not only what he modestly calls 'a small collection of articles on "practical stylistics"' (Leech, 2008, p. viii), but also gives an indispensable overview of the history of stylistics through a variety of hands-on analyses of the language of poems, narrative fiction and dramatic texts with an emphasis on foregrounding. He moves both chronologically and from small-scale to large-scale stylistic investigations and provides the reader with stylistic-informed studies of works of authors like Dylan Thomas, John Keats, Percy B. Shelley, Samuel Johnson and Virginia Woolf. This volume also shows the theoretical and methodological challenges stylistics has faced. For example, as the collection shows, in the course of his stylistic career, Leech has worked on the relationship between stylistics and rhetoric, on the interplay between analysis and interpretation and 'Stylistics and Functionalism'.

Leech has also introduced the distinction between a variety of norms that are necessary to measure and describe foregrounding at all levels of language (these are external and internal norms, primary, secondary and tertiary norms). He stresses the role of the text as a corrective and a multi-levelled coding-system, which has to be meticulously analysed in order to be able to make valid interpretations (Leech, 2008, pp. 180–2). Also, Leech's work in corpus linguistics has been innovatively and challengingly fused with his interest in literary language. For example, most recently, he has discussed the methodological and theoretical implications of applying corpus stylistic tools to literary texts (e.g., his Wmatrix analysis of Woolf's 'The Mark on the Wall' in Leech, 2008) and elaborated on the character of reference corpora for stylistic text comparison.

Style in Fiction (Leech and Short, 1981; 2nd edition, 2007) which he co-authored with Mick Short and which was awarded the prize as most influential book in stylistics by the members of the *Poetics and Linguistics Association* (*PALA*; see entry) in 2005, is pioneering in its systematic and detailed account of the levels of analysis crucial for a stylistic analysis. It also introduces a stylistic tool kit for the analysis of the language of the main literary genres, which has furthermore been applied to a variety of non-literary text types. Similarly, the Leech and Short (1981) model of analysing discourse presentation is a landmark, whose influence goes beyond that of stylistics and which has been applied to genres other than literary ones (see Semino and Short, 2004).

His work within the field of pragmatics (see, for example, Leech, 1983), notably in politeness and socio-pragmatics, has been highly influential within stylistic investigation of play texts and fictional dialogue (see Leech, 1992). The same holds true for his work on grammar (Quirk et al., 1985), spoken discourse (Leech, 2002, with Svartvik) and corpus linguistics (Leech, 2008).

Further reading

Leech, G. (1969), *A Linguistic Guide to English Poetry*. London: Longman.

Leech, G. (1983), *Principles of Pragmatics*. London: Longman.

Leech, G. (2008), *Language in Literature. Style and Foregrounding*. Harlow: Pearson Longman.

Leech, G. and Short, M. (2007), *Style in Fiction. A Linguistic Introduction to English Fictional Prose*. 2nd ed. Harlow: Pearson Longman. 1st edition 1981.

Walter Nash

Walter Nash is Emeritus Professor of English Language at the University of Nottingham from where he retired in 1991. His interests range from the teaching of English literature and medievalist studies, to being involved in academic matters carrying more linguistic weight such as teaching phonetics, analysing rhetoric, jargon and literary language. Walter Nash is currently still publishing and, although he is mainly focused on fictional work, his research also continues to appear in scholarly volumes (Nash, 2000, 2008a, 2008b).

Looking at Nash's *Language in Popular Fiction* (1990) can help illustrate the academic proficiency of this scholar and can similarly exemplify his rather personal writing style which evidences his creative side, on the one hand, and a jocular affability in his dealing with academic matters, on the other. For instance, when discussing the evaluative, descriptive terms generally employed to characterize the male counterparts to female heroines in romantic fiction, Nash concludes that male characters tend to be represented in a positive, albeit rather unrealistic, light:

> Poised symmetrically with her is her symmetrical mate, he whose hairline cannot recede, whose jaw has immaculate definition, whose ears, discretely proportioned and tastefully whorled, lie close to his skull, whose nose runs true, whose eyebrows are well-aligned, whose tie is becomingly knotted and lies in direct descent from his Adam's apple and the roguish cleft in his chin. (Nash, 1990, p. 8)

Nash eloquently characterizes a particular kind of male in romantic fiction but he also deftly pinpoints a certain prototypicality and repetitiveness in the creation of such figures in this type of popular genre. This unique combination of skills makes Nash's publications stand out among fellow stylisticians. Furthermore, the creativity with which he presents his arguments does in no way detract from the seriousness with which academic concerns are discussed. One other example in which his creative prowess is combined with a humorous take can be found in Nash's discussion of the discoursal features of graffiti:

> 'Kick the Pope', it used to say, in withered whitewash, on the wall by the forecourt of an old Lube and Krypton Tuning garage that I occasionally passed on my way to work. Further, this sweet and lovely wall announced, 'Chelsea fans are wankers', a disparaging comment on the sporting successes of Chelsea's football club; and then – on a political note – 'Tories get stuffed', to which had been added, in a different hand, 'at the taxpayer's expense', followed by a subsidiary gloss, 'but not on the NHS'. (Nash, 2000, p. 1)

The playful tone of this chapter, however, is complemented by an insightful analysis of graffiti as contextualized pieces of language, ephemeral and yet still firmly situated in well-defined social and temporal parameters.

Nash's sensitivity to matters concerning poetic style is also evident in the many pieces he has produced on poetry (1982, 1986b, 1993b, 2008a). Moreover, Nash's pedagogical preoccupations also find their way into his work:

> These responses to the acoustics of the poem are not mere fancies; they are reasonably based on what is demonstrable from textual fact. But is it then fanciful to suggest a connection between such recurrent shift of vowel quantity and quality and the prevalent 'mood' or 'feeling' of the

> poem, its conveyed sense of a talkative hesitation and doubt turning at last to epigrammatic certainty? We here confront the problem that so often vexes beginners in the art of literary stylistics: how can we be sure that the writer intended, or indeed was aware of, the 'effects' that we, as readers, are so ready to perceive? (Nash, 1993b, p. 49)

Nash underscores the danger that stylistics practitioners need to be aware of if they want to avoid drawing unfounded conclusions in relation to how form and effect relate to one another. Moreover, he concludes that passing on that awareness to 'beginners in the art of literary stylistics' (Nash, 1993b, p. 49) should be a top priority for more established stylistics scholars.

Further reading

Carter, R. and Nash, W. (1990), *Seeing through Language: Guide to Styles of English Writing*. Oxford: Basil Blackwell.

Nash, W. (1985), *The Language of Humour*. London: Longman.

Nash, W. (1986a), *English Usage: A Guide to First Principles*. London: Routledge.

Nash, W. (1992), *An Uncommon Tongue: The Uses and Resources of English*. London: Routledge.

Nash, W. (1993a), *Jargon: Its Uses and Abuses*. Oxford: Basil Blackwell.

Nash, W. (1998), *Language and the Creative Illusion: The Writing Game*. London: Longman.

Ferdinand de Saussure (1857–1913)

Ferdinand de Saussure was a Swiss linguist whose ideas about language have had an immense impact on modern linguistics. Saussure studied at universities in Geneva, Berlin and Leipzig (where he was awarded his doctorate in 1880) and taught at the universities of Leipzig and Paris. In 1891 he returned to the University of Geneva to take up a university chair in Sanskrit and Indian-European languages (1901–11) and in general linguistics (1907–11). In his lifetime, Saussure did not publish much. His most famous and influential work, *Cours de linguistique générale* (1916) (Engl. *Course in General Linguistics*), was based on lecture notes made by some of his students and published after his death. In 1996, a manuscript by Saussure was found in his family house in Geneva. The manuscript, which turned out to be based on

Saussure's lectures and thus covering the same ground as *Cours de linguistique générale*, was published in 2002 as *Écrits de linguistique générale* (Engl. *Writings in General Linguistics*) and helps clarify some of the uncertainties of the former work.

A central element of Saussure's theory of language is his concept of the sign. According to Saussure, a linguistic sign does not correspond directly to an object in the real world, but consists of two inseparable components: the 'signifier' and the 'signified'. The signifier is the physical realization of the sign in the shape of, e.g., the marks on the page of the written word or the sound of the spoken word. The signified, in turn, is the mental concept that the signifier expresses. The relation between the sign and real-world objects and phenomena is called 'signification', but this is an aspect of Saussure's model of the sign which receives very little attention due to his overriding interest in the nature of the sign itself. In Saussure's view, the relation between the signifier and the signified is arbitrary and conventional. Arbitrary means that no inherent natural connection exists between the two. While the word 'table' is a linguistic sign which consists of lettering or sound (the signifier) as well as the mental concept of a table (the signified), the relationship between the two is determined by convention rather than by natural relation, since there is no 'tableness' about the signifier 'table'. It should be noted that Saussure's concept of the sign extends beyond the linguistic sign as he envisaged a more general science of signs, a *semiology*, which, while based on the laws of linguistics, would apply to all sign systems.

According to Saussure, meaning does not reside in the individual sign, but in a complex system of oppositions of which the sign is a part. It is thus not the substance of the sign, but its relations to and difference from other signs that give the sign meaning. Saussure further argued that there are two basic types of relationship between linguistic units: (a) a relationship of choice on the vertical axis and (b) a relationship of chain or combination on the horizontal axis. Choice relations are referred to as 'paradigmatic relations', while relations of chain or combination are referred to as 'syntagmatic relations'. Constituents such as subject, predicator, object and adverbial thus combine syntagmatically into sentences, yet, for the selection of each constituent, the interlocutor must choose from paradigms of several possible options: 'Peter'/'my friend'/'the boy'/'the lazy bastard'/etc. + 'slept'/'snoozed'/'dozed'/etc. + 'awhile'/'for ages'/'a bit'/etc. The value (*valeur*) of a sign is determined by the syntagmatic as well as the paradigmatic relations it enters into.

In addition to his work on the nature of the sign, Saussure also reflected on the object of study in linguistics. In this connection, he emphasized the importance of distinguishing between particular instances of language use (*parole*) and the underlying system of a language (*langue*) which enables interlocutors to produce and understand utterances. A third concept employed is that of *langage*, which refers to the universal phenomenon of language that is characteristic of human beings. In Saussure's view, the aim of the linguist is to deduce from *parole* the rules and conventions that underlie the language system. Following Saussure, generations of linguists have focused mainly on *langue* rather than *parole*; on the system rather than instances of language use.

Saussure further pointed out that linguistics can either be studied diachronically, i.e., focusing on linguistic change over time, or synchronically, i.e., as a system of meaning at a given point in time. Before Saussure, linguistics was characterized by diachronic investigations of language(s), but Saussure's seminal work on synchrony made the linguistic pendulum swing almost entirely away from diachrony for a considerable period of time.

In many respects, Saussure's pioneering work in linguistics has had an impact on fields outside linguistics. In particular, his thinking was central to the development of European structuralism which flourished in fields as diverse as linguistics, anthropology, psychoanalysis, sociology, history and literary theory in the second half of the twentieth century. Thus, for instance, Saussure's ideas about signs and sign systems and about *langue* and *parole* were transferred to many fields in the humanities, where human culture more generally was seen and examined as systems of signs, and where cultural phenomena, i.e., instances of *parole*, were seen as realizations of the underlying structures, i.e., the *langue*, of a particular culture. In stylistics, Saussure's concepts of sign, signifier and signified have been widely adopted, as has his distinction between *langue* and *parole* and his general focus on structures, systems and the relations between signs within a sign system.

Further reading

Culler, J. (1976), *Saussure*. Glasgow: Fontana/Collins.

Sanders, C. (ed.) (2004), *The Cambridge Companion to Saussure*. Cambridge: Cambridge University Press.

Saussure, F. de (1916), *Cours de linguistique générale*. C. Bally and A. Sechehaye (eds). Lausanne and Paris: Payot. Translated by W. Baskin, (1977), *Course in General Linguistics*. Glasgow: Fontana/Collins.

Saussure, F. de (2002), *Écrits de linguistique générale*. Simon Bouquet and Rudolf Engler (eds). Paris: Gallimard. Translated by M. Pires, (2006), *Writings in General Linguistics*. Oxford: Oxford University Press.

Mick Short

Mick Short is Professor of English Language and Literature and teaches in the Department of Linguistics and English Language at Lancaster University. He holds a BA from Lancaster, an MA from Birmingham University and a PhD from Lancaster University. Ever since the publication of *Style in Fiction* (1981; 2nd edition, 2007), which he wrote in collaboration with Geoffrey Leech and which was awarded the prize as most influential book in stylistics by the members of the *Poetics and Linguistics Association* (*PALA*; see entry) in 2005, Short has played an influential role in the advancement and formation of what stylistics is today. In the introduction to one of his more recent books, *Exploring the Language of Poems, Plays and Prose* (1996), Short identifies himself both as a linguist and a literary critic. Also, he has managed to bridge the gap between literary critics and stylisticians and to comprehensively outline stylistics' potential for a systematic, retrievable and rigorous investigation of texts; even in times of heavy attacks (see also his defence against the Mackay (1996) attack (Short and van Peer, 1999)).

Mick Short has illustrated what stylistics is and has crossed disciplinary boundaries in many of his publications, including *Exploring the Language of Drama: From Text to Context* (which he co-edited in 1998), as well as a number of books and articles, in which he has written about such diverse topics as stylistics and its relationship to critical theory, the theory of foregrounding, or more recently, *Corpus Stylistics: Speech, Writing and Thought Presentation in a Corpus of English Writing* (published with Elena Semino in 2004). Mick Short was founding editor (1992) of *Language and Literature,* the international journal of the *Poetics and Linguistics Association* (*PALA*; see entry), of which he was one of the founding members.

Short's didactic expertise is illustrated in various publications on teaching stylistics, such as *Reading, Analysing and Teaching Literature* (which he edited in 1989). He has always stressed the potential of stylistics in general, for (English) language teaching and for helping students to be more precise, systematic and more analytic in their analyses. His quest for transparent and clear didactic concepts and tool kits that students can use finds its expression in the famous 'Short Checklists' which can be found in his 1996 volume, for example.

He received the prestigious National Teaching Fellowship Scheme award in 2000 from the UK Institute for Learning and Teaching in Higher Education, and is one of the leading stylisticians of the English Subject Centre. He also developed a comprehensive web-based stylistics course (see http://www.lancs.ac.uk/fass/projects/stylistics/), intended as a bundle of introductory stylistics techniques applicable to the main literary genres. The web-based course, which Short has applied in various teaching environments and which has also been used in a variety of international settings (see Short et al., 2006), is a useful tool for online as well as blended learning environments.

Short's further academic work is particularly influential in the area of the stylistic analysis of narrative fiction, play texts and in corpus stylistics. He was one of the first stylisticians to apply pragmatics findings to the analysis of drama (Short, 1989), which resulted in a specific toolkit developed for dramatic texts and which also served to underscore the concepts of foregrounding and style as motivated choice. His model of the discourse levels of drama (see *pragmatic stylistics*) is an additional example of the way in which Short's proposals have successfully been incorporated by many other stylisticians. Most recently, he has illustrated the usefulness of the stylistic approach to the analysis of film.

With Leech in *Style in Fiction* (1981/2007), he was among the first scholars to give a systematic and detailed account of the levels of analysis as well as provide a stylistician's tool kit for the analysis of the language of narrative fiction. The Leech and Short (1981) model of discourse presentation (that is speech, thought and writing presentation; see entry) is a landmark whose influence goes beyond stylistics. Within a corpus linguistic framework (Semino and Short, 2004), Short has elaborated on the model proposed in 1981 and introduced various new sub-categories as well as the category of writing presentation which was missing from the original. He has shown the advantages of corpus linguistic methodology to interplay with and complement the stylistician's intuition. At the same time, he has also discussed the usefulness of employing tagged and annotated corpora for a complex discoursal phenomenon like discourse presentation. More recently Short (2007a) has elaborated on the functions of thought presentation, speech summary and embedded discourse presentation.

In addition, a discussion of the usefulness of cognitive approaches to the analysis of narrative fiction is equally paramount to his research profile (see Leech and Short, 1981; also chapters 11 and 12 of *Style in Fiction*, 2007, 2nd edition). Short was also in charge of finalizing the unfinished manuscript by the cognitive linguist Paul Werth, *Text Worlds: Representing Conceptual Space in Discourse* (1999) after Werth's sudden death in 1997.

Further reading

Busse, B. and Plummer, P. (2007), 'Mick Short (Lancaster University) in discussion with Patricia Plummer (University of Mainz) and Beatrix Busse (University of Mainz)'. *Anglistik*, 18, (1), 135–51.

Leech, G. and Short, M. (1981), *Style in Fiction*. London: Longman.

Leech, G. and Short, M. (2007), *Style in Fiction*. 2nd ed. London: Longman.

Semino, E. and Short, M. (2004), *Corpus Stylistics: Speech, Writing and Thought Presentation in a Corpus of English Writing*. London: Routledge.

Short, M. (1993), 'To analyse a poem stylistically: "To Paint a Water Lily" by Ted Hughes', in P. Verdonk (ed.), *Twentieth-century Poetry: From Text to Context*. London: Routledge, pp. 7–20.

Short, M. (1996), *Exploring the Language of Poems, Plays and Prose*. London: Longman.

Paul Simpson

Paul Simpson is currently Professor of English Language in the School of English at Queen's University, Belfast, after having held a lectureship at the University of Liverpool. His professional and academic career includes his current post as Director of Research in English Language and Linguistics at the University of Belfast, his recently-concluded editorial position in the journal *Language and Literature*, and several other responsibilities as consultant editor for a series of publications among which we find the *Routledge Encyclopedia of Narrative Theory* (Herman, 2005b).

One of the many strengths of this scholar's research output is the amiability and clarity with which his academic work is delivered. His research interests are wide-ranging although they faithfully abide by the same principle of academic accessibility, as clearly pointed out by Toolan (2006b) when reviewing Simpson's *Stylistics: A Resource Book for Students* (2004):

> The present volume amply demonstrates his gifts: it is invariably clear, readable, well-paced, stimulating, informative, and wide-ranging in its topics and texts. It should race to the top of the charts among the Introductions to Stylistics designed to induct students at the level of first- or second-year undergraduates of a UK honours degree in English, or their rough equivalent around the world, into the subtle complexities of literary construction. (Toolan, 2006b, p. 409)

His research covers a diversity of aspects on language and linguistics such as accent variation in pop songs, the pragmatics of advertising discourse, satire, humour and irony, stylistics, critical linguistics and linguistic analyses of narratives, to name but a few.

Among Simpson's publications, his linguistic analysis of fictional narratives in *Language, Ideology and Point of View* (1993) deserves special attention. Quoted and referenced by more than three hundred scholarly pieces, this monograph continues to provide interesting linguistic and stylistic insights into the nature of narratives. Simpson builds on the work of previous stylisticians (namely Uspensky and Fowler) to devise his own 'modal grammar of point of view in narrative fiction' (see *narrator*) which combines primarily narratological perspectives such as a typology of narrators and focalizers with linguistic categories such as modality. Furthermore, he incorporates the systemic-functional tradition of looking at the ideational function of language via transitivity, applies pragmatic principles to newspaper language and researches issues of gender, ideological and point of view all in furtherance of an understanding of narrative.

Simpson's *On the Discourse of Satire: Towards a Stylistic Model of Satirical Humour* (2003) illustrates the versatility of this academic in as much as this monograph expertly deals with issues significantly disparate from the work he had previously published. He is here concerned with devising a theoretical model for the study of satirical discourse, broadly understood so that both written and pictorial humour can be accounted for. His aim is primarily comprehensive as an overview on existent theories of humour from a variety of perspectives informs his own stylistic take on the discourse of satire. Further proof of Simpson's far-reaching expertise comes from his analysis of the interface of literature and film (Simpson and Montgomery, 1995), his pedagogical approaches to the teaching of stylistics (Simpson, 2007) and his critical linguistic analyses (Simpson, 1990; Simpson and Mayr, 2009).

Further reading

Carter, R. and Simpson, P. (eds) (1989), *Language Discourse and Literature: An Introductory Reader in Discourse Stylistics*. London: Routledge.

Simpson, P. (1993), *Language, Ideology and Point of View*. London: Routledge.

Simpson, P. (1997), *Language through Literature*. London: Routledge.

Simpson, P. (1999), 'Language, culture and identity: With (another) look at accents in pop and rock singing'. *Multilingua: Journal of Cross-Cultural and Interlanguage Communication*, 18, (4), 343–68.

Simpson, P. (2000), 'Satirical humour and cultural context: With a note on the curious case of Father Todd Unctuous', in T. Bex, M. Burke and P. Stockwell (eds), *Contextualized Stylistics*. Amsterdam, Atlanta: Rodopi, pp. 243–66.

Simpson, P. (2003), *On the Discourse of Satire. Towards a Stylistic Model of Satirical Humour*. Amsterdam: Benjamins.

John Sinclair (1933–2007)

John Sinclair is one of the leading figures in modern (English) linguistics. John Sinclair was Professor at the Department of English Language and Literature at the University of Birmingham, where he held the Foundation Chair in Modern English Language from 1965 until 2000. After his retirement, he was co-founder and director of the Tuscan Word Centre in Italy, which provides foundational courses in corpus linguistics. He was awarded a variety of honorary memberships in international linguistic associations, such as the Linguistics Association of Great Britain, and held – among others – honorary professorships at the Universities of Jiao Tong, Shanghai and Glasgow.

Sinclair's publications and research foci are numerous and wide-ranging. He wrote and edited over 30 books and over 100 articles that dealt with fields as diverse as grammar, vocabulary, discourse analysis, lexicography, stylistics, language teaching and corpus linguistics. What he is probably most famous for is his introduction of two new fields: that of discourse analysis in the 1970s and of corpus linguistics in the 1980s. He totally recast studies of spoken discourse with *Towards an Analysis of Discourse* (1975, written with Malcolm Coulthard), founded the corpus-driven investigation of large-scale corpora in the 1980s COBUILD research project and, thereby, he also recast, both in theory and practice, the computational analysis of lexis, grammar and patterns of discourse. Sinclair produced the 400 million word Bank of English corpus, which was used to produce a set of highly creative and innovative dictionaries, grammars and teaching materials. His description of language was so innovative because it was based on large-scale corpora and corpus-driven lexicography: 'The language looks different when you look at a lot of it at once' (Sinclair, 1991, p. xvii). He opposed the Chomskyan approach to intuition-based and non-quantitative language research.

Sinclair's earlier papers were in the area of stylistics and included theoretical reflections on the interplay between language and literature and analyses of Larkin, Wordsworth, Shakespeare sonnets and a range of fictional texts. In an obituary for John Sinclair published in the Newsletter of the *Poetics and Linguistics Association* (*PALA*; see entry) in 2007, Carter stresses:

> He was one of the first to show the possibilities of linguistic analysis of literary texts in the 1960s, laid foundations for the development of the discipline world wide and contributed much to understandings that all texts, whether literary or non-literary, can be trusted to yield their most hidden meanings only after the most detailed and exhaustive linguistic treatment. (Carter, 2007b)

As can be seen, for example, in one of his famous stylistic articles 'Taking a Poem to Pieces' (Sinclair, 1966), he considers stylistics to be a legitimate area of linguistic investigation, which can be approached empirically and from a quantitative angle. Also, for Sinclair, literature is a valid source of data: 'no systematic apparatus can claim to describe a language if it does not embrace the literature also; and not as a freakish development, but as a natural specialization of categories which are required in other parts of the descriptive system' (Sinclair, 2004, p. 51).

His central and groundbreaking concepts of, for example, describing the interplay between lexis and grammar, are now compiled in *Trust the Text: Language, Corpus and Discourse* (2004), which is a collection of some of his most important articles. The articles collected in this volume, which are placed within a Firthian tradition, also show his influence on stylistics, practical analysis, theory and teaching. Among the concepts propounded by this scholar we find:

(a) the inseparability of form and meaning, of competence and performance
(b) the inseparability of lexis and grammar and the notion that an accurate description of meaning relies on lexical constraints and semantic prosody (Louw, 1993; Hunston, 2006)

(c) the concept of a lexical grammar and an elaboration of the notions of 'collocation' and 'colligation'
(d) the inclusion of natural language data and of extended examples; one of his key-words is 'evidence', because the language, in a corpus-driven approach, tells us how it functions
(e) the investigation of patterns in large amounts of data, as patterns appear everywhere in the lexical concordances generated from the corpus
(f) the notion of trusting the text and of 'prospection' and 'encapsulation', or 'anaphora' and 'cataphora', which means that sentences are strings which are connected to one another (see also McIntyre 2007b)

Sinclair's work in corpus linguistics is indispensable for approaches in corpus stylistics and beyond. His notion of trusting the text including prospection and encapsulation anticipates what has been stressed by Emmot (1997), for example, as a primed frame in cognitive poetics. Also, it addresses the stylistic interest in online processing. He also elaborates on the relationship between language and literature in his concept of the 'planes of discourse' (Sinclair, [1982] 2004, p. 52). Echoing Halliday's interpersonal and ideational function of language, he distinguishes between the 'interactive plane of discourse' and the 'autonomous plane of discourse', that which is a 'developing record of experience' (Sinclair, [1982] 2004, p. 52). In the former, the writer attempts to create some kind of relationship with the reader; the latter plane can, for example, be seen in long expository texts where the reader is not given any interactive clues. Reporting in fiction bridges the two planes and is seen as a property of fiction in the sense that 'an unspecified author said that one of his characters said' (Sinclair, [1982] 2004, p. 52). This model is closely related to work on discourse presentation (Semino and Short, 2004; see entry) and text world theory (Werth, 1999; see entry) and examines the author's position with reference to the text.

The ways Sinclair elaborates on the differences between spoken and written language are fruitful for stylistics because he discusses the notion of 'posture' and 'speaker change', which reverberates work on point of view, for example (McIntyre, 2007b, p. 570). In 'A tool for text explanation' (Sinclair, 2004, p. 116), he elaborates on the use of corpora for critical discourse analysis. However, Sinclair (2004, p. 190) is critical of manual annotation and tagging, a practice that has been employed by stylisticians, such as Semino and Short (2004) and Busse (2010a). Sinclair stresses that no matter what caution one takes, 'the original text cannot be reliably retrieved' (Sinclair,

2004, p. 191). Despite these strong arguments put forward by Sinclair, which should clearly be accounted for, stylisticians argue that complex discoursal phenomena such as discourse presentation, which are not lexically based, cannot yet be systematically and quantitatively retrieved and then contextually interpreted by a computer programme.

Further reading

McIntyre, D. (2007b), 'Trusting the text: Corpus linguistics and stylistics'. *International Journal of Corpus Linguistics*, 12, (4), 563–75.

Sinclair, J. (1966), 'Taking a poem to pieces', in R. Fowler (ed.), *Essays on Style and Language: Linguistic and Critical Approaches to Literary Style*. London: Routledge and Kegan Paul, pp. 68–81.

Sinclair, J. (2004), *Trust the Text. Language, Corpus and Discourse*. London and New York: Routledge.

Sinclair, J. (2005), 'Corpus and text: Basic principles', in M. Wynne (ed.), *Developing Linguistic Corpora: A Guide to Good Practice*. Oxford: Oxbow Books, pp. 1–16.

Michael Toolan

Michael Toolan is a British stylistician and integrational linguist with a particular interest in narrative analysis and corpus stylistics. He studied at Edinburg University (MA in Language and Literature) and Oxford University (D. Phil. in English), has held academic positions at the University of Washington and the National University of Singapore and is now Professor of English Language at the University of Birmingham. He is a founding member of the *International Association for the Integrational Study of Language and Communication (IAISLC)*, Chair of the *International Association of Literary Semantics (IALS)* (2006–current) and editor of the *Journal of Literary Semantics* (2002–current).

Toolan's facet as a narrative stylistician is informed by his interest in bringing together notions that have traditionally been dealt with in narratological circles and the linguistic concerns that characterize stylistics. This marriage can be said to have started with his doctorate work which resulted in the publication of *The Stylistics of Fiction* (1990). His *Narrative. A Critical Linguistic Introduction* (1988; 2nd edition, 2001), however, is the main materialization of his linguistic take on narrative although it is patently alive in many other publications, too (e.g., Toolan, 1990, 1995). The informative combination of elements from various disciplines achieved in his narrative analyses can be illustrated by, for instance, his discussion of free indirect discourse (FID) (see *discourse presentation*). Toolan succeeds in looking into FID, first, from the perspective that Banfield's (1982) theory of 'unspeakable sentences' had put forward; secondly, from the more linguistically-informed take of Leech and Short (1981; 2nd edition, 2007); and finally, from the corpus-driven perspectives of scholars such as Semino and Short (2004).

Toolan has recently devoted his attention to the potential of corpus stylistic methods to illuminate how narrative progression and narrativity are created (Toolan, 2006d, 2009). The assumption is that in narratives, in order to answer the question 'What next?', readers are guided in their experience and expectations while reading, and that the core ingredients of narrativity (suspense, surprise, secrecy or gaps, mystery, tension, obscurity) are created as a result of implicit and explicit textual elements. The approach is also tested against readers' responses.

Toolan (2009, p. 2) aims at understanding how the lexico-grammatical patterning contributes to narrativity and how useful a corpus approach is when the sequentiality of a text is the main issue. His corpus consists of a set of representative twentieth-century short stories, and he makes use of *WordSmith Tools* (Scott, 2004) and *Wmatrix* (Rayson, 2007) as well as a programme, which helps track distributions of recurring words and new words across a text (Youman's (1994) *Vocabulary Management Profile*).

A corpus stylistic approach involves the rapid searching and sorting of electronic versions of texts. These are often compared against a variety of so-called reference corpora. Toolan (2009, pp. 25–8) problematizes the choice of the comparator corpus and stresses that the investigation of the elements which create narrative texts also necessitates a move away from language to psychology, social history and culture. In addition, he considers it important to include what the reader brings to the text: inferences, schemas, genre expectations and background or cultural knowledge. However, it seems to be the case that background can only be described once a systematic textual analysis has been attended to (Toolan, 2009, p. 5).

This new approach to narrative progression allows Toolan to identify eight crucial features to which 'high narrativity prospection' can be attributed, that is features of texts which draw the reader's attention to the progression of the narrative. These are (Toolan, 2009, chapters 7 and 8):

- sentences containing high-frequency keyword character names
- sentences with narrative-tense finite verbs in character-depicting action clauses
- opening sentences of narrative paragraphs
- sentences carrying lexical keywords and clusters
- sentences carrying characters' represented thought
- prospective direct speech
- negated proposition
- projecting modal or mental process verbs

Toolan (2009, pp. 3–12) gives a useful account of the variety of disciplines and research frameworks involved when studying narrative progression. Also, he critically discusses the potential of a corpus stylistic bottom-up approach and lists its advantages and disadvantages when trying to place on a sounder footing a complex discoursal phenomenon such as narrative progression. He stresses, for example, that collocational studies are objective and bottom-up and counteract the stylistician's reliance on intuition, but also points out that it takes a human analyst to analyse, interpret and contextualize the patterns identified by the respective programme. He stresses the usefulness of Hoey's (2005) theory of 'lexico-grammatical priming', but stresses that it is more difficult to interpret lexical patterns and priming theory in literary texts because of the shifting points of view in such texts.

Further reading

Toolan, M. (1988), *Narrative. A Critical Linguistic Introduction*. London: Routledge (2nd edition: 2001).

Toolan, M. (1990), *The Stylistics of Fiction. A Literary-Linguistic Approach*. London and New York: Routledge.

Toolan, M. (1998), *Language in Literature. An Introduction to Stylistics*. London: Arnold.

Toolan, M. (2007), 'Trust and text, text as trust', in R. Moon (ed.), *Words, Grammar and Text: Revisiting the Works of John Sinclair. Special Issue of the International Journal of Corpus Linguistics*, 12, (2), 269–88.

Toolan, M. (2009), *Narrative Progression in the Short Story. A Corpus-Stylistic Approach*. Amsterdam and Philadelphia: John Benjamins.

Theo van Leeuwen

Theo van Leeuwen is one of the founding fathers of the social semiotic approach to visual communication and multimodality. His social semiotic framework is now employed in multimodal stylistics for the systematic description and analysis of texts which in addition to wording make use of modes such as typography, layout, colour and visual images for their meaning-making. Born in Holland, van Leeuwen worked as a film and television producer in Holland and Australia before he started his academic career. He studied linguistics and semiotics in Australia at Macquarie University and the University of Sydney. After teaching communication theory at Macquarie University, van Leeuwen moved on to a number of prestigious positions in the academic world, first as Professor of Communication Theory at the London College of Printing, then as Director of the Centre for Language and Communication at the University of Cardiff (where he now holds the title of Honorary Professor), and finally as Dean of the Faculty of Humanities and Social Sciences at the University of Technology, Sydney. Van Leeuwen is furthermore one of the founding editors of the journal *Visual Communication*.

Inspired by Halliday's view of language (see *M. A. K. Halliday*), van Leeuwen, in collaboration with Gunther Kress, set out to explore whether and to what extent the ideas and concepts of Hallidayan linguistics could be applicable to visual communication. This resulted in the publication of *Reading Images. The Grammar of Visual Design* (1996), a comprehensive – yet according to the authors also provisional – theory of visual communication which demonstrates how ideational, interpersonal and compositional (Halliday's 'textual') meanings are also found in visual communication and may be described as systematically as those of verbal language. Subsequently, van Leeuwen ventured to explore different semiotic modes of meaning such as sound (van Leeuwen, 1999), typography (van Leeuwen, 2006b) and colour (Kress and van Leeuwen, 2002), and to focus more explicitly on the ways in which the different modes interact in meaning-making, which is seen as always and invariably multimodal (van Leeuwen, 2005a). In *Multimodal Discourse – The Modes and Media of Contemporary Communication* (2001), Kress and van Leeuwen take a slightly different approach to the concept of multimodality, focusing on four different strata – discourse, design, production and distribution – which are involved in the construction of meaning and may be meaning-making in their own right.

With its focus on and systematic approach to multimodal meaning-making, van Leeuwen's work is applied by stylisticians in the field of multimodal stylistics, including the stylistics of film and drama performance as well as stylistic work done on the interplay of various semiotic modes such as wording, layout, typography and sometimes also colour and visual images in literary texts.

Further reading

Kress, G. and van Leeuwen, T. (1996), *Reading Images – The Grammar of Visual Design*. London: Routledge.

Kress, G. and van Leeuwen, T. (2001), *Multimodal Discourse – The Modes and Media of Contemporary Communication*. London: Arnold.

van Leeuwen, T. (1999), *Speech, Music, Sound*. London: Macmillan.

van Leeuwen, T. (2005a), *Introducing Social Semiotics*. London: Routledge.

Willie van Peer

Willie van Peer is Professor of Literary Studies and Intercultural Hermeneutics at the University of Munich after having held several other positions elsewhere in Europe. He is the former President of *IGEL* (*International Society for the Empirical Study of Literature and Media*) and former Chair of *PALA* (*Poetics and Linguistics Association*; see entry). He is the editor of the *Linguistic Approaches to Literature* series, John Benjamins, and was a member of the international Advisory Board for the *Utrecht Publications in General and Comparative Literature* series, also with Benjamins; he is furthermore a member of the editorial board for the journal *Language and Literature*. He has written several books, has edited or co-edited more than ten volumes and has published more than 165 articles on a variety of topics. His research interests range from the study of narrative, the literary canon in education, stylistics and psychology, stylistics and pragmatics, empirical studies of literature and the quality of literary texts. His first monograph, *Stylistics and Psychology: Investigations of Foregrounding* (1986) already established the premises of what was to become one of his core lines of investigation, the theory of foregrounding (see entry):

> In English, the term 'foregrounding' has come to mean several things at once. First of all, it is used to indicate the (psycholinguistic) processes by which – during the reading act – something may be given special

> prominence. Second, it may refer to specific devices (as produced by the author) located in the text itself. It is also employed to indicate the specific poetic effect on the reader. Furthermore, it may be used as an analytic category in order to evaluate literary texts, or to situate them historically, or to explain their importance and cultural significance. Finally, it is also employed in order to differentiate literature from other varieties of language use, such as everyday conversations or scientific reports. Thus the term covers a wide area of meaning. (van Peer and Hakemulder, 2006, p. 547)

Van Peer's fortunate marriage of stylistic and psychological aspects represented the initial steps of foregrounding theory which, nonetheless, has subsequently developed to embrace more than its initial linguistic definition: 'in sentence structure, it then refers to new information, in contrast to elements in the sentence that form the background against which new elements are to be understood by the listener or reader' (van Peer and Hakemulder, 2006, p. 547). Van Peer's determination to bring literary studies in line with other social sciences by endowing them with the kind of rigour existing in disciplines such as psychology, cognitive studies, anthropology or sociology illustrates his second major line of research. His tenacity and unyielding belief in the need for rigour in literary studies has been exemplary and has inspired many others to take on the same empirical stance towards literature. As van Peer et al. (2007) clarify, empirical refers to 'a kind of reasoning and a kind of research that is based on real evidence, that is, on evidence from the real world, which can be inspected by anyone' (van Peer et al., 2007, p. 7). Most of the empirical research currently published is linked in one way or another to *IGEL* (*International Society for the Empirical Study of Literature and Media*) but some of its members are quick to point out that van Peer's belief in empiricism well preceded the foundation of the association in 1987 (Zyngier et al., 2008, p. xi). See the further reading section for some selected publications and his personal webpage for the full list.

Further reading

van Peer, W. (1986), *Stylistics and Psychology: Investigations of Foregrounding*. London: Croom Helm.

van Peer, W. (ed.) (2008), *The Quality of Literature. Linguistic Studies in the Evaluation of Literary Texts.* Amsterdam and Philadelphia: John Benjamins.

van Peer, W. and Chatman, S. (eds) (2001), *New Perspectives on Narrative Perspective*. Albany, NY: SUNY Press.

van Peer, W. and Louwerse, M. (eds) (2003), *Thematics. Interdisciplinary Studies*. Amsterdam and Philadelphia: John Benjamins.

van Peer, W. and Renkema, J. (eds) (1984), *Pragmatics and Stylistics*. Amersfoort: Acco.

van Peer, W., Zyngier, S. and Hakemulder, F. (2007), 'Foregrounding: Past, Present, Future', in D. Hoover and S. Lattig (eds), *Stylistics: Prospect and Retrospect*. Amsterdam and New York: Rodopi, pp. 1–22.

Peter Verdonk

Peter Verdonk is Emeritus Professor of Stylistics at the University of Amsterdam where he started lecturing in the early 1970s. Although retired, Professor Verdonk is still research active and engaged with academic matters as his recent plenary conference at the Roosevelt Academy (*PALA* conference, Middelburg, The Netherlands; July 2009) proves. His research interests lie in rhetoric, literary criticism, discourse analysis, narratology and cognitive stylistics, all of them areas on which he has published. He is a member of the editorial board of *Language and Literature* and of the advisory editorial board (previously series editor) of the *Linguistic Approaches to Literature* series for Benjamins. He is the sole author of four books, has edited and co-edited another four and was honoured in his retirement with a festschrift entitled *Contextualized Stylistics* (2000) where colleagues past and present published pieces to highlight the academic worth of the honouree.

Verdonk is primarily associated with literary stylistics, that is, he has mainly focused on the interface of language and literature. Of the many strengths of Verdonk's work, his capability to marry older trends in literary analysis with new developments needs special mentioning. His background in rhetoric and literary criticism has aided to endow his work with a historical perspective but he has similarly been prompt to acknowledge those areas where new approaches needed to be incorporated. For instance, his 'Liberation of the icon: A brief summary from classical rhetoric to cognitive stylistics' (1999) succeeds in sufficiently crediting the classical rhetoricians' contributions to stylistics while also highlighting the state of negligence that the role of the reader has traditionally tended to endure:

> Though [. . .] rhetoric in its widest scope is definitely audience directed, it is remarkable that its huge theoretical apparatus does not mention a single word about the possibility of an active role of the audience in the process of meaning production. The audience was only the passive object of the intended persuasive effects of the text [. . .]. The British and American pioneers of stylistics also left the reader out in the cold. It was not until the seventies that postformalist theories were advanced in which the literary text was no longer seen as an autonomous object, but as a discourse, that is, as a contextualised sociocognitive interaction in which meaning is not unidirectional but rather a matter of negotiation between speakers or writers on the one hand and listeners or readers on the other. (Verdonk, 1999, pp. 294, 296)

Verdonk is referring here to the rise of cognitive approaches to literature (he goes on to analyse a poem by Philip Larkin from a schema theory perspective; see *schema theory*). The advantages of understanding the literary artefact from a discoursal perspective in which the text, the context of its production and the recipient of that text need to be borne in mind seem conclusive enough for this stylistician who, consequently, advocates for an inclusion of any new development on language analysis that may underscore the mental component of meaning construction via the role of the reader.

His latest monograph published to date, *Stylistics* (2002), is a relatively short volume which still manages to present the novice reader with a considerable amount of theoretical as well as practical tools in a totally affordable and accessible style. Prior to this publication, Verdonk had already confirmed his all-rounder status by working on poetry (1987, 1993), drama (1998, with Culpeper and Short) and fiction (1995, with Weber) alike and this volume further confirms that standing by also discussing issues such as the nature of literature as discourse, the relationship of stylistics to literary criticism as well as ideological positions in literary texts.

Further reading

Sell, Roger and Verdonk, P. (eds) (1994), *Literature and the New Interdisciplinarity: Poetics, Linguistics, History*. Amsterdam: Rodopi.

Verdonk, P. (1980), *Making Sense of Sentences*. Amsterdam: University of Amsterdam.

Verdonk, P. (1982), *The Language of Poetry: A Seminar on Literary Stylistics, 1981–82*. Amsterdam: University of Amsterdam.

Katie Wales

Katie Wales is Professor of English language at Nottingham University and she held professorships at Sheffield, London and Leeds universities. She is a founding member of the *Poetics and Linguistics Association* (*PALA*; see entry) and one of its former chairs. She was also the editor of the journal *Language and Literature* and is now a member of the editorial board. Katie Wales is a versatile and prolific linguist who has worked on such areas as *Personal Pronouns in Present-Day English* (Wales, 1996) and *Northern English. A Social and Cultural History* (Wales, 2006a). She is also a writer of children's books, such as *Santa's Christmas Joke Book* (Wales, 1989, with Kevin Smith) or *The Elephant Joke Book* (Wales, 1985, with Mark Burgess). Katie Wales's work in stylistics covers a variety of fields, such as the stylistics of poetry, the language of James Joyce, diachronic stylistics with articles on Shakespeare's language, the intersections between rhetoric and stylistics and critical discourse analysis.

In Wales's (1993) article 'Teach yourself "rhetoric": An analysis of Philip Larkin's "Church Going"' she illustrates the roots of stylistics in classical rhetoric and shows how stylistics can focus on textuality in relation to readerly affect, interpretation and context of production.

In a collection of essays on female writing edited by Wales (1994), female scholars investigate not only the advantages, but also the necessity, of looking at feminism from the perspective afforded by linguistic means:

> [The articles] present an original and close analysis of a 'literary' text, or range of texts, by applying the methodology or framework of linguistic (grammatical, lexical, pragmatic, discourse) theories, in order to address directly questions and ideas that have been raised in feminist literary theory, criticism and linguistics about gender and style. (Wales, 1994, p. vii)

Her *Dictionary of Stylistics* (2001, 2nd ed.) is a landmark and an important reference tool for any stylistician because it is one of the first attempts to give a comprehensive overview of the main features of stylistics, its versatility and interdisciplinarity.

Further reading

Wales K. (1992), *The Language of James Joyce*. Basingstoke: Macmillan.

Wales, K. (1993), 'Teach yourself "rhetoric": An analysis of Philip Larkin's "Church Going"', in P. Verdonk (ed.), *Twentieth-Century Poetry: From Text to Context*. London: Routledge, pp. 134–58.

Wales, K. (2001), *A Dictionary of Stylistics*. 2nd ed. Harlow: Longman.

Wales, K. (2006b), 'Stylistics', in K. Brown (ed.), *Encyclopaedia of Language and Linguistics*. Amsterdam: Elsevier Science, pp. 213–7.

Paul Werth

Paul Werth gained his professorship from the University of Amsterdam after having been a lecturer at the University of Hull, in the United Kingdom and the Université Libre de Bruxelles, Belgium. His untimely death stopped him from actually putting together the final version of the monograph for which he is best known, *Text Worlds: Representing Conceptual Space in Discourse* (1999). This volume only saw the light thanks to the investigative and editorial efforts of Mick Short (Lancaster University) (see *Mick Short*) jointly working with other friends and colleagues from several institutions. Werth began publishing in the 1970s when his work had still not developed the cognitive dimension it later took on. For instance, in 1981 he edited a collection of papers on the nature of conversation and discourse, which widely ranged from applications of Sinclair and Coulthard's (1975) discourse-analytical model and Grice's (1975) notion of implicature to insights into Sacks, Schegloff and Jefferson's (1974) ethnomethodological approach to the study of conversation and Austin's (1962) and Searle's (1969) proposals on speech act theory. Werth initiates his journey into cognitive explorations via the discussion of some of the generativist matters prevalent at the time, but soon departs from these theoretical tenets (see his *Focus, Coherence and Emphasis*, 1984) by proposing a move from the sentence-grammar focus of generativism and onto the discourse grammar he subsequently develops in text world theory (see entry). His dissatisfaction with the types of analyses carried out by generativists is evident in the following:

> We have tried to provide evidence in support of the thesis that an extension of grammatical theory in the direction of discourse will solve many of the problems of sentence-grammar in a unified and natural way. As

> we see it, a D-grammar is not a device equivalent to a S-grammar except that it has texts rather than sentences at its output [. . .]. We propose that a D-grammar is a S-grammar with additional constraints [. . .]. By 'discourse', we refer not only to the text (the verbal context) but also to the situational and community knowledge shared by the speakers, and specifically informing a given text. (Werth, 1984, p. 259)

The discourse worlds (see *text world theory*) of text world theory are incipiently suggested in this quotation which highlights Werth's conviction of the need for a more comprehensive grammar than was available via generativist tenets at the time. The defence for a discourse-oriented framework of analysis is finally concretized in his 1999 monograph as follows:

> Then our starting-point in this equation must be the discourse, since it is a term which characterises actual stretches of language. We can say, therefore, that a discourse is a complete language event, i.e. one with a perceived beginning and an end. In practice, a discourse can be as short as a single word, such as 'Fire!' or as long as a written record spanning many generations of authors, like the *Anglo-Saxon Chronicle*. The point is that it should be perceived as a single language event. (Werth, 1999, p. 1)

Considering language as a discourse event, rather than a sentence event facilitates the move towards a cognitivist stance. Werth defends that the reader (in the case of written communication) is as essential a part as any other component in the discourse event. Meaning is only created via the combination of textual prompts and the inferences made by this reader from such textual clues; the result is the creation of certain mental worlds which Werth names 'text worlds':

> My main thesis is that all of semantics and pragmatics operates within a set of stacked cognitive spaces, termed 'mental worlds' [. . .]. The text world, though, is a total construct, so therefore negotiated by the participants through the medium of discourse, again backed up by relevant knowledge. Since it is a construct, it is dependent on resources of memory and imagination, rather than direct perception. (Werth, 1999, p. 17)

Text world theory's three-layered structure is complemented by sub-worlds or mental spaces indicating wishes, desires, attitudes, temporal and location shifts, etc. This framework, although not finalized by its author himself, has nonetheless had considerable impact on practitioners of cognitive stylistics who embrace it as one of the more solid frameworks of the cognitive approaches to language (Gavins, 2003, 2007; Montoro, 2006a).

Further reading

Werth, P. (1980), 'Articles of association: Determiners and context', in J. van der Auwera (ed.), *The Semantics of Determiners*. London: Croom Helm, pp. 250–89.

Werth, P. (1986), 'A functional approach to presupposition', in A. Bossuyt (ed.), *Functional Approaches to Linguistics*. Brussels: Presses Universitaires de Bruxelles, pp. 239–79.

Werth, P. (1994), 'Extended metaphor: A text-world account'. *Language and Literature*, 3, (2), 79–103.

Werth, P. (1995a), 'How to build a world (in a lot less than six days and using only what's in your head)', in K. Green (ed.), *New Essays on Deixis: Discourse, Narrative, Literature*. Amsterdam: Rodopi, pp. 49–80.

Werth, P. (1995b), '"World enough and time": Deictic space and the interpretation of prose', in P. Verdonk and J. J. Weber (eds), *Twentieth Century Fiction: From Text to Context.* London: Routledge, pp. 181–205.

Henry G. Widdowson

Henry G. Widdowson is Emeritus Professor of Education, University of London. He has previously held professorships at the universities of Essex and Vienna. He is the Applied Linguistics adviser to Oxford University Press and series adviser of Oxford Bookworms Collection. Widdowson is co-editor of the series *Language Teaching: A Scheme for Teacher Education* (Oxford University Press). He is the series editor of *Oxford Introductions to Language Study* and the author of *Linguistics* (Widdowson, 1996a) in that series.

Following an approach to stylistics which he calls 'practical stylistics', Widdowson has published on the stylistics of poetry (Widdowson, 1992), but his work also has to be situated within pedagogical stylistics (Widdowson, 1992; Rubik and Widdowson, 2000). Widdowson's (Widdowson, 1975) early work in stylistics has successfully and provocatively played a role in establishing stylistics as a discipline which mediates dynamically between linguistics and literary criticism. In a famous article from 1972, he explains the points of intersection between stylistics and literary criticism, and identifies the significance of particular uses of language: 'Widdowson differentiates linguistic deviance from literary deflection, in order to demonstrate that stylisticians can have things to say about literary value and significance' (Carter and Stockwell, 2008, p. 29). Widdowson (2002) discusses a number of issues that are related to verbal art and stresses that personal meanings are more central than social meanings in literary communication.

Furthermore, Widdowson criticized critical discourse analysis (see entry) for always applying a pre-fabricated interpretation to the text before the actual analysis; he has especially debated over these issues with Norman Fairclough (Widdowson, 1996b, 2000). The methodological intersections between stylistics, on the one hand, and critical discourse analysis (CDA), on the other, are described in the 'Key Branches' entry on *critical stylistics* and in the 'Key Terms' entry on *critical discourse analysis*.

Further reading

Widdowson, H. G. (1972), 'On the deviance of literary discourse'. *Style*, 6, (3), 294–306.

Widdowson, H. G. (1975), *Stylistics and the Teaching of Literature*. Harlow, Essex: Longman.

Widdowson, H. G. (1992), *Practical Stylistics: An Approach to Poetry*. Oxford: Oxford University Press.

Widdowson, H. G. (2004), *Text, Context, Pretext. Critical Issues in Discourse Analysis*. Oxford: Blackwell.

Key Texts in Stylistics

Abbott, H. P. (2008), *The Cambridge Introduction to Narrative*. Cambridge: Cambridge University Press.

Abelson, R. (1987), 'Artificial intelligence and literary appreciation: How big is the gap?', in L. Hálàsz (ed.), *Literary Discourse: Aspects of Cognitive and Social Psychological Approaches*. Berlin: de Gruyter, pp. 1–37.

Adamson, S. (1995), 'From empathetic deixis to empathetic narrative: Stylisation and (de-)subjectivisation as processes of language change', in S. Wright and D. Stein (eds), *Subjectivity and Subjectivisation*. Cambridge: Cambridge University Press, pp. 195–224.

Adamson, S. (2001), 'The rise and fall of empathetic narrative', in W. van Peer and S. Chatman (eds), *New Perspectives on Narrative Perspective*. New York: State University of New York Press, pp. 83–99.

Adolphs, S. and Carter, R. A. (2002), 'Point of view and semantic prosodies in Virginia Woolf's *To the Lighthouse*'. *Poetica*, 58, 7–20.

Allan, K. (2001), *Natural Language Semantics*. Oxford: Blackwell.

Allen, R. (1999), 'Psychoanalytic film theory', in T. Miller and R. Stam (eds), *A Companion to Film Theory*. Oxford: Blackwell Publishing, pp. 123–45.

Andringa, E. (1998), 'The empirical study of literature: Its development and future', in S. Janssen and N. van Dijk (eds), *The Empirical Study of Literature and the Media: Current Approaches and Perspectives*. Rotterdam: Waalwijk van Doorn, pp. 12–23.

Archer, D. and McIntyre, D. (2005), 'A computational approach to mind style', paper presented at the 25th Conference of the Poetics and Linguistics Association, July 2005, University of Huddersfield.

Attridge, D. (1982), *The Rhythms of English Poetry*. London: Longman.

Austin, J. L. (1962), *How to Do Things with Words*. Oxford: Oxford University Press.

Bache, C. and Davidsen-Nielsen, N. (1997), *Mastering English. An Advanced Grammar for Non-native and Native Speakers*. Berlin and New York: Mouton de Gruyter.

Bakhtin, M. M. (1981), 'Discourse in the novel', in M. Holquist (ed.), *The Dialogic Imagination. Four Essays by M. M. Bakhtin*, 12th ed., trans. by C. Emerson and M. Holquist. Austin: The University of Texas Press, pp. 259–422.

Bal, M. (1997), *Narratology: Introduction to the Theory of Narrative*. Toronto: University of Toronto Press.

Baldry, A. (2004), 'Phase and transition, type and instance: Patterns in media texts as seen through a multimodal concordancer', in K. O'Halloran (ed.), *Multimodal Discourse Analysis: Systemic Functional Perspectives*. London: Continuum, pp. 83–108.

Baldry, A. and Thibault, P. (2006), *Multimodal Transcription and Text Analysis*. London: Equinox.

Banfield, A. (1982), *Unspeakable Sentences*. New York: Routledge and Kegan Paul.

Barbiers, S., van der Wurff, W. and Beukema, F. (eds) (2002), *Modality and its Interaction with the Verbal System*. Amsterdam and Philadelphia: John Benjamins.

Barthes, R. ([1966] 1977), 'Introduction to the structural analysis of narratives', in *Image-Music-Text*. London: Fortuna, pp. 79–124.

Bartlett, F. Ch. (1932), *Remembering: A Study in Experimental and Social Psychology*. Cambridge: Cambridge University Press.

Baş, I. and Freeman, D. C. (eds) (2007), *Challenging the Boundaries*. (*PALA Papers 2*). Amsterdam and New York: Rodopi.

Bell, A. (2007), 'Do you want to hear about it?' Exploring possible worlds in Michael Joyce's Hyperfiction, Afternoon, a story', in M. Lambrou and P. Stockwell (eds), *Contemporary Stylistics*. London: Continuum, pp. 43–55.

Bell, A. (2010), *The Possible Worlds of Hypertext Fiction*. Basingstoke: Palgrave Macmillan.

Bell, A. (fc), 'Ontological boundaries and conceptual leaps: The significance of possible worlds for hypertext fiction (and Beyond)', in B. Thomas and R. Page (eds), *New Narratives: Stories and Storytelling in the Digital Age*. Lincoln, Nebraska: University of Nebraska Press.

Bex, T., Burke, M. and Stockwell, P. (eds) (2000), *Contextualized Stylistics*. Amsterdam: Rodopi.

Biber, D., Conrad, S. and Cortes, V. (2004), 'If you look at…: Lexical bundles in university teaching and textbooks'. *Applied Linguistics*, 25, (3), 371–405.

Biber, D., Stig, J., Leech, G., Conrad, S. and Finegan, E. (1999), *Longman Grammar of Spoken and Written English*. London: Longman.

Birch, D. (1991), *The Language of Drama*. London: Macmillan.

Birch, D. J. and O'Toole, L. M. (1988), *Functions of Style*. London and New York: Pinter Publishers.

Black, E. (1993), 'Metaphor, simile and cognition in Golding's *The Inheritors*'. *Language and Literature*, 2, (1), 37–48.

Black, E. (2006), *Pragmatic Stylistics*. Edinburg: Edinburgh University Press.

Blum-Kulka, S., House, J. and Kasper, G. (1989), *Cross-cultural Pragmatics: Requests and Apologies*. Norwood, NJ: Ablex.

Boase-Beier, J. (2003), 'Mind style translated'. *Style*, 37, (3), 253–65.

Bockting, I. (1994), 'Mind style as an interdisciplinary approach to characterisation in Faulkner'. *Language and Literature*, 3, (3), 157–74.

Boeriis, M. (2008), 'A mode instantiation model', in N. Nørgaard (ed.), *Systemic Functional Linguistics in Use, Odense Working Papers in Language and Communication*, 29, 237–50.

Boeriis, M. and Nørgaard, N. (fc), 'The multimodal construal of humour and intertextuality in Tele2's Small Bill/Big Bill Campaign', in A. Baldry and E. Montagna (eds), *Interdisciplinary Perspectives on Multimodality: Theory and Practice*. Campobasso: Palladino.

Bortolussi, M. and Dixon, P. (2003), *Psychonarratology: Foundations for the Empirical Study of Literary Response*. Cambridge: Cambridge University Press.

Bousfield, D. (2007), 'Never a truer word said in jest': A pragmastylistic analysis of impoliteness as banter in *Henry IV, Part I*, in M. Lambrou and P. Stockwell (eds), *Contemporary Stylistics*. London: Continuum, pp. 210–20.

Bousfield, D. (2008), *Impoliteness in Interaction*. Amsterdam and Philadelphia: John Benjamins.

Bradford, R. (1994), *Roman Jakobson. Life, Language, Art*. London and New York: Routledge.

Bray, J. (2007), 'The dual voice of free indirect discourse: A reading experiment'. *Language and Literature*, 16, (1), 37–52.

Brewer, W. F. (1995), 'Discourse force and empirical study of literature', in G. Rusch (ed.), *Empirical Approaches to Literature. Proceedings of the Fourth Biannual Conference of the International Society for the Empirical Study of Literature*. Siegen: Lumis Publications, pp. 89–95.

Brinton, L. J. (2001), 'Historical discourse analysis', in D. Schiffrin, D. Tannen and H. E. Hamilton (eds), *Handbook of Discourse Analysis*. Oxford: Blackwell, pp. 138–60.

Brown, K. (ed.) (2006), *Encyclopaedia of Language and Linguistics*. Amsterdam: Elsevier Science.

Brown, R. W. and Ford, M. (1961), 'Address in American English'. *Journal of Abnormal and Social Psychology*, 62, 375–85.

Brown, R. W. and Gilman, A. (1958), 'Who says "tu" to "whom"'. *A Review of General Semantics*, 15, 169–74.

Brown, R. W. and Gilman, A. (1960), 'The pronouns of power and solidarity', in T. Sebeok (ed.), *Style in Language*. Cambridge, Mass.: MIT Press, pp. 253–76.

Brown, P. and Levinson, S. C. (1987), *Politeness. Some Universals in Language Use*. Cambridge: Cambridge University Press.

Brumfit, C. J. and Carter, R. A. (1986), *Literature and Language Teaching*. Oxford: Oxford University Press.

Bühler, K. (1934), *Sprachtheorie: Die Darstellungsfunktion der Sprache*. Jena, Germany: Fischer.

Bühler, K. (1982), 'The deictic field of language and deictic words', in R. Jarvella and W. Klein (eds), *Speech, Place and Action: Studies in Deixis and Related Topics*. New York: Wiley, pp. 9–30.

Burke, M. (2001), 'Iconicity and literary emotion'. *European Journal of English Studies*, 5, (1), 31–46.

Burke, M. (2006a), 'Cognitive stylistics', in K. Brown (ed.), *Encyclopaedia of Language and Linguistics*. Amsterdam: Elsevier Science, pp. 218–21.

Burke, M. (2006b), 'Emotion: Stylistic approaches' in K. Brown (ed.), *Encyclopaedia of Language and Linguistics*. Amsterdam: Elsevier Science, pp. 127–9.

Burke, M. (2010), *Literary Reading, Cognition and Emotion: An Exploration of the Oceanic Mind*. London: Routledge.

Burton, D. (1973), *The Exploitation of 'the word' in Concrete Poetry*. Unpublished MA Thesis, University of Birmingham.

Burton, D. (1978a), *Dialogue and Discourse*. Unpublished PhD Thesis, University of Birmingham.

Burton, D. (1978b), 'Towards an analysis of casual conversation'. *Nottingham Linguistic Circular*, 17, (2), 131–59.

Burton, D. (1980), *Dialogue and Discourse: A Sociolinguistic Approach to Modern Drama Dialogue and Naturally Occurring Conversation*. London: Routledge and Kegan Paul.

Burton, D. (1981a) 'The sociolinguistic analysis of spoken discourse', in P. French and M. MacLure (eds), *Adult-Child Conversation*. London: Croom Helm, pp. 21–46.

Burton, D. (1981b), 'Analysing spoken discourse', in M. Coulthard and M. Montgomery (eds), *Studies in Discourse Analysis*. London and Boston: Routledge and Kegan Paul, pp. 61–81.

Burton, D. (1982), 'Through glass darkly: Through dark glasses', in R. Carter (ed.), *Language and Literature. An Introductory Reader in Stylistics*. London: George Allen and Unwin, pp. 195–214.

Burton, D. (1984), 'A feminist reading of Lewis Grassic Gibbon's *A Scots Quair*', in J. Hawthorn (ed.), *The British Working-Class Novel in the Twentieth Century*. London: Edward Arnold, pp. 35–46.

Burton, D. and Stubbs, M. W. (1976), 'On speaking terms: Analysing conversational data'. *Midland Association of Linguistic Studies*, 2, (2), 22–44.

Busse, B. (2006a), 'Linguistic aspects of sensuality: A corpus-based approach to will-construing contexts in Shakespeare's works', in C. Houswitschka, G. Knappe and A. Müller (eds), *Anglistentag 2005 Bamberg Proceedings*. Trier: WVT 2006, pp. 123–42.

Busse, B. (2006b), *Vocative Constructions in the Language of Shakespeare*. Amsterdam and Philadelphia: John Benjamins.

Busse, B. (2007), 'The stylistics of drama: An Early Modern English example', in P. Stockwell and M. Lambrou (eds), *Contemporary Stylistics*. London: Continuum, pp. 232–43.

Busse, B. (2010a), 'Recent trends in new historical stylistics', in D. McIntyre and B. Busse (eds), *Language and Style*. London: Palgrave.

Busse, B. (2010b), 'Adverbial expressions of stance in Early Modern "spoken" English', in J. Helbig (ed.), *Anglistentag 2009 Klagenfurt Proceedings*. Trier: WVT.

Busse, B. and Plummer, P. (2007), 'Mick Short (Lancaster University) in discussion with Patricia Plummer (University of Mainz) and Beatrix Busse (University of Mainz)'. *Anglistik*, 18, (1), 135–51.

Butler, C. S. (2004), 'Corpus studies and functional linguistic theories'. *Functions of Language*, 11, (2), 147–86.

Bybee, J. and Fleischman, S. (eds) (1995), *Modality in Grammar and Discourse*. Amsterdam and Philadelphia: John Benjamins.

Calvo, C. (1994), 'In defence of Celia: Discourse analysis and women's discourse in *As You Like It*', in K. Wales (ed.), *Feminist Linguistics in Literary Criticism*. Woodbridge, England: Boydell and Brewer, pp. 91–116.

Cameron, L. (2003), *Metaphor in Educational Discourse*. London: Continuum.

Canning, P. (2008), '"The bodie and the letters both": "blending" the rules of early modern religion'. *Language and Literature*, 17, (3), 187–203.

Carroll, N. (1996a), *Theorizing the Moving Image*. Cambridge: Cambridge University Press.

Carroll, N. (1996b), 'Prospects for film theory: A personal assessment', in D. Bordwell and N. Carroll (eds), *Post-Theory. Reconstructing Film Studies*. Madison: University of Wisconsin Press, pp. 37–70.

Carter, R. A. (1982), 'Style and interpretation in Hemingway's "Cat in the Rain"', in R. A. Carter (ed.), *Language and Literature. An Introductory Reader in Stylistics*. London: Unwin Hyman, pp. 64–80.

Carter, R. A. (1993), 'Between languages: Grammar and lexis in Thomas Hardy's "The Oxen"' in P. Verdonk (ed.), *Twentieth-century Poetry: From Text to Context.* London: Routledge, pp. 57–67.

Carter, R. A. (2004), *Language and Creativity. The Art of Common Talk*. London: Routledge.

Carter, R. A (2007a), 'Foreword', in G. Watson and S. Zyngier (eds), *Literature and Stylistics for Language Learners*. London: Palgrave, pp. 1–3.

Carter, R. (2007b), 'Obituary for John Sinclair' published in *Parlance*, October 2007.

Carter, R. A. and Burton, D. (1982), *Literary Text and Language Study*. London: Edward Arnold.

Carter, R. A. and McRae, J. (1996), *Language, Literature and the Learner: Creative Classroom Practice*. Harlow: Longman.

Carter, R. A. and Nash, W. (1990), *Seeing through Language: Guide to Styles of English Writing*. Oxford: Basil Blackwell.

Carter, R. A. and Simpson, P. (eds) (1989), *Language, Discourse and Literature. An Introductory Reader in Discourse Stylistics*. London: Unwin Hyman.

Carter, R. A. and Stockwell, P. (eds) (2008), *The Language and Literature Reader*. London: Routledge.

Chapman, R. (1973), *Linguistics and Literature. An Introduction to Literary Stylistics*. London: Edward Arnold.

Chatman, S. (1978), *Story and Discourse*. Ithaca, New York: Cornell University Press.

Chomsky, N. (1957), *Syntactic Structures*. London: Mouton.

Chomsky, N. (1965), *Aspects of the Theory of Syntax*. Cambridge: MIT Press.

Chomsky, N. (1972a), *Language and Mind*. New York: Harcourt, Brace and World.

Chomsky, N. (1972b), *Studies on Semantics in Generative Grammar*. The Hague: Mouton.

Chomsky, N. (1986), *Knowledge of Language: Its Nature, Origin and Use*. New York: Praeger.

Chomsky, N. (1995), *The Minimalist Program*. Cambridge: MIT Press.

Chomsky, N. and Halle, M. (1968), *The Sound Pattern of English*. New York: Harper and Row.

Clark, H. H. and Clark, E. V. (1977), *Psychology and Language. An Introduction to Psycholinguistics*. USA: Harcourt Brace Jovanovich.

Coates, J. (1983), *The Semantics of the Modal Auxiliaries*. London: Croom Helm.

Cockcroft, R. (2004), 'Putting Aristotle to the proof: Style, substance and the EPL group'. *Language and Literature*, 13, (3), 195–215.

Cockcroft, R. (2005), 'Who talks whose language? George Herbert and the reader's world'. *Language and Literature*, 14, (3), 245–58.

Cohn, D. (1978), *Transparent Minds. Narrative Modes for Presenting Consciousness in Fiction*. Princeton, New Jersey: Princeton University Press.

Collins, J. (2008), *Chomsky: A Guide for the Perplexed*. London: Continuum.

Cook, G. (1994), *Discourse and Literature: The Interplay of Form and Mind*. Oxford: Oxford University Press.

Cook, G. (2000), *Language Play. Language Learning*. Oxford: Oxford University Press.

Cornils, A. and Schernus, W. (2003), 'On the relationship between the theory of the novel, narrative and narratology', in T. Kindt and H. Müller (eds), *What is Narratology?: Questions and Answers Regarding the Status of a Theory*. Berlin and New York: Walter de Gruyter, pp. 137–74.

Coulson, S. (2001), *Semantic Leaps*. Cambridge: Cambridge University Press.

Coulson, S. (2006), 'Conceptual blending in thought, rhetoric, and ideology', in G. Kristiansen, M. Achard, R. Dirven, F. J. Ruiz de Mendoza Ibáñez (eds), *Cognitive Linguistics: Current Applications and Future Perspectives*. Berlin and New York: Mouton de Gruyter, pp. 187–208.

Coulson, S. and Oakley, T. (2000), 'Blending basics'. *Cognitive Linguistics*, 11, (3–4), 175–96.

Crisp, P. (2008), 'Between extended metaphor and allegory: Is blending enough?'. *Language and Literature*, 17, (4), 291–308.

Culler, J. (1975), *Structuralist Poetics*. London: Routledge and Kegan Paul.

Culler, J. (1976), *Saussure*. Glasgow: Fontana/Collins.

Culler, J. (1981), *The Pursuit of Signs: Semiotics, Literature, Deconstruction*. Ithaca: Cornell University Press.

Culpeper, J. (1996), 'Towards an anatomy of impoliteness'. *Journal of Pragmatics*, 25, (3), 349–67.

Culpeper, J. (1998), '(Im)politeness in drama', in J. Culpeper, P. Verdonk and M. Short (eds), *Exploring the Language of Drama: From Text to Context*. London: Routledge, pp. 83–95.

Culpeper, J. (2000), 'A cognitive approach to characterization: Katherina in Shakespeare's *The Taming of the Shrew*'. *Language and Literature*, 9, (4), 291–316.

Culpeper, J. (2001), *Language and Characterisation: People in Plays and other Texts*. Harlow: Longman.

Culpeper, J. and Archer, D. (2008), 'Requests and directness in Early Modern English trial proceedings and play texts, 1640–1760', in A. H. Jucker and I. Taavitsainen (eds), *Speech Acts in the History of English* (Pragmatics and Beyond New Series 176). Amsterdam and Philadelphia: John Benjamins, pp. 45–84.

Culpeper, J., Bousfield, D. and Wichmann, A. (2003), 'Impoliteness revisited: With special reference to dynamic and prosodic aspects'. *Journal of Pragmatics*, 35, (10–11), 1545–79.

Culpeper, J., Short, M. and Verdonk, P. (1998), *Exploring the Language of Drama: From Text to Context*. London: Routledge.

Cupchik, G. C. and Leonard, G. (2001), 'High and popular culture from the viewpoints of psychology and cultural studies', in D. Schram and G. Steen (eds), *The Psychology and Sociology of Literature. In Honor of Elrud Ibsch. Philadelphia*. Amsterdam and Philadelphia: John Benjamins, pp. 421–41.

Currie, G. (2004), 'Cognitivism', in T. Miller and R. Stam (eds), *A Companion to Film Theory*. Oxford: Blackwell Publishing, pp. 105–22.

Damasio, A. (1999), *The Feeling of What Happens: Body and Emotion in the Making of Consciousness*. New York: Harcourt Brace.

Dancygier, B. (2005), 'Blending and narrative viewpoint: Jonathan Raban's travels through mental spaces'. *Language and Literature*, 14, (2), 99–127.

Dancygier, B. (2006), 'What can blending do for you?'. *Language and Literature*, 15, (1), 5–15.

Darby, D. (2001), 'Form and context: An essay in the history of narratology'. *Poetics Today*, 22, (4), 829–52.

De Cuypere, L. (2008), *Limiting the Iconic. From the Metatheoretical Foundations to the Creative Possibilities of Iconicity in Language*. Amsterdam and Philadelphia: John Benjamins.

Deignan, A. (1999), 'Corpus-based research into metaphor', in L. Cameron and G. Low (eds), *Researching and Applying Metaphor*. Cambridge: Cambridge University Press, pp. 177–99.

Deignan, A. (2005), *Metaphor and Corpus Linguistics*. Amsterdam and Philadelphia: John Benjamins.

Dillon, G. (1978), *Language Processing and the Reading of Literature. Towards a Model of Comprehension*. Bloomington and London: Indiana University Press.

Doležel, L. (1988), 'Mimesis and possible worlds'. *Poetics Today*, 9, (3), 475–97.

Doležel, L. (1989), 'Possible worlds and literary fictions', in S. Allen (ed.), *Possible Worlds in Humanities, Arts and Sciences*. New York: de Gruyter, pp. 221–42.

Doležel, L. (1998a), *Heterocosmica: Fiction and Possible Worlds*. Baltimore, MD: John Hopkins University Press.

Doležel, L. (1998b), 'Possible worlds of fiction and history'. *New Literary History*, 29, (4), 785–809.

Douthwaite, J. (2000), *Towards a Linguistic Theory of Foregrounding*. Allessandria: Edizioni dell'Orso.

Downes, W. (2000), 'The language of felt experience: Emotional, evaluative and intuitive'. *Language and Literature*, 9, (2), 99–121.

Duchan, J. F., Bruder, G. A. and Hewitt, L. E. (eds) (1995), *Deixis in Narrative. A Cognitive Science Perspective*. Hillsday, NJ: Lawrence Erlbaum Associates, Inc.

Eaton, T. (1966), *The Semantics of Literature*. The Hague: Mouton.

Eco, U. (1979), *The Role of the Reader: Explorations in the Semiotics of Texts*. Bloomington: Indiana University Press.

Edwards, A. D. and Westgate, D. P. G. (1994), *Investigating Classroom Talk*. London: The Falmer Press.

Eggins, S. (1994), *An Introduction to Systemic Functional Linguistics*. Great Britain: Pinter.

Eggins, S. (2004), *An Introduction to Systemic Functional Linguistics*. (2nd edition). London: Continuum.

Eggins, S. and Slade, D. (2005), *Analysing Casual Conversation*. London: Equinox.

Emmott, C. (1992), 'Splitting the referent: An introduction to narrative enactors', in M. Davies and L. J. Ravelli (eds), *Advances in Systemic Linguistics: Recent Theory and Practice*. London: Pinter, pp. 221–8.

Emmott, C. (1994), 'Frames of reference: Contextual monitoring and narrative discourse', in R. M. Coulthard (ed.), *Advances in Written Text Analysis*. London: Routledge, pp. 157–66.

Emmott, C. (1995), 'Consciousness and context-building: Narrative inferences and anaphoric theory', in K. Green (ed.), *New Essays in Deixis*. Amsterdam: Rodopi, pp. 81–97.

Emmott, C. (1996), 'Real grammar in fictional contexts'. *Glasgow Review*, 4, 9–23.

Emmott, C. (1997), *Narrative Comprehension: A Discourse Perspective*. Oxford: Oxford University Press.

Emmott, C. (2002a), 'Responding to style. Cohesion, foregrounding and thematic interpretation', in M. Louwerse and W. van Peer (eds), *Thematics: Interdisciplinary Studies*. Amsterdam and Philadelphia: John Benjamins, pp. 91–117.

Emmott, C. (2002b), '"Split selves" in fiction and in medical "life stories": Cognitive linguistic theory and narrative practice', in E. Semino and J. Culpeper (eds), *Cognitive Stylistics. Language and Cognition in Text Analysis*. Amsterdam and Philadelphia: John Benjamins, pp. 153–81.

Emmott, C. (2003a), 'Reading for pleasure: A cognitive poetic analysis of "twists in the tale" and other plot reversals in narrative texts', in J. Gavins and G. Steen (eds), *Cognitive Poetics in Practice*. London: Routledge, pp. 145–59.

Emmott, C. (2003b), 'Constructing social space: Sociocognitive factors in the interpretation of character relations', in D. Herman (ed.), *Narrative Theory and the Cognitive Sciences*. Stanford, CA: CSLI, pp. 295–321.

Emmott, C. and Sanford, A. J. (2002) *The STACS Project*. http://www.gla.ac.uk/departments/englishlanguage/research/researchprojects/stacsproject/#d.en.53663

Emmott, C., Sanford, A. J. and Dawydiak, E. J. (2007), 'Stylistics meets cognitive science: Studying style in fiction and readers' attention from an interdisciplinary perspective'. *Style*, 41, (2), 204–24.

Emmott, C., Sanford, A. J. and Morrow, L. I. (2006), 'Capturing the attention of readers? Stylistic and psychological perspectives on the use and effect of text fragmentation in narratives'. *Journal of Literary Semantics*, 35, (1), 1–30.

Ermida, I. (2006), 'Linguistic mechanisms of power in *Nineteen-Eighty Four*: Applying politeness theory to Orwell's world'. *Journal of Pragmatics*, 38, (6), 842–62.

Evans, V. and Green, M. (2006), *Cognitive Linguistics: An Introduction*. Edinburgh: Edinburgh University Press.

Fab, N. (1997), *Linguistics and Literature. Language in the Verbal Arts of the World*. Oxford and Massachusetts: Blackwell.

Facchinetti, R., Krug, M. and Palmer, F. (eds) (2003), *Modality in Contemporary English*. Berlin: Mouton de Gruyter.

Fairclough, N. (1989), *Language and Power*. London: Longman.

Fairclough, N. (1995), *Critical Discourse Analysis*. London: Longman.

Fairclough, N. (1997), 'A reply to Henry Widdowson's "Discourse analysis: A critical view"'. *Language and Literature*, 5, (1), 49–56.

Fairclough, N. (2000), *New Labour, New Language*. London: Routledge.

Fauconnier, G. (1994), *Mental Spaces. Aspects of Meaning Construction in Natural Language*. Cambridge: Cambridge University Press.

Fauconnier, G. (1997), *Mappings in Thought and Language*. Cambridge and New York: Cambridge University Press.

Fauconnier, G. and Turner, M. (1998), 'Conceptual integration networks'. *Cognitive Science*, 22, (2), 133–87.

Fauconnier, G. and Turner, M. (2002), *The Way We Think: Conceptual Blending and the Mind's Hidden Complexities*. New York: Basic Books.

Firth, J. R. (1957), *Papers in Linguistics 1934–1951*. London: Oxford University Press.

Fish, S. (1970), 'Literature in the reader. Affective stylistics'. *New Literary History*, 2, 123–62.

Fish, S. E. (1973), 'What is stylistics and why are they saying such terrible things about it?', in J. J. Weber (ed.) (1996), *The Stylistic Reader. From Roman Jakobson to the Present.* London: Arnold, pp. 94–116.

Fish, S. E. (1980), *Is There a Text in This Class? The Authority of Interpretive Communities*. Cambridge, Mass.: Harvard University Press.

Fitzmaurice, S. (2000), 'Tentativeness and insistence in the expression of politeness in Margaret Cavendish's *Sociable Letters*'. *Language and Literature*, 9, (1), 7–24.

Fitzmaurice, S. and Taavitsainen, I. (eds) (2007), *Methods in Historical Pragmatics.* Berlin: Mouton de Gruyter.

Fludernik, M. (1993), *The Fictions of Language and the Languages of Fiction: The Linguistic Representation of Speech and Consciousness*. London: Routledge.

Fludernik, M. (1996), *Towards a 'Natural' Narratology*. London: Routledge.

Fludernik, M. (1998), 'Sprachwissenschaft und Literaturwissenschaft: Paradigmen, Methoden, Funktionen und Anwendungsmöglichkeiten', in A. Nünning (ed.), *Literaturwissenschaftliche Theorien, Modelle und Methoden*. Trier: WVT, pp. 119–36.

Fludernik, M. (2009), *An Introduction to Narratology*. London: Routledge.

Forceville, C. (1996), *Pictorial Metaphor in Advertising*. London and New York: Routledge.

Forceville, C. (1999), 'The metaphor COLIN IS A CHILD in Ian McEwan's, Harold Pinter's, and Paul Schrader's *The Comfort of Strangers*'. *Metaphor and Symbol*, 14, (3), 179–98.

Forceville, C. (2002a), 'The conspiracy in *The Comfort of Strangers*: Narration in the novel and the film'. *Language and Literature*, 11, (2), 119–35.

Forceville, C. (2002b), 'The identification of target and source in pictorial metaphors'. *Journal of Pragmatics*, 34, (1), 1–14.

Forceville, C. (2005a), 'Visual representations of the idealized cognitive model of ANGER in the Asterix album *La Zizanie*'. *Journal of Pragmatics*, 37, (1), 69–88.

Forceville, C. (2005b), 'Cognitive linguistics and multimodal metaphor', in K. Sachs-Hombach (ed.), *Bildwissenschaft: zwischen Reflektion und Anwendung*. Cologne: von Halem, pp. 264–84.

Forceville, C. (2006a), 'Non-verbal and multimodal metaphor in a cognitivist framework: Agendas for research', in G. Kristiansen, M. Achard, R. Dirven and F. J. Ruiz de Mendoza Ibáñez (eds), *Cognitive Linguistics: Current*

Applications and Future Perspective. Berlin and New York: Mouton de Gruyter, pp. 379–402.

Forceville, C. (2007), 'Multimodal metaphor in ten Dutch TV commercials'. *The Public Journal of Semiotics*, 1, (1), 19–51.

Forceville, C. and Urios-Aparisi, E. (eds) (2009), *Multimodal Metaphor*. Berlin: Walter de Gruyter.

Fowler, R. (ed.) (1966), *Essays on Style and Language*. London: Routledge and Kegan Paul.

Fowler, R. (1971), *The Languages of Literature*. London: Routledge and Kegan Paul.

Fowler, R. (1972), 'Style and the concept of deep structure'. *Journal of Literary Semantics*, 1, 5–24.

Fowler, R. (ed.) (1975), *Style and Structure in Literature: Essays in the New Stylistics*. Oxford: Basil Blackwell.

Fowler, R. (1977), *Linguistics and the Novel*. London: Methuen.

Fowler, R. (1979), 'Anti-language in fiction', *Style*, 13, 259–78.

Fowler, R. (1983), 'Polyphony and problematic in *Hard Times*', in R. Giddings (ed.), *The Changing World of Charles Dickens*. New York: Barnes and Noble.

Fowler, R. (1986), *Linguistic Criticism*. Oxford and New York: Oxford University Press.

Fowler, R. (1991), *Language in the News: Discourse and Ideology in the Press*. London: Routledge.

Fowler, R. (1996), *Linguistic Criticism*. 2nd edition. Oxford: Oxford University Press.

Fowler, R., Hodge, R., Kress, G. and Trew, T. (1979), *Language and Control*. London: Routledge and Kegan Paul.

Frawley, W. (ed.) (2006), *The Expression of Modality*. Berlin: Mouton de Gruyter.

Freeman, D. C. (ed.) (1970), *Linguistics and Literary Style*. New York: Holt, Rinehart and Winston, Inc.

Freeman, D. C. (1993), '"According to my bond": *King Lear* and re-cognition'. *Language and Literature*, 2, (1), 1–18.

Freeman, D. C. (1995), '"Catch(ing) the nearest way: Macbeth and cognitive metaphor"'. *Journal of Pragmatics*, 24, (6), 689–708.

Freeman, M. H. (1995), 'Metaphor making meaning: Dickinson's conceptual universe'. *Journal of Pragmatics*, 24, (6), 643–66.

Freeman, M. H. (2003), 'Poetry and the scope of metaphor: Toward a cognitive theory of literature', in A. Barcelona (ed.), *Metaphor and Metonymy at the Crossroads*. Berlin: Mouton de Gruyter, pp. 253–81.

Freeman, M. H. (2005), 'The Poem as complex blend: Conceptual mappings of metaphor in Sylvia Plath's "The Applicant"'. *Language and Literature*, 14, (1), 25–44.

Freeman, M. H. (2006), 'Blending: A response'. *Language and Literature*, 15, (1), 107–17.

Fucks, W. (1955), *Mathematische Analyse von Sprachelementen, Sprachstil und Sprachen*. Köln/Opladen: Westdeutscher Verlag.

Fucks, W. (1968), *Nach allen Regeln der Kunst*. Stuttgart: Deutsche Verlags-Anstalt.

Fucks, W. (1970/71), 'Über den Gesetzesbegriff einer exakten Literaturwissenschaft, erläutert an Sätzen und Satzfolgen'. *Zeitschrift fuer Literaturwissenschaft und Linguistik*, 1, 113–37.

Galbraith, M. (1995), 'Deictic shift theory and the poetics of involvement in narrative', in J. F. Duchan, G. A. Bruder and L. E. Hewitt (eds), *Deixis in Narrative. A Cognitive Science Perspective*. Hillsday, NJ: Lawrence Erlbaum Associates, Inc., pp. 19–59.

Gavins, J. (2003), 'Too much blague? An exploration of the text worlds of Donald Barthelme's *Snow White*', in J. Gavins and G. Steen (eds), *Cognitive Poetics in Practice*. London: Routledge, pp. 129–44.

Gavins, J. (2007), *Text World Theory. An Introduction*. Edinburgh: Edinburgh University Press.

Gavins, J. and Steen, G. (eds) (2003), *Cognitive Poetics in Practice*. London and New York: Routledge.

Genette, G. (1972), *Figures III*. Paris: Seuil.

Genette, G. (1980), *Narrative Discourse*. Ithaca: Cornell University Press.

Genette, G. (1982), *Figures of Literary Discourse*. New York: Columbia University Press.

Gibbons, A. (2010), '"I contain multitudes": Narrative multimodality and the book that bleeds', in R. Page (ed.), *New Perspectives on Narrative and Multimodality*. New York and London: Routledge, pp. 99–114.

Gibbs, R. W. Jr (2003), 'Prototypes in dynamic meaning construal', in J. Gavins and G. Steen (eds), *Cognitive Poetics in Practice*. London: Routledge, pp. 27–40.

Gibbs, R. W., Leggitt, J. S. and Turner E. A. (2002), 'What's special about figurative language in emotional communication?', in S. R. Fussel (ed.),

The Verbal Communication of Emotions. Interdisciplinary Perspectives. Mahwah, NJ: Erlbaum, pp. 125–49.

Givón, T. (1979), *On Understanding Grammar.* New York, San Francisco and London: Academic Press.

Goffman, E. (1955), 'On face-work: An analysis of ritual elements in social interaction'. *Psychiatry*, 18, 213–31.

Goffman, E. (1967), *Interactional Ritual: Essays in Face-to-Face Behaviour.* Chicago: Aldine.

Grady, J. (2005), 'Primary metaphors as inputs to conceptual integration'. *Journal of Pragmatics*, 37, 1595–614.

Grady, J., Oakley, T. and Coulson, S. (1999), 'Blending and metaphor', in R. W. Gibbs and G. Steen (eds), *Metaphor in Cognitive Linguistics.* Amsterdam and Philadelphia: John Benjamins, pp. 101–24.

Green, K. (1992), 'Deixis and the poetic persona'. *Language and Literature*, 1, (2), 121–34.

Green, K. (ed.) (1995), *New Essays on Deixis.* Amsterdam: Rodopi.

Greenbaum, S. and Quirk, R. (1990), *A Student's Grammar of the English Language.* Great Britain: Longman.

Gregoriou, C. (2003), 'Criminally minded: The stylistics of justification in contemporary American crime fiction'. *Style*, 37, (2), 144–59.

Greimas, A. (1966), *Sémantique Structurale.* Paris: Larousse.

Grice, H. P. (1975), 'Logic and conversation', in P. Cole and J. Morgan (eds), *Syntax and Semantics 3: Speech Acts.* New York: Academic Press, pp. 41–58.

Groeben, N. (1994), 'Literaturwissenschaft als empirisch-interdisziplinäre Kulturwissenschaft', in L. Jäger and B. Switalla (eds), *Germanistik in der Mediengeselschaft.* München: Fink, pp. 79–109.

Gross, S. (2000), 'Intentionality and the markedness model in literary codeswitching'. *Journal of Pragmatics*, 32, (9), 1283–303.

Hakemulder, J. F. (2000), *The Moral Laboratory: Experiments Examining the Effects of Reading Literature on Social Perception and Moral Self-Concept.* Amsterdam and Philadelphia: John Benjamins.

Hakemulder, J. F. (2004), 'Foregrounding and its effect on readers' perception'. *Discourse Processes*, 38, (2), 193–218.

Hakemulder, J. F. (2006), 'Literature: Empirical studies', in K. Brown (ed.), *Encyclopaedia of Language and Linguistics.* Amsterdam: Elsevier Science, pp. 274–80.

Hall, G. (2005), *Literature in Language Education*. London: Palgrave Macmillan.

Hall, G. (2009), 'Texts, readers – and real readers'. *Language and Literature*, 18, (3), 333-9.

Hall, G. (2008), 'A grammarian's funeral: On Browning, post-structuralism, and the state of stylistics', In G. Watson (ed.), *The State of Stylistics.* Amsterdam and Philadelphia: John Benjamins, pp. 31–44.

Hall, G. (2008), 'Empirical research into the processing of free indirect discourse and the imperative of ecological validity', in S. Zyngier, M. Bortolussi, A. Chesnolova, and J. Auracher, J. (eds), *Directions in Empirical Literary Studies*. Amsterdam and Philadelphia: John Benjamins, pp. 21–34.

Halliday, M. A. K. (1971), 'Linguistic function and literary style: An inquiry into the language of William Golding's *The Inheritors*', in D. C. Freeman (ed.) (1981), *Essays in Modern Stylistics*. London and New York: Methuen, pp. 325–60.

Halliday, M. A. K. (1994), *An Introduction to Functional Grammar*. London and Sydney: Arnold.

Halliday, M. A. K. (2004), *An Introduction to Functional Grammar*, 3rd edition. London: Arnold.

Halliday, M. A. K. and Hasan, R. (1976), *Cohesion in English.* London and New York: Longman.

Hanauer, D. I. (2001), 'What we know about reading poetry: Theoretical positions and empirical research', in D. Schram and G. Steen (eds), *The Psychology and Sociology of Literature. In Honor of Elrud Ibsch*. Amsterdam and Philadelphia: John Benjamins, pp. 107–28.

Hayes, C. W. (1966), 'A study in prose styles: Edward Gibbon and Ernest Hemingway'. *Texas Studies in Literature and Language*, 7, 371–86.

Herman, D. (2001), 'Spatial reference in narrative domains'. *Text*, 21, (4), 515–41.

Herman, D. (2002), *Story Logic: Problems and Possibilities of Narrative.* Nebraska: University of Nebraska Press.

Herman, D. (2005a), 'Histories of narrative theory (I): A genealogy of early developments', in J. Phelan and P. Rabinowitz (eds), *A Companion to Narrative Theory*. Malden, MA: Blackwell, pp. 19–35.

Herman, D. (ed.) (2005b), *Routledge Encyclopedia of Narrative Theory.* London and New York: Routledge.

Herman, D. (2006a), 'Narrative: Cognitive approaches', in K. Brown (ed.), *Encyclopaedia of Language and Linguistics.* Amsterdam: Elsevier Science, pp. 452–9.

Herman, D. (2006b), 'Genette meets Vygotsky: Narrative embedding and distributed intelligence'. *Language and Literature*, 15, (4), 357–80.

Herman, D. (ed.) (2007a), *The Cambridge Companion to Narrative*. Cambridge: Cambridge University Press.

Herman, D. (2007b), 'Narratology', in D. Herman (ed.), *The Cambridge Companion to Narrative*. Cambridge: Cambridge University Press, p. 280.

Herman, D. (2009), *Basic Elements of Narrative*. Malden, MA and Oxford: Wiley-Blackwell.

Herman, D., Jahn, M. and Ryan, M. L. (2005), 'Extradiegetic narrator', in D. Herman, J. Manfred and M. L. Ryan (eds), *Routledge Encyclopedia of Narrative Theory*. London and New York: Routledge, p. 156.

Herman, V. (1995), *Dramatic Discourse: Dialogue as Interaction in Plays*. London: Routledge.

Hidalgo-Downing, L. (2002), 'Creating things that are not: The role of negation in the poetry of Wisława Szymborska'. *Journal of Literary Semantics*, 31, 113–32.

Hidalgo-Downing, L. (2003), 'Negation as a stylistic feature in Joseph Heller's *Catch-22*: A corpus study'. *Style*, 37 (3), 318–41.

Hochberg, J. and Brooks, V. (1996), 'Movies in the mind's eye', in D. Bordwell and N. Carroll (eds), *Post-Theory. Reconstructing Film Studies*. Madison: University of Wisconsin Press, pp. 368–87.

Hoey, M. (2005), *Lexical Priming. A New Theory of Words and Language*. London: Routledge.

Holland, N. (1968), *The Dynamics of Literary Response*. New York: Oxford University Press.

Holland, N. (1975), *5 Readers Reading*. London: Yale University Press.

Hoover, D. L. (1999), *Language and Style in The Inheritors*. Lanham: University Press of America.

Hoover, D. L. (2004), 'Altered texts, altered worlds, altered styles'. *Language and Literature*, 13, (2), 99–118.

Hoover, D. L., Culpeper, J. and Louw, B. (2007), *Approaches to Corpus Stylistics. The Corpus, the Computer and the Study of Literature*. London: Routledge.

Hori, M. (2004), *Investigating Dickens's Style. A Collocational Analysis*. London: Palgrave.

Horn, L. (1988), 'Pragmatic theory', in F. J. Newmeyer (ed.), *Linguistics. The Cambridge Survey*. Vol. 1. Cambridge: Cambridge University Press, pp. 113–45.

Hoye, L. (1997), *Adverbs and Modality in English*. London and New York: Longman.

Hunston, S. (2006), 'Corpus linguistics', in K. Brown (ed.), *Encyclopedia of Language and Linguistics*. Vol. 3. Amsterdam, Elsevier, pp. 234–48.

Hunston, S. and Francis, G. (1999), *Pattern Grammar. A Corpus-Driven Approach to the Lexical Grammar of English*. Amsterdam and Philadelphia: John Benjamins.

Ibsch, E. (1994), 'Das Selbstverständnis der Literaturwissenschaft in den Niederlanden', in A. Barsch, G. Rusch and R. Viehoff (eds), *Empirische Literaturwissenschaft in der Diskussion*. Frankfurt: Suhrkamp, pp. 39–54.

Ibsch, E. (1998), 'Statement within plenary discussion on methods', paper presented at the Fifth Biennial IGEL Conference, Utrecht University.

Iser, W. (1978), *The Act of Reading: A Theory of Aesthetic Response*. Baltimore: Johns Hopkins University Press.

Jackson, S. (1993), 'Love and romance as objects of feminist knowledge', in M. Kennedy, C. Lubelska and V. Walsh (eds), *Making Connections: Women's Studies, Women's Movements, Women's Lives*. London and Washington: Taylor and Francis, pp. 39–50.

Jacobs, A. and Jucker, A. H. (1995), 'The historical perspective in pragmatics', in A. H. Jucker (ed.), *Historical Pragmatics: Pragmatic Development in the History of English* (Pragmatics and Beyond. New Series 35). Amsterdam and Philadelphia: John Benjamins, pp. 3–36.

Jahn, M. (2007), 'Focalization', in D. Herman (ed.), *The Cambridge Companion to Narrative*. Cambridge: Cambridge University Press, pp. 94–108.

Jäkel, O. (1999), 'Kant, Blumemberg, Weinrich: Some forgotten contributions to the cognitive theory of metaphor', in R. W. Gibbs Jr. and G. J. Steen (eds), *Metaphor in Cognitive Linguistics*. Amsterdam and Philadelphia: John Benjamins, pp. 9–27.

Jakobson, R. (1956), 'Two aspects of language and two types of aphasic disturbances', in R. Jakobson and M. Halle (1956), *Fundamentals of Language*. The Hague: Mouton, pp. 69–96.

Jakobson, R. (1960), 'Closing Statement: Linguistics and poetics', in T. A. Sebeok (ed.), *Style in Language*. Cambridge, Mass.: MIT Press, pp. 350–77.

Jakobson, R. (1987), *Language in Literature* (edited by K. Pomorska and S. Rudy). Cambridge, Mass.: Belknap Press.

Jakobson, R. and Jones, L. G. (1970), *Shakespeare's Verbal Art in 'Th' Expense of Spirit*. The Hague: Mouton.

Jakobson, R. and Lévi-Strauss, C. (1962), '"Les Chats" de Charles Baudelaire'. *L'Homme*, 2, 5–21. (English translation in M. Lane (ed.) (1970), *Structuralism: A Reader*. London: Jonathan Cape).

Jefferson, A. (1981), 'The place of free indirect discourse in the poetics of fiction: With examples from Joyce's "Eveline"'. *Essays in Poetics*, 5, (1), 36–47.

Jeffries, L. (1994), 'Language in common: Apposition in contemporary poetry by women', in K. Wales (ed.), *Feminist Linguistics in Literary Criticism*. Woodbridge, England: Boydell and Brewer, pp. 21–50.

Jeffries, L. (2000), 'Point of view and the reader in the poetry of Carol Ann Duffy', in L. Jeffries and P. Sansom (eds), *Contemporary Poems: Some Critical Approaches*. Huddersfield: Smith/Doorstop Press, pp. 54–68.

Jeffries, L. (2001), 'Schema affirmation and white asparagus: Cultural multilingualism among readers of texts'. *Language and Literature*, 10, (4), 325–43.

Jeffries, L. (2007), *Textual Construction of the Female Body. A Critical Discourse Approach*. Houndmills, Basingstoke: Palgrave Macmillan.

Jeffries, L. (2008), 'The role of style in reader-involvement: Deictic shifting in contemporary poems'. *Journal of Literary Semantics*, 37, 69–85.

Jeffries, L. (2010), *Critical Stylistics. The Power of English*. Houndmills, Basingstoke: Palgrave Macmillan.

Jespersen, O. (1917), *Negation in English and Other Languages*. Copenhagen: Det Kgl. Danske Videnskabernes Selskab.

Jones, A. (1986), 'Mills & Boon meets feminism', in J. Radford (ed.), *The Progress of Romance. The Politics of Popular Fiction*. London and New York: Routledge, pp. 195–218.

Jucker, A. H. and Taavitsainen, I. (2000), 'Diachronic speech act analysis: Insults from flyting to flaming'. *Journal of Historical Pragmatics*, 1, (1), 67–95.

Jucker, A. H. and Taavitsainen, I. (eds) (2008), *Speech Acts in the History of English*. Amsterdam and Philadelphia: John Benjamins

Kant, E. ([1787] 1963), *Critique of Pure Reason*. London: Macmillan.

Kellner, D. (1999), 'Cultural industries', in T. Miller and R. Stam (eds), *A Companion to Film Theory*. Oxford: Blackwell Publishing, pp. 202–20.

Kennedy, C. (1982), 'Systemic grammar and its use in literary analysis', in R. Carter (ed.), *Language and Literature: An Introductory Reader in Stylistics*. London: George Allen and Unwin, pp. 83–99.

Kindt, T. and Müller, H. (2003), 'Preface', in T. Kindt and H. Müller (eds), *What Is Narratology?: Questions and Answers Regarding the Status of a Theory*. Berlin and New York: Walter de Gruyter, pp. v–vii.

Kohnen, T. (2000), 'Explicit Performatives in Old English'. *Journal of Historical Pragmatics*, 1, (2), 301–21.

Kortman, B. (2005), *English Linguistics: Essentials*. Berlin: Cornelsen.

Kövecses, Z. (2002), *Metaphor. A Practical Introduction*. Oxford: Oxford University Press.

Kress, G. and van Leeuwen, T. (1996), *Reading Images – The Grammar of Visual Design*. London: Routledge.

Kress, G. and van Leeuwen, T. (2001), *Multimodal Discourse – The Modes and Media of Contemporary Communication*. London: Arnold.

Kress, G. and van Leeuwen, T. (2002), 'Colour as a semiotic mode: Notes for a grammar of colour'. *Visual Communication*, 1, (3), 343–68.

Kripke, S. (1972), *Naming and Necessity*. Oxford: Blackwell.

Krug, M. G. (2000), *Emerging English Modals. A Corpus-Based Study of Grammaticalization*. Berlin: Mouton de Gruyter.

Labov, W. (1972), *Language in the Inner City*. Philadelphia: University of Pennsylvania Press.

Labov, W. (1997), 'Some further steps in narrative analysis'. *Journal of Narrative and Life History*, 7, (1–4), 395–415.

Labov, W. and Waletzky, J. (1967), 'Narrative analysis. Oral versions of personal experience', in J. Helm (ed.), *Essays on Verbal and Visual Arts*. Seattle: University of Washington Press for the American Ethnological Society, pp. 12–44.

Lakoff, G. (2004), *Don't Think of an Elephant! Know Your Values and Frame the Debate: The Essential Guide for Progressives*. Vermont: Chelsea Green Publishing.

Lakoff, G. and Johnson, M. (1980), *Metaphors We Live By*. Chicago: University of Chicago Press.

Lakoff, G. and Johnson, M. (1998), *Philosophy in the Flesh*. Chicago, IL and London: University of Chicago Press.

Lakoff, G. and Johnson, M. (2003), *Metaphors We Live By*. 2nd edition. Chicago: University of Chicago Press.

Langacker, R. W. (1987), *Foundations of Cognitive Grammar. Vol I: Theoretical Perspectives*. Stanford, CA: Stanford University Press.

Langacker, R. W. (1991), *Foundations of Cognitive Grammar. Vol II: Descriptive Application*. Stanford, CA: Stanford University Press.

Langer, S. K. (1953), *Feeling and Form: A Theory of Art*. New York: Charles Scribner's.

Langer, S. K. (1967), *Mind: An Essay on Human Feeling*. Baltimore, MD: Johns Hopkins University Press.

Leech, G. (1965), '*This Bread I Break*: Language and interpretation'. *Review of English Literature*, 6, (2), 66–75.

Leech, G. (1966), 'Linguistics and the figures of rhetoric', in R. G. Fowler (ed.), *Essays in Style and Language*. London: Routledge and Kegan Paul, pp. 135–56.

Leech, G. (1969), *A Linguistic Guide to English Poetry*. London: Longman.

Leech, G. (1983), *Principles of Pragmatics*. London: Longman.

Leech, G. (1987), 'Stylistics and functionalism', in N. Fabb, D. Attridge, A. Durant and C. MacCabe (eds), *The Linguistics of Writing: Arguments between Language and Literature*. Manchester: Manchester University Press, pp. 76–88.

Leech, G. (1992), 'Pragmatic principles in Shaw's *You Never Can Tell*', in M. Toolan (ed.), *Language, Text and Context: Essays in Stylistics*. London: Routledge, pp. 259–79.

Leech, G. (1999), 'The distribution and function of vocatives in American and British English conversation', in H. Hasselgard and S. Oksefjell (eds), *Out of Corpora. Studies in Honour of Stig Johansson*. Amsterdam: Rodopi, pp. 107–18.

Leech, G. (2007), 'Style in fiction revisited: The beginning of *Great Expectations*'. *Style*, 41, (2), 117–32.

Leech, G. (2008), *Language in Literature. Style and Foregrounding*. Harlow, England: Pearson Longman.

Leech, G. and Short, M. (1981), *Style in Fiction: A Linguistic Introduction to English Fictional Prose*. London: Longman.

Leech, G. and Short, M. (2007), *Style in Fiction. A Linguistic Introduction to English Fictional Prose*. 2nd edition. Harlow: Pearson Longman.

Leech, G. and Svartvik, J. (2002), *A Communicative Grammar of English*. Harlow: Pearson Limited.

Levinson, S. C. (1983), *Pragmatics*. Cambridge: Cambridge University Press.

Lewis, D. (1973), *Counterfactuals*. Cambridge: Cambridge University Press.

Litosseliti, L. and Sunderland, J. (2002), *Gender Identity and Discourse Analysis*. Amsterdam and Philadelphia: John Benjamins.

Lodge, D. (1977), *The Modes of Modern Writing. Metaphor, Metonomy, and the Typology of Modern Literature*. London: Edward Arnold.

Louw, B. (1997), 'The role of corpora in critical literary appreciation', in A. Wichman, S. Fligelstone, T. McEnery and G. Knowles (eds), *Teaching and Language Corpora*. London: Longman, pp. 240–52.

Louw, W. E. (2000), 'Contextual prosodic theory. Bringing semantic prosodies to life', in C. Heffener and H. Sauntson (eds), *Words in Context*. Birmingham: Birmingham University Press, pp. 48–94.

Louw, W. E. (2006), 'Literary worlds as collocation', in G. Watson and S. Zyngier (eds), *Literature and Stylistics for Language Learners. Theory and Practice*. London: Palgrave, pp. 91–105.

Low, G (2003), 'Validating metaphoric models in applied linguistics', *Metaphor and Symbol*, 18, (4), 239-54.

Lyons, J. (1977), *Semantics: Volume I*. Cambridge: Cambridge University Press.

Lyons, J. (1977), *Semantics: Volume II*. Cambridge: Cambridge University Press.

Mackay, R. (1996), 'Mything the point: A critique of objective stylistics'. *Language and Communication*, 16, (1), 81–93.

Mahlberg, M. (2006), 'Lexical cohesion: Corpus linguistic theory and its application in English language teaching'. International Journal of Corpus Linguistics, 11, (3), 227-47.

Mahlberg, M. (2007), 'Corpus stylistics. Bridging the gap between linguistic and literary studies', in M. Hoey, M. Mahlberg and M. Stubbs (eds), *Text, Discourse and Corpora*. London: Continuum, pp. 219–46.

Mahon, J. E. (1999), 'Getting your sources right. What Aristotle didn't say', in L. Cameron and G. Low (eds), *Researching and Applying Metaphor*. Cambridge: Cambridge University Press, pp. 69–80.

Mandala, S. (2007), *Twentieth-Century Drama Dialogue as Ordinary Talk: Speaking Between the Lines*. Aldershot: Ashgate.

Marmaridou, S. (2000), *Pragmatic Meaning and Cognition*. Amsterdam and Philadelphia: John Benjamins.

McAllister, S. (2006), '"The explosive devices of memory": Trauma and the construction of identity in narrative'. *Language and Literature*, 15, (1), 91–106.

McCarthy, M. and Carter, R. (1994), *Language as Discourse. Perspectives for Language Teaching*. London: Longman.

McCarthy, M. and Carter, R. A. (2006), *Cambridge Grammar of English. A Comprehensive Guide Spoken and Written English Grammar and Usage*. Cambridge: Cambridge University Press.

McFarlane, B. (1996), *Novel to Film. An Introduction to the Theory of Adaptation*. Oxford: Clarendon Press.

McFarlane, B. (2000), 'It wasn't like that in the book'. *Literature/Film Quarterly*, 28, (3), 163–9.

McGilvray, J. (1999), *Chomsky: Language, Mind, and Politics*. Cambridge: Polity Press.

McHale, B. (1978), 'Free indirect discourse. A survey of recent accounts'. *Poetics and Theory of Literature*, 3, 249–87.

McHale, B. (2007), 'Introduction to Bell's chapter', in M. Lambrou and P. Stockwell (eds), *Contemporary Stylistics*. London: Continuum, pp. 43–4.

McIntyre, D. (2004), 'Point of view in drama: A socio-pragmatic analysis of Dennis Potter's *Brimstone and Treacle*'. *Language and Literature*, 13, (2), 139–60.

McIntyre, D. (2005), 'Logic, reality and mind style in Alan Bennett's *The Lady in the Van*'. *Journal of Literary Semantics*, 34, (1), 21–40.

McIntyre, D. (2006), *Point of View in Plays. A Cognitive Stylistic Approach to Viewpoint in Drama and Other Text-Types*. Amsterdam and Philadelphia: John Benjamins.

McIntyre, D. (2007a), 'Deixis, cognition and the construction of viewpoint', in M. Lambrou and P. Stockwell (eds), *Contemporary Stylistics*. London: Continuum, pp. 118–30.

McIntyre, D. (2007b), 'Trusting the text: Corpus linguistics and stylistics'. *International Journal of Corpus Linguistics,* 12, (4), 565–77.

McIntyre, D. (2008), 'Integrating multimodal analysis and the stylistics of drama: A multimodal perspective on Ian McKellen's *Richard III*'. *Language and Literature*, 17, (4), 309–34.

Mey, J. L. (1999), *When Voices Clash. A Study in Literary Pragmatics*. Berlin and New York: Mouton de Gruyter.

Miall, D. and Kuiken, D. (1994a), 'Foregrounding, defamiliarization, and affect. Response to literary stories'. *Poetics*, 22, 389–407.

Miall, D. S. and Kuiken, D. (1994b), 'Beyond text theory: Understanding literary response'. *Discourse Processes*, 17, (3), 337–52.

Miller, D. R. and Turci, M. (2007), *Language and Verbal Art Revisited. Linguistic Approaches to the Study of Literature*. London and Oakville: Equinox.

Mills, S. (1995), *Feminist Stylistics*. London: Routledge.

Mills, S. (2006), 'Feminist stylistics', in K. Brown (ed.), *Encyclopaedia of Language and Linguistics*. Amsterdam: Elsevier Science, pp. 221–3.

Montoro, R. (2006a), 'Text world theory and cinematic discourse', paper presented at the Annual Conference of the Poetics and Linguistics Association, July 2006. University of Joensuu, Finland.

Montoro, R. (2006b), 'Analysing literature through films', in G. Watson and S. Zyngier (eds), *Literature and Stylistics for Language Learners: Theory and Practice*. Basingstoke: Palgrave, pp. 48–59.

Montoro, R. (2007), 'The stylistics of popular fiction: A socio-cognitive perspective', in M. Lambrou and P. Stockwell (eds), *Contemporary Stylistics*. London: Continuum, pp. 68–80.

Montoro, R. (2010a), 'A multimodal approach to mind style: Semiotic metaphor vs. multimodal conceptual metaphor', in R. Page (ed.), *New Perspectives on Narrative and Multimodality*. New York and London: Routledge, pp. 31–49.

Montoro, R. (2010b), 'Cinematic mind style and modal systems', in R. Piazza, F. Rossi, M. Bednarek (eds), *Telecinematic Discourse: An Introduction to the Fictional Language of Cinema and Television*. Amsterdam and Philadelphia: John Benjamins.

Montoro, R. (2011, fc), *The Stylistics of Chick Lit. An Analysis of Cappuccino Fiction*. London: Continuum.

Nanajec, L. (2009), 'Negation and the creation of implicit meaning in poetry'. *Language and Literature*, 18, (2), 109–27.

Nänny, M. and Fischer, O. (eds) (2003), *Iconicity in Language and Literature*. Amsterdam and Philadelphia: John Benjamins.

Nash, W. (1982), 'On a passage from Lawrence's "Odour of Chrysanthemums"', in R. Carter (ed.), *Language and Literature: An Introductory Reader in Stylistics*. London: Allen and Unwin, pp. 201–20.

Nash, W. (1985), *The Language of Humour*. London: Longman.

Nash, W. (1986a), *English Usage: A Guide to First Principles*. London: Routledge.

Nash, W. (1986b), 'Sound and the pattern of poetic meaning', in T. D'haen (ed.), *Linguistics and the Study of Literature*. Amsterdam: Rodopi, pp. 128–51.

Nash, W. (1990), *Language in Popular Fiction*. London: Routledge.

Nash, W. (1992), *An Uncommon Tongue: The Uses and Resources of English*. London: Routledge.

Nash, W. (1993a), *Jargon: Its Uses and Abuses*. Oxford: Basil Blackwell.

Nash, W. (1993b), 'The lyrical game: C. Day Lewis's "Last Words"', in P. Verdonk (ed.), *Twentieth-Century Poetry: From Text to Context*. London: Routledge, pp. 46–56.

Nash, W. (1998), *Language and the Creative Illusion: The Writing Game*. London: Longman.

Nash, W. (2000), 'The writing on the wall', in T. Bex, M. Burke and P. Stockwell (eds), *Contextualized Stylistics*. Amsterdam: Rodopi, pp. 1–14.

Nash, W. (2008a), 'A matter of versifying: Tradition, innovation and the sonnet form in English', in S. Zyngier, M. Bortolussi, A. Chesnokova and J. Auracher (eds), *Directions in Empirical Literary Studies*. Amsterdam and Philadelphia: John Benjamins, pp. 329–42.

Nash, W. (2008b), 'The value of Juvenal', in W. van Peer (ed.), *The Quality of Literature*. Amsterdam and Philadelphia: John Benjamins, pp. 139–58.

Nølke, H. (2006), 'The semantics of polyphony (and the pragmatics of realization)'. *Acta Linguistica Hafniensia*, 38, 2–25.

Nørgaard, N. (2003), *Systemic Functional Linguistics and Literary Analysis. A Hallidayan Approach to Joyce – a Joycean Approach to Halliday*. Odense, Denmark: University Press of Southern Denmark.

Nørgaard, N. (2007), 'Disordered collarettes and uncovered tables. Negative polarity as a stylistic device in Joyce's "Two Gallants"'. *Journal of Literary Semantics*, 36, 35–52.

Nørgaard, N. (2009), 'The semiotics of typography in literary texts. A multimodal approach'. *Orbis Litterarum*, 64, (2), 141–60.

Nørgaard, N. (2010a), 'Multimodality and the literary text: Making sense of Safran Foer's *Extremely Loud and Incredibly Close*', in R. Page (ed.), *New Perspectives on Narrative and Multimodality*. New York and London: Routledge, pp. 115–26.

Nørgaard, N. (2010b), 'Multimodality: Extending the stylistic tool kit', in D. McIntyre and B. Busse (eds), *Language and Style*. Houndmills, Basingstoke: Palgrave.

Nørgaard, N. (2010c, fc), 'Teaching multimodal stylistics', in L. Jeffries and D. McIntyre (eds), *Teaching Stylistics*. London: Palgrave Macmillan.

Nuyts, J. (2001), *Epistemic Modality, Language and Conceptualization. A Cognitive-Pragmatic Perspective.* Amsterdam and Philadelphia: John Benjamins.

O'Halloran, K. (2004), 'Visual semiosis in film', in K. O'Halloran (ed.), *Multimodal Discourse Analysis: Systemic Functional Perspectives*. London: Continuum, pp. 109–30.

Oatley, K., Kelter, D. and Jenkins, J. M. (2006), *Understanding Emotions*. Malden, MA and Oxford: Blackwell Publishing.

OED = Oxford English Dictionary, http://www.oed.com

Ohmann, R. (1964), 'Generative grammars and the concept of literary style'. *Word*, 20, 423–39.

Ohmann, R. (1966), 'Literature as sentences'. *College English*, 27, 261–7.

O'Regan, T. (1999), 'Cultural exchange', in T. Miller R. Stam (eds), *A Companion to Film Theory*. Oxford: Blackwell Publishing, pp. 262–94.

O'Toole, M. (1994), *The Language of Displayed Art*. London: Leicester University Press.

Owens, M. and Reinfurt, D. (2005), 'Pure data: moments in a history of machine-readable type', *Visual Communication*, 4, (2), 144-50.

Page, N. (1973), *Speech in the English Novel*. London: Longman.

Page, R. (2006), 'Feminist narratology', in K. Brown (ed.), *Encyclopaedia of Language and Linguistics.* Amsterdam: Elsevier Science, pp. 482–4.

Page, R. (2007a), '*Bridget Jones's Diary* and feminist narratology', in M. Lambrou and P. Stockwell (eds), *Contemporary Stylistics*. London: Continuum, pp. 93–105.

Page, R. (2007b), 'Gender', in D. Herman (ed.), *The Cambridge Companion to Narrative*. Cambridge: Cambridge University Press, pp. 189–202.

Palmer, A. (2004), *Fictional Minds*. Lincoln and London: University of Nebraska Press.

Palmer, F. R. (1986), *Mood and Modality*. Cambridge: Cambridge University Press.

Palmer, F. R. (1990), *Modality and the English Modals*. Harlow: Longman.

Palmer, F. R. (2001), *Mood and Modality*. 2nd edition. Cambridge: Cambridge University Press.

Papafragou, A. (2002), 'Modality and theory of mind. Perspectives from language development and autism', in S. Barbiers, W. van der Wurff and F. Beukema (eds), *Modality and its Interaction with the Verbal System*. Amsterdam and Philadelphia: John Benjamins, pp. 185–204.

Pascal, R. (1977), *The Dual Voice*. Manchester: Manchester University Press.

Pavel, T. G. (1986), *Fictional Worlds*. London: Harvard University Press.

Peirce, C. S. (1931–58), *Collected Papers*. Cambridge: Harvard University Press.

Perkins, M. R. (1983), *Modal Expressions in English*. London: Frances Pinter.

Plantinga, A. (1979), 'Actualism and possible worlds'. *Loux*, 253-73.

Plummer, P. and Busse, B. (2006), 'E-learning and *Language and Style* in Mainz and Münster'. *Language and Literature*, 15, (3), 257–76.

Pope, R. (1994), *Textual Intervention: Critical and Creative Strategies for Literary Studies*. London: Routledge.

Pope, R. (2002), *The English Studies Book*. 2nd edition. London: Routledge.

Portner, P. (2009), *Modality*. Oxford: Oxford University Press.

Prince, G. (2003a), *A Dictionary of Narratology*. Lincoln: University of Nebraska Press.

Prince, G. (2003b), 'Surveying narratology', in T. Kindt and H. (eds), *What Is Narratology?: Questions and Answers Regarding the Status of a Theory.* Berlin and New York: Walter de Gruyter, pp. 1–16.

Propp, V. ([1928] 1968), *Morphology of the Folktale*. Austin, Texas: University of Texas Press.

Pun, B. O. K. (2008), 'Metafunctional analyses of sound in film communication', in L. Unsworth (ed.), *Multimodal Semiotics. Functional Analysis in Contexts of Education*. London: Continuum, pp. 105– 21.

Punday, D. (2005), 'Creative accounting: Role-playing games, possible-worlds theory, and the agency of imagination'. *Poetics Today*, 26, (1), 113–39.

Quigley, J. (2000), *The Grammar of Autobiography: A Developmental Account*. Mahwah, NJ: Lawrence Erlbaum Associates.

Quirk, R., Greenbaum, S., Leech, G. and Svartvik, J. (1985), *A Comprehensive Grammar of the English Language*. Essex: Longman.

Ramachandran, V. S. and Blakeslee, S. (1998), *Phantoms in the Brain: Probing the Mysteries of the Human Mind*. New York: William Morrow.

Rayson, P. (2007), *Wmatrix: A Web-based Corpus Processing Environment*. Lancaster: Computing Department, Lancaster University, http://ucrel.lancs.ac.uk/wmatrix/

Rescher, N. (1979), 'The ontology of the possible'. *Loux*, 166-81.

Richards, I. A. (1936), *The Philosophy of Rhetoric*. Oxford: Oxford University Press.

Riffaterre, M. (1959), 'Criteria for style analysis'. *Word*, 15, 154–74.

Riffaterre, M. (1966), 'Describing poetic structures: Two approaches to Baudelaire's "Les Chats"'. *Yale French Studies*, 36/37, 200–42.

Rimmon-Kenan, Sh. (1983), *Narrative Fiction. Contemporary Poetics*. London and New York: Routledge.

Rimmon-Kenan, Sh. (2002), *Narrative Fiction. Contemporary Poetics*. 2nd edition. London and New York: Routledge.

Rubik, M. and Widdowson, H. G. (2000), 'The stylistic intersection: On an integrated course in language and literature'. *AAA*, 25, (1), 5–28.

Rudanko, J. (2006), 'Aggravated impoliteness and two types of speaker intention in an episode in Shakespeare's *Timon of Athens*'. *Journal of Pragmatics*, 38, (6), 829–41.

Rumelhart, D. E. (1975), 'Notes on a schema for stories', in D. G. Bobrow and A. Collins (eds), *Representation and Understanding*. New York: Academic Press, pp. 211–36.

Rumelhart, D. E. (1980), 'Schemata: The building blocks of cognition', in R. J. Spiro, B. Bruce and W. Brewer (eds), *Theoretical Issues in Reading Comprehension: Perspectives from Cognitive Psychology, Linguistics, Artificial Intelligence and Education*. Hillsdale, NJ: Lawrence Erlbaum Associates, pp. 33–58.

Rumelhart, D. E. (1984), 'Schemata and the cognitive system', in R. S. Wyer and T. K. Srull (eds), *Handbook of Social Cognition, vol. 1*. Hillsdale, NJ: Lawrence Erlbaum Associates, pp. 161–88.

Rumelhart, D. E. and Norman, D. A. (1978), 'Accretion, tuning and restructuring: Three modes of learning', in J. W. Cotton and R. L. Klatzky (eds), *Semantic Factors in Cognition*. Hillsdale, NJ: Lawrence Erlbaum Associates, pp. 37–53.

Rumelhart, D. E. and Ortony, A. (1977), 'The representation of knowledge in memory', in R. C. Anderson, R. J. Spiro and W. E. Montague (eds), *Schooling and the Acquisition of Knowledge*. Hillsdale, NJ: Lawrence Erlbaum Associates, pp. 99–135.

Ryan, M. L. (1991a), *Possible Worlds, Artificial Intelligence and Narrative Theory*. Bloomington: Indiana University Press.

Ryan, M. L. (1991b), 'Possible worlds and accessibility relations: A semantic typology of fiction'. *Poetics Today*, 12, (3), 553–76.

Ryan, M. L. (1992), 'Possible worlds in recent literary theory'. *Style*, 26, (4), 528–52.

Ryan, M. L. (1998), 'The text as world versus the text as game: Possible worlds semantics and postmodern theory'. *Journal of Literary Semantics*, 27, (3), 137–63.

Ryan, M. L. (2006), 'From parallel universes to possible worlds: Ontological pluralism in physics, narratology, and narrative'. *Poetics Today*, 27, (4), 633–74.

Ryan, M. L. (2007), 'Toward a definition of narrative', in D. Herman (ed.), *The Cambridge Companion to Narrative*. Cambridge: Cambridge University Press, pp. 22–35.

Ryder, M. E. (1999), 'Smoke and mirrors: Event patterns in the discourse structure of a romance novel'. *Journal of Pragmatics*, 31, (8), 1067-80.

Ryder, M. E. (1999), 'Bankers and blue-chippers: an account of -er formations in Present-day English'. *English Language and Linguistics*, 3, (2), 269-97.

Sacks, H., Schegloff, E. and Jefferson, G. (1974), 'A simplest systematics for the organization of turn-taking in conversation'. *Language*, 50, 696–735.

Sacks, H., Schegloff, E. and Jefferson, G. (1978), 'A simplest systematics for the organization of turn-taking for conversation', in J. Schenkein (ed.), *Studies in the Organization of Conversational Interaction*. New York: Academic, pp. 7–55.

Saeed, J. L. (1997), *Semantics*. Malden, MA: Blackwell.

Sanders, C. (ed.) (2004), *The Cambridge Companion to Saussure*. Cambridge: Cambridge University Press.

Sanders, J. and Redeker, G. (1996), 'Perspective and the representation of speech and thought in narrative discourse', in G. Fauconnier and E. Sweetser (eds), *Spaces, Worlds and Grammar*. Chicago and London: The University of Chicago Press, pp. 290–317.

Sanford, A. J. S, Sanford, A. J., Molle, J. and Emmott, C. (2006), 'Shallow processing and attention capture in written and spoken discourse'. *Discourse Processes*, 42, (2), 109–30.

Saussure, F. de (1916), *Cours de linguistique générale*. C. Bally and A. Sechehaye (eds), Lausanne and Paris: Payot. Translated by W. Baskin (1977), *Course in General Linguistics*. Glasgow: Fontana/Collins.

Saussure, F. de (2002), *Écrits de linguistique générale*. Simon Bouquet and Rudolf Engler (eds), Paris: Gallimard. Translated by M. Pires (2006), *Writings in General Linguistics*. Oxford: Oxford University Press.

Schank, R. C. (1982a), *Dynamic Memory: A Theory of Reminding and Learning in Computers and People*. Cambridge: Cambridge University Press.

Schank, R. C. (1982b), *Reading and Understanding: Teaching from the Perspective of Artificial Intelligence*. Hillsdale, NJ: Lawrence Erlbaum Associates.

Schank, R. C. (1984), *The Cognitive Computer*. Reading, MA: Addison-Wesley.

Schank, R. C. (1986), *Explanation Patterns*. Hillsdale, NJ: Lawrence Erlbaum Associates.

Schank, R. C. and Abelson, R. (1977), *Scripts, Plans, Goals and Understanding*. Hillsdale, NJ: Lawrence Erlbaum Associates.

Schiffrin, D. (1987), *Discourse Markers*. Cambridge: Cambridge University Press.

Schneider, R. (2005a), 'Reader constructs', in D. Herman, M. Jahn and M. L. Ryan (eds), *Routledge Encyclopedia of Narrative Theory*. London and New York: Routledge, pp. 482–3.

Schneider, R. (2005b), 'Reader response theory', in D. Herman, M. Jahn and M. L. Ryan (eds), *Routledge Encyclopedia of Narrative Theory*. London and New York: Routledge, pp. 484–6.

Schneider, R. (2005c), 'Reception theory', in D. Herman, M. Jahn and M. L. Ryan (eds), *Routledge Encyclopedia of Narrative Theory*. London and New York: Routledge, pp. 492–3.

Schram, D. H. and Steen, G. J. (eds) (2001a), *The Psychology and Sociology of Literature. In Honor of Elrud Ibsch*. Amsterdam and Philadelphia: John Benjamins.

Schram, D. H. and Steen, G. J. (2001b), 'The empirical study of literature', in D. H. Schram and G. J. Steen (eds), *The Psychology and Sociology of Literature*. Amsterdam and Philadelphia: John Benjamins, pp. 1–16.

Schreier, M. (2001), 'Qualitative methods in studying text reception', in D. Scham and G. Steen (eds), *The Psychology and Sociology of Literature. In Honor of Elrud Ibsch*. Amsterdam and Philadelphia: John Benjamins, pp. 35–56.

Scott, M. (2004), *WordSmith Tools* version 4. Oxford: Oxford University Press.

Searle, J. R. (1969), *Speech Acts: An Essay in the Philosophy of Language*. Cambridge: Cambridge University Press.

Searle, J. R. (1976), 'A classification of illocutionary acts'. *Language in Society*, 5, 1–23.

Searle, J. R. (1979), *Expression and Meaning: Studies in the Theory of Speech Acts*. Cambridge: Cambridge University Press.

Segal, E. M. (1995), 'Narrative comprehension and the role of deictic shift theory', in J. F. Duchan, G. A. Bruder and L. E. Hewitt (eds), *Deixis in Narrative. A Cognitive Science Perspective*. Hillsdale, New Jersey: Lawrence Erlbaum Associates, pp. 3-17.

Sell, R. and Verdonk, P. (eds) (1994), *Literature and the New Interdisciplinarity: Poetics, Linguistics, History*. Amsterdam: Rodopi.

Semino, E. (1995), 'Schema theory and the analysis of text worlds in poetry'. *Language and Literature*, 4, (2), 79–108.

Semino, E. (1997), *Language and World Creation in Poems and other Texts*. London and New York: Longman.

Semino, E. (2002), 'A cognitive stylistic approach to mind style in narrative Fiction', in E. Semino, and J. Culpeper (eds), *Cognitive Stylistics. Language and Cognition in Text Analysis*. Amsterdam and Philadelphia: John Benjamins, pp. 95–122.

Semino, E. (2003), 'Possible worlds and mental spaces in Hemingway's "A Very Short Story"', in J. Gavins and G. Steen (eds), *Cognitive Poetics in Practice*. London: Routledge, pp. 107–15.

Semino, E. (2006a), 'Mind style', in K. Brown (ed.), *Encyclopaedia of Language and Linguistics*. Amsterdam and Philadelphia: Elsevier Science, pp. 142–8.

Semino, E. (2006b), 'Possible worlds: Stylistic applications', in K. Brown (ed.), *Encyclopaedia of Language and Linguistics.* Amsterdam: Elsevier Science, pp. 777–82.

Semino, E. (2006c), 'Blending and characters' mental functioning in Virginia Woolf's "Lappin and Lapinova"'. *Language and Literature*, 15, (1), 55–72.

Semino, E. (2006d), 'Metaphor and fictional minds', in R. Benczes and S. Csábi (eds), *The Metaphors of Sixty*. Budapest: Eötvös Loránd, pp. 227–35.

Semino, E. (2007), 'Mind style 25 years on'. *Style*, 41, (2), 153–73.

Semino, E. (2008), *Metaphor in Discourse*. Cambridge: Cambridge University Press.

Semino, E. and Culpeper, J. (eds.) (2002), *Cognitive Stylistics: Language and Cognition in Text Analysis*. Amsterdam and Philadelphia: John Benjamins.

Semino, E. and Short, M. (2004), *Corpus Stylistics. Speech, Writing and Thought Presentation in a Corpus of English Narratives*. London: Routledge.

Semino, E. and Swindlehurst, K. (1996), 'Metaphor and mind style in Ken Kesey's *One Flew over the Cuckoo's Nest*'. *Style*, 30, (1), 143–66.

Shen, D. (2005), 'How stylisticians draw on narratology: Approaches, advantages and disadvantages'. *Style*, 39, (4), 381–95.

Shklovsky, V. (1917), 'Art as technique'. English translation in D. Lodge (1988), *Modern Criticism and Theory. A Reader.* London and New York: Longman, pp. 16–30.

Shklovsky, V. ([1925]1990), *Theory of Prose*. Elmwood Park, IL: Dalkey Archive Press.

Short, M. (1981), 'Discourse analysis and the analysis of drama'. *Applied Linguistics*, 180–202.

Short, M. (ed.) (1989), *Reading, Analysing and Teaching Literature*. London: Longman.

Short, M. (1993), 'To analyse a poem stylistically: "To Paint a Water Lily" by Ted Hughes', in P. Verdonk (ed.), *Twentieth-century Poetry: From Text to Context*. London: Routledge, pp. 7–20.

Short, M. (1996), *Exploring the Language of Poems, Plays and Prose*. London: Longman.

Short, M. (1998), 'From dramatic text to dramatic performance', in J. Culpeper, M. Short and P. Verdonk (eds), *Exploring the Language of Drama. From Text to Context*. London: Routledge, pp. 6–18.

Short, M. (2000), 'Graphological deviation, style variation and point of view in *Marabou Stork Nightmares* by Irvine Welsh'. *Journal of Literary Studies/ Tydskrif vir Literatuur Wetenskap*, 15, (3–4), 305–23.

Short, M. (2007a), 'Thought presentation twenty-five years on'. *Style*, 41, (2), 227–41.

Short, M. (2007b), 'How to make a drama out of a speech act: The speech act of apology in the film *A Fish Called Wanda*', in D. Hoover and S. Lattig (eds), *Stylistics: Retrospect and Prospect*. Amsterdam and Philadelphia: John Benjamins, pp. 169–89.

Short, M. (2007c), 'Language and Style – A web-based course' http://www.lancs.ac.uk/fass/projects/stylistics/

Short, M. (2008), 'Discourse analysis and drama', in R. Carter and P. Stockwell (eds), *The Language and Literature Reader*. London: Routledge, pp. 70–82.

Short, M., Busse, B. and Plummer, P. (2006), 'Preface: The web-based *Language and Style* Course: E-learning and stylistics'. *Language and Literature*, 15, (3), 219–35.

Short, M., Freeman, D. C., van Peer, W. and Simpson, P. (1998), 'Stylistics, criticism and mythrepresentation again: squaring the circle with Ray Mackay's subjective solution for all problems'. *Language and Literature*, 7, (1), 39-50.

Short, M. and van Peer, W. (1999), 'A reply to Mackay'. *Language and Literature*, 8, (3), 269–75.

Simpson, P. (1989), 'Politeness phenomena in Ionesco's *The Lesson*', in R. Carter and P. Simpson (eds), *Language, Discourse and Literature: An Introductory Reader in Discourse Stylistics*. London: Unwin Hyman, pp. 169-92.

Simpson, P. (1990), 'Modality in literary-critical discourse', in W. Nash (ed.), *The Writing Scholar. Studies in Academic Discourse.* Newbury Park: Sage Publications, pp. 63–94.

Simpson, P. (1993), *Language, Ideology and Point of View.* London: Routledge.

Simpson, P. (1997), *Language through Literature. An Introduction*. London and New York: Routledge.

Simpson, P. (1998), 'Odd talk: Studying discourses of ambiguity', in J. Culpeper, M. Short and P. Verdonk (eds), *Exploring the Language of Drama. From Text to Context*. London: Routledge, pp. 34–53.

Simpson, P. (1999), 'Language, culture and identity: With (another) look at accents in pop and rock singing'. *Multilingua: Journal of Cross-Cultural and Interlanguage Communication*, 18, (4), 343–68.

Simpson, P. (2000), 'Satirical humour and cultural context: With a note on the curious case of Father Todd Unctuous', in T. Bex, M. Burke and P. Stockwell (eds), *Contextualized Stylistics*. Amsterdam and Atlanta: Rodopi, pp. 243–66.

Simpson, P. (2001), '"Reason" and "Tickle" as pragmatic constructs in the discourse of advertising'. *Journal of Pragmatics*, 33, (4), 589–607.

Simpson, P. (2003), *On the Discourse of Satire: Towards a Stylistic Model of Satirical Humour*. Amsterdam and Philadelphia: John Benjamins.

Simpson, P. (2004), *Stylistics: A Resource Book for Students*. London: Routledge.

Simpson, P. (2007), 'Non-standard grammar in the teaching of language and style', in G. Watson and S. Zyngier (eds), *Literature and Stylistics for Language Learners. Theory and Practice*. Basingstoke, Houndmills: Palgrave Macmillan, pp. 140–54.

Simpson, P. and Mayr, A. (2009), *Language and Power: A Resource Book for Students*. London: Routledge.

Simpson, P. and Montgomery, M. (1995), 'Language, literature and film. The stylistics of Bernard MacLaverty's *Cal*', in P. Verdonk and J. J. Weber (eds), *Twentieth-Century Fiction: From Text to Context*. London: Routledge, pp. 138–64.

Sinclair, J. (1966), 'Taking a poem to pieces', in R. Fowler (ed.), *Essays on Style and Language: Linguistic and Critical Approaches to Literary Style*. London: Routledge and Kegan Paul, pp. 68–81.

Sinclair, J. (1991), *Corpus, Concordance, Collocation*. Oxford: Oxford University Press.

Sinclair, J. ([1982] 2004), 'Planes of discourse', in S. N. A. Rizvi (ed.), *The Two-fold Voice: Essays in Honour of Ramesh Mohan*. India: Pitambar Publishing Co, 1982; reprinted in J. Sinclair. *Trust the Text. Language, Corpus and Discourse*. London and New York: Routledge, 2004, pp. 51–66.

Sinclair, J. (2004), *Trust the Text. Language, Corpus and Discourse*. London and New York: Routledge.

Sinclair, J. (2005), 'Corpus and text: Basic principles', in M. Wynne (ed.), *Developing Linguistic Corpora: A Guide to Good Practice*. Oxford: Oxbow Books, pp. 1–16.

Sinclair, J. and Coulthard, M. (1975), *Toward an Analysis of Discourse: The English Used by Teachers and Pupils*. Oxford: Oxford University Press.

Smith, N. (2004), *Chomsky: Ideas and Ideals*. Cambridge: Cambridge University Press.

Sopcak, P. (2004), *Approaches to the Development of Literariness in Drafts to James Joyce's* Ulysses: *A Foregrounding Study*. Unpublished M.A. thesis, Ludwig Maximilian University: Munich.

Sotirova, V. (2004), 'Connectives in free indirect style: Continuity or shift?'. *Language and Literature*, 13, (3), 216–34.

Sotirova, V. (2005), 'Repetition in Free Indirect Style: A Dialogue of Minds?'. *Style*, 39, (2), 123–36.

Sperber, D. and Wilson, D. (1996), *Relevance. Communication and Cognition*. Oxford: Blackwell.

Stanzel, F. K. (1984), *A Theory of Narrative*, (trans. C. Goedsche). Cambridge: Cambridge University Press.

Steen, G. (1994), *Understanding Metaphor in Literature: An Empirical Approach*. London: Longman.

Steen, G. (1999), 'From linguistic to conceptual metaphor in five steps', in R.W. Gibbs Jr. and G. Steen (eds), *Metaphor in Cognitive Linguistics*. Amsterdam and Philadelphia: John Benjamins, pp. 57–78.

Steen, G. (2003), 'A historical view of empirical poetics: Trends and possibilities'. *Empirical Studies of the Arts*, 21, (1), 51–67.

Stockwell, P. (2000), *The Poetics of Science Fiction*. Harlow: Longman.

Stockwell, P. (2002), *Cognitive Poetics: An Introduction*. London: Routledge.

Stockwell, P. (2003), 'Schema poetics and speculative cosmology'. *Language and Literature*, 12, (3), 252–71.

Stockwell, P. (2006), 'Schema theory: Stylistic applications ', in K. Brown (ed.), *Encyclopaedia of Language and Linguistics*. Amsterdam: Elsevier Science, pp. 8–13.

Stubbs, M. (2005), 'Conrad in the computer. Examples of quantitative stylistics methods'. *Language and Literature*, 14, (1), 5–24.

Sweetser, E. (2000), 'Blended spaces and performativity'. *Cognitive Linguistics*, 11, (3–4), 305–34.

Sweetser, E. (2006), 'Whose rhyme is whose reason? Sound and sense in *Cyrano de Bergerac*'. *Language and Literature*, 15, (1), 29–54.

Taavitsainen, I. and Fitzmaurice, S. (2007), 'Historical pragmatics: What it is and how to do it', in S. M. Fitzmaurice and I. Taavitsainen (eds), *Methods in Historical Pragmatics*. Berlin and New York: de Gruyter, pp. 11–36.

Talmy, L. (2000), *Toward a Cognitive Semantics. Vol. I: Concept Structuring Systems. Vol. II: Typology and Process in Concept Structuring*. Cambridge, MA, and London: MIT Press.

Taylor, T. J. and Toolan, M. (1984), 'Recent trends in stylistics'. *Journal of Literary Semantics*, 13, (1), 57–79.

Thomas, B. (2000), '"Piecing together a Mirage": Adapting *The English Patient* for the screen', in R. Giddins and E. Sheen (eds), *The Classic Novel.*

From Page to Screen. Manchester and New York: Manchester University Press, pp. 197–232.

Thomas, J. (1995), *Meaning in Interaction*. London and New York: Longman.

Thompson, G. (1996a), *Introducing Functional Grammar*. Great Britain: Arnold.

Thompson, G. (1996b), 'Voices in the text: Discourse perspectives on language reports'. *Applied Linguistics*, 17, (4), 501–30.

Thorne, J. P. (1965), 'Stylistics and generative grammars'. *Journal of Linguistics*, 1, 49–59.

Tobin, V. (2006), 'Ways of reading *Sherlock Holmes*: The entrenchment of discourse blends'. *Language and Literature*, 15, (1), 73–90.

Todorov, T. (1969), *Grammaire du Décaméron*. The Hague: Mouton.

Todorov, T. (1977), *The Poetics of Prose*. Oxford: Blackwell.

Tomashevsky, B. (1965), 'Thematics', in L. T. Lemon and M. J. Reis (eds), *Russian Formalist Criticism: Four Essays*. Lincoln, Nebraska: University of Nebraska Press, pp. 61–98.

Toolan, M. (1988), *Narrative. A Critical Linguistic Introduction*. London: Routledge.

Toolan, M. (1990), *The Stylistics of Fiction. A Literary-Linguistic Approach*. London and New York: Routledge.

Toolan, M. (ed.) (1992), *Language, Text and Context. Essays in Stylistics*. London and New York: Routledge.

Toolan, M. (1995), 'Discourse style makes viewpoint: The example of Carver's narrator in "Cathedral'", in P. Verdonk and J. J. Weber (eds), *Twentieth-Century Fiction: From Text to Context*. London: Routledge, pp. 126–37.

Toolan, M. (1998), *Language in Literature. An Introduction to Stylistics*. London: Arnold.

Toolan, M. (2000), '"What makes you think you exist?": A speech move schematic and its application to Pinter's *The Birthday Party*'. *Journal of Pragmatics*, 32, 177-201.

Toolan, M. (2001), *Narrative. A Critical Linguistic Introduction*. 2nd edition. London: Routledge.

Toolan, M. (2006a), 'Narrative. Linguistic and structural theories', in K. Brown (ed.), *Encyclopedia of Language and Linguistics*. Amsterdam: Elsevier Science, pp. 459–73.

Toolan, M. (2006b), 'Review of Simpson's *Stylistics: A Resource Book for Students* (2004)'. *Language and Literature*, 15, (4), 409–11.

Toolan, M. (2006c), 'Speech and Thought: Representation of', in K. Brown (ed.), *Encyclopedia of Language and Linguistics.* Amsterdam: Elsevier Science, pp. 698–710.

Toolan, M. (2006d), 'Top keyword abridgements of short stories: A corpus linguistic resource?'. *Journal of Literary Semantics*, 35, 181–94.

Toolan, M. (2007), 'Trust and text, text as trust', in R. Moon (ed.), *Words, Grammar and Text: Revisiting the Works of John Sinclair. Special Issues of the International Journal of Corpus Linguistics*, 12, (2), 269–88.

Toolan, M. (2009), *Narrative Progression in the Short Story. A Corpus Stylistic Approach.* Amsterdam and Philadelphia: John Benjamins.

Traugott, E. C. and Pratt, M. L. (1980), *Linguistics for Students of Literature.* New York, London and Sydney: Hartcourt Brace Jovanovich.

Tredell, N. (ed.) (2002), *Cinemas of the Mind. A Critical History of Film Theory.* Cambridge: Icon Books, UK.

Tseng, C. (2008), 'Coherence and cohesive harmony in filmic text', in L. Unsworth (ed.), *Multimodal Semiotics. Functional Analysis in Contexts of Education*. London: Continuum, pp. 87–104.

Tsur, R. (1978), 'Emotions, emotional qualities and poetry'. *Psychocultural Review*, 2, 165–80.

Tsur, R. (1992), *Toward a Theory of Cognitive Poetics*. Amsterdam: Elsevier.

Tsur, R. (1998), *Poetic Rhythm: Structure and Performance. An Empirical Study in Cognitive Poetics.* Bern: Peter Lang.

Tsur, R. (2002), 'Aspect of cognitive poetics', in E. Semino and J. Culpeper (eds), *Cognitive Stylistics: Language and Cognition in Text Analysis*. Amsterdam and Philadelphia: John Benjamins, pp. 280–318.

Tsur, R. (2003), 'Deixis and abstractions: Adventures in space and time', in J. Gavins and G. Steen (eds), *Cognitive Poetics in Practice*. London: Routledge, pp. 41–54.

Tsur, R. (2008), *Toward a Theory of Cognitive Poetics*. Sussex: Sussex Academic Press.

Turner, M. (2001), *Cognitive Dimensions of Social Science*. Oxford: Oxford University Press.

Turner, M. (2006), 'Compression and representation'. *Language and Literature*, 15, (1), 17–27.

Uspensky, B. (1973), *A Poetics of Composition*. Berkeley: University of California Press.

van Dijk, T. A. (1993), 'Principles of critical discourse analysis'. *Discourse and Society*, 4, (2), 249–83.

van Leeuwen, T. (1999), *Speech, Music, Sound*. London: Macmillan.

van Leeuwen, T. (2005a), *Introducing Social Semiotics*. London: Routledge.

van Leeuwen, T. (2005b), 'Typographic meaning'. *Visual Communication*, 4, (2), 137–43.

van Leeuwen, T. (2006a), 'Critical discourse analysis', in K. Brown (ed.), *Encyclopedia of Language and Linguistics*. Amsterdam: Elsevier Science, pp. 290-4.

van Leeuwen, T. (2006b), 'Towards a semiotics of typography'. *Information Design Journal + Document Design*, 14, (2), 139–55.

van Leeuwen, T. and Wodak, R. (1999), 'Legitimizing immigration control. A discourse historical analysis'. *Discourse Studies*, 1, (1), 83–118.

van Peer, W. (1986), *Stylistics and Psychology: Investigations of Foregrounding*. London: Croom Helm.

van Peer, W. (1997), 'Towards a poetics of emotion', in M. Hjort and S. Laver (eds), *Emotion and The Arts*. Oxford: Oxford University Press, pp. 215–24.

van Peer, W. (2002), 'Where do literary themes come from?', in M. Louwerse and W. van Peer (eds), *Thematics: Interdisciplinary Studies*. Amsterdam and Philadelphia: John Benjamins, 253–63.

van Peer, W. (2007), 'Introduction to foregrounding: A state of the art'. *Language and Literature*, 16, (2), 99–104.

van Peer, W. (ed.) (2008), *The Quality of Literature. Linguistic Studies in the Evaluation of Literary Texts*. Amsterdam and Philadelphia: John Benjamins.

van Peer, W. and Chatman, S. (eds) (2001), *New Perspectives on Narrative Perspective*. Albany: State University of New York Press.

van Peer, W. and Graf, E. (2002), 'Between the lines: Spatial language and its developmental representation in Stephen King's *IT*', in E. Semino and J. Culpeper (eds), *Cognitive Poetics. Language and Cognition in Text Analysis*. Amsterdam and Philadelphia: John Benjamins, pp. 123–52.

van Peer, W. and Hakemulder, J. (2006), 'Foregrounding', in K. Brown (ed.), *Encyclopaedia of Language and Linguistics*. Amsterdam: Elsevier Science, pp. 546–50.

van Peer, W. and Louwerse, M. (eds) (2003), *Thematics. Interdisciplinary Studies*. Amsterdam and Philadelphia: John Benjamins.

van Peer, W. and Renkema, J. (eds) (1984), *Pragmatics and Stylistics*. Amersfoort: Acco.

van Peer, W., Hakemulder, J. and Zyngier, S. (2007), *Muses and Measures. Empirical Research Methods for the Humanities*. Newcastle: Cambridge Scholars Publications.

van Peer, W., Zyngier, S. and Hakemulder, J. (2007), 'Foregrounding: Past, present, future', in D. Hoover and S. Lattig (eds), *Stylistics: Prospect and Retrospect*. Amsterdam and New York: Rodopi, pp. 1–22.

Verdonk, P. (1980), *Making Sense of Sentences*. Amsterdam: University of Amsterdam.

Verdonk, P. (1982), *The Language of Poetry: A Seminar on Literary Stylistics, 1981–82*. Amsterdam: University of Amsterdam.

Verdonk, P. (1987), '"We have art in order that we may not perish from truth": The universe of discourse in Auden's "Musée des Beaux Arts"'. *Dutch Quarterly Review of Anglo-American Letters*, 17, (2), 77–96.

Verdonk, P. (ed.) (1993), *Twentieth-Century Poetry: From Text to Context*. London: Routledge.

Verdonk, P. (1999), 'The liberation of the icon: A brief survey from classical rhetoric to cognitive stylistics'. *Journal of Literary Studies*, 15, (3–4), 291–304.

Verdonk, P. (2002), *Stylistics*. Oxford: Oxford University Press.

Verdonk, P. and Weber, J. J. (eds) (1995), *Twentieth-Century Fiction: From Text to Context*. London: Routledge.

Voloshinov, V. N. (1973), *Marxism and the Philosophy of Language*, trans. L. Matejka and I. R. Titunik. New York: Seminar Press.

Wales K. (1992), *The Language of James Joyce*. Basingstoke: Macmillan.

Wales, K. (1993), 'Teach yourself "rhetoric": An analysis of Philip Larkin's "Church Going"', in P. Verdonk (ed.), *Twentieth-Century Poetry: From Text to Context*. London: Routledge, pp. 134–58.

Wales, K. (ed.) (1994), *Feminist Linguistics in Literary Criticism*. Woodbridge, England: Boydell and Brewer.

Wales, K. (1996), *Personal Pronouns in Present-Day English*. Cambridge: Cambridge University Press.

Wales, K. (2001), *A Dictionary of Stylistics*. 2nd edition. Harlow: Longman.

Wales, K. (2006a), *Northern English. A Social and Cultural History*. Cambridge: Cambridge University Press.

Wales, K. (2006b), 'Stylistics', in K. Brown (ed.), *Encyclopaedia of Language and Linguistics*. Amsterdam: Elsevier Science, pp. 213–7.

Walsh, C. (2001), *Gender and Discourse: Language and Power in Politics, the Church and other Organisations*. Harlow: Longman.

Walton, K. (1990), *Mimesis as Make-Believe: On the Foundations of the Representational Arts*. Cambridge, MA: Harvard University Press.

Wareing, S. (1994), 'And then he kissed her: The reclamation of female characters to submissive roles', in K. Wales (ed.), *Feminist Linguistics in Literary Criticism*. Woodbridge, England: Boydell and Brewer, pp. 117–36.

Watson, G. and Zyngier, S. (eds) (2007), *Literature and Stylistics for Language Learners. Theory and Practice*. London: Palgrave.

Watts, R. (2003), *Politeness*. Cambridge: Cambridge University Press.

Waugh, L. (1995), 'Reported speech in journalistic discourse. The relation between function and text'. *Text*, 15, (1), 129–73.

Weber, J. J. (1992), *Critical Analysis of Fiction*. Amsterdam and Atlanta: Rodopi.

Weber, J. J. (1996), *The Stylistics Reader. From Roman Jakobson to the Present*. London and New York: Arnold.

Weber, J. J. (2004), 'A new paradigm for literary studies, or: The teething troubles of cognitive poetics'. *Style*, 38, (4), 515–34.

Werkhofer, K. T. (2005), 'Traditional and modern views: The social constitution and power of politeness', in R. Watts, S. Ide and K. Ehlich (eds), *Politeness in Language Studies in its History, Theory and Practice*. Berlin: Mouton de Gruyter, pp. 155-201.

Werth, P. (1980), 'Articles of association: Determiners and context', in J. van der Auwera (ed.), *The Semantics of Determiners*. London: Croom Helm, pp. 250–89.

Werth, P. (ed.) (1981), *Conversation and Discourse: Structure and Interpretation*. London: Croom Helm.

Werth, P. (1984), *Focus, Coherence and Emphasis*. Kent: Croom Helm Ltd.

Werth, P. (1986), 'A functional approach to presupposition', in A. Bossuyt (ed.), *Functional Approaches to Linguistics*. Brussels: Presses Universitaires de Bruxelles, pp. 239–79.

Werth, P. (1994), 'Extended metaphor – A text-world account'. *Language and Literature*, 3, (2), 79–103.

Werth, P. (1995a), 'How to build a world (in a lot less than six days and using only what's in your head)', in K. Green (ed.), *New Essays on Deixis: Discourse, Narrative, Literature*. Amsterdam: Rodopi, pp. 49–80.

Werth, P. (1995b), '"World enough and time": Deictic space and the interpretation of prose', in P. Verdonk and J. J. Weber (eds), *Twentieth Century Fiction: From Text to Context*. London: Routledge, pp. 181–205.

Werth, P. (1999), *Text Worlds: Representing Conceptual Space in Discourse*. London: Longman.

Whelehan, I. (1999), 'Adaptations: The contemporary dilemmas', in D. Cartmell and I. Whelehan (eds), *Adaptations. From Text to Screen, Screen to Text*. London and New York: Routledge, pp. 3–19.

Whiteley, S. (2008), 'Real readers, text world theory & emotional response', paper presented at the Annual Conference of the Poetics and Linguistics Association, July 2008, University of Sheffield, UK.

Widdowson, H. G. (1972), 'On the deviance of literary discourse'. *Style*, 6, (3), 294–306.

Widdowson, H. G. (1975), *Stylistics and the Teaching of Literature*. Harlow, Essex: Longman.

Widdowson, H. G. (1992), *Practical Stylistics: An Approach to Poetry*. Oxford: Oxford University Press.

Widdowson, H. (1995), 'Discourse analysis. A critical view'. *Language and Literature*, 4, (3), 157–72.

Widdowson, H. (1996a), *Linguistics*. Oxford: Oxford University Press.

Widdowson, H. (1996b), 'Reply to Fairclough: Discourse and interpretation: Conjectures and refutations'. *Language and Literature*, 5, (3), 57–69.

Widdowson, H. (2000), 'On the limitations of linguistics applied'. *Applied Linguistics*, 21, (1), 3–25.

Widdowson, H. G. (2002), 'Verbal art and social practice: A reply to Weber'. *Language and Literature*, 11, (2), 161–7.

Widdowson, H. G. (2004), *Text, Context, Pretext. Critical Issues in Discourse Analysis*. Oxford: Blackwell.

Wierzbicka, A. (1987), *English Speech Act Verbs: A Semantic Dictionary*. Sydney: Academic Press.

Willems, K. and De Cuypere, L. (eds) (2008), *Naturalness and Iconicity in Language*. Amsterdam and Philadelphia: John Benjamins.

Wimsatt, W. K. and Beardsley, M. C. (1954), 'The affective fallacy', in W. K. Wimsatt (ed.), *The Verbal Icon*. Lexington: University of Kentucky Press, pp. 21–39.

Wodak, R. and Meyer, M. (2001), *Methods for Critical Discourse Analysis*. London: Sage Publications; 2nd edition 2009.

Wodak, R., Novak, P. and Pelikan, J. (1990), *'Wir sind alle unschuldige Täter'. Diskurshistorische Studien zum Nachkriegsantisemitismus*. Frankfurt: Suhrkamp.

Youman, G. (1994), 'The Vocabulary Management Profile in Two Stories by Faulkner.' *Empirical Studies in the Arts*, 12, (2), 113–30.

Yule, G. (1996), *Pragmatics*. Oxford: Oxford University Press.

Ziegeler, D. (2006), 'Mood and modality in grammar', in K. Brown (ed.), *Encyclopaedia of Language and Linguistics*. Amsterdam: Elsevier, pp. 259–67.

Zyngier, S., Bortolussi, M., Chesnolova, A. and Auracher, J. (eds) (2008), *Directions in Empirical Literary Studies*. Amsterdam and Philadelphia: John Benjamins.

Primary sources

This bibliography lists the primary sources quoted in the book. Where relevant, original dates of publication are provided according to the following system: ([original year of publication] year of edition quoted).

Austen, J. ([1816] 1985), *Emma*. Ed. Ronald Blythe. London: Penguin.

Auster, P. (2006), *The Brooklyn Follies*. New York: Henry Holt.

Baudelaire, C. (1847), 'Les Chats', in R. Jakobson and C. Lévi-Strauss (1962), '"Les Chats" de Charles Baudelaire'. *L'Homme*, 2, 5–21.

Bynner, W. (trans.) (1920), *The Jade Mountain: A Chinese Anthology*. New York: Knopf.

Camus, A. ([1942] 1989), *The Stranger* (translated from French *L'Etranger* by M. Ward). New York: Random House.

Chada, G. (2002), *Bend it Like Beckham*, Helkon SK, Fox Searchlight Pictures.

Conrad, J. ([1907] 2007), *The Secret Agent*. London: Penguin.

Dawood, N. J. (trans.) (1954), *Arabian Nights: Tales from the Thousand and One Nights*. London: Penguin.

Dickens, C. ([1837] 1966), *Oliver Twist*. Ed. Kathleen Tillotson. Oxford: Oxford University Press.

Dickens, C. ([1860] 1999), *Great Expectations*. Ed. Edgar Rosenberg. New York: Norton.

Evans, B. G. and Tobin, J. J. M. (eds) (1997), *The Riverside Shakespeare*. 2nd edition. Boston: Houghton Mifflin.

Faulkner, W. ([1929] 1978), *The Sound and the Fury*. Middlesex and New York: Penguin.

Foer, J. S. (2005), *Extremely Loud and Incredibly Close*. New York: Houghton Mifflin.

Golding, W. ([1955] 2005), *The Inheritors*. London: Faber and Faber.

Hardy, T. ([1891] 1975), *Jude the Obscure*. Ed. P. N. Furbank. The New Wessex Edition 2. London: Macmillan.

Herbert, G. ([1633] 1983), 'Easter Wings', in A. W. Allison, H. Barrows, C. R. Blake, A. J. Carr, A. M. Eastman, H. M. English jr. (eds), *The Norton Anthology of Poetry.* 3rd edition. London and New York: W. W. Norton and Company, p. 254.

Joyce, J. ([1914] 1992), 'Two Gallants', in *Dubliners*. London, New York and Victoria: Penguin.

Joyce, J. ([1922]1993), *Ulysses*. London and New York: Vintage Books.

Joyce, J. ([1939]1992), *Finnegans Wake*. London, New York and Toronto: Penguin.

Keats, J. ([1820] 1983), 'To Autumn', in A. W. Allison, H. Barrows, C. R. Blake, A. J. Carr, A. M. Eastman, H. M. English jr. (eds), *The Norton Anthology of Poetry.* 3rd edition. London and New York: W. W. Norton and Company, p. 664.

McEwan, I. (1981), *The Comfort of Strangers*. London: Jonathan Cape.

McEwan, I. (1992), *Black Dogs*. London: Vintage.

Milton, J. ([1667] 1983), 'Paradise Lost', in A. W. Allison, H. Barrows, C. R. Blake, A. J. Carr, A. M. Eastman, H. M. English jr. (eds), *The Norton Anthology of Poetry.* 3rd edition. London and New York: W. W. Norton and Company, p. 295.

Pinter, H. (1957), *The Dumb Waiter*. London: Samuel French Ltd.

Plath, S. (1963), *The Bell Jar*. London: HarperCollins.

Poe, E. A. ([1849] 1983), 'Annabel Lee', in A. W. Allison, H. Barrows, C. R. Blake, A. J. Carr, A. M. Eastman, H. M. English jr. (eds), *The Norton Anthology of Poetry.* 3rd edition. London and New York: W. W. Norton and Company, p. 697.

Schrader, P. (1990), *The Comfort of Strangers*. Skoura Pictures: USA.

Shakespeare, W. ([1599] 2006), *As You Like It*. London: Arden Shakespeare.

Shelley, P. B. ([1820] 1983), 'The Cloud', in A. W. Allison, H. Barrows, C. R. Blake, A. J. Carr, A. M. Eastman, H. M. English jr. (eds), *The Norton*

Anthology of Poetry. 3rd edition. London and New York: W. W. Norton and Company, p. 622.

Sterne, T. ([1759–1767] 1978), *The Life and Opinions of Tristram Shandy*. London: Penguin.

Szymborska, W. (1999), *Wisława Szymborska. Poems New and Collected (1957–1997).* Translation from the Polish by S. Baraczak and C. Cavanagh. London: Faber and Faber.

Thomas, D. ([1936] 2003), *Collected Poems*. Ed. W. Davies and R. Maud. London: Phoenix.

Wales, K. and Smith, K. (1998), *Santa's Christmas Joke Book*. New York: Red Fox.

Wales, K. and Burgess, M. (1985), *The Elephant Joke Book*. Quebec: Beaver Books.

Wilde, O. ([1890] 1994), *Picture of Dorian Gray*. London: Penguin.

Woolf, V. ([1927] 1996), *To the Lighthouse*. London and New York: Penguin.

Wordsworth, W. ([1805] 1983), 'The Prelude', in A. W. Allison, H. Barrows, C. R. Blake, A. J. Carr, A. M. Eastman, H. M. English jr. (eds), *The Norton Anthology of Poetry* (3rd edition). London and New York: W. W. Norton and Company, p. 538.

Index

Note: Numbers in **bold** indicate main entry for the term in question.

Lightning Source UK Ltd.
Milton Keynes UK
UKHW021555270819
348688UK00008B/692/P

9 780826 419484